D1327508

EXILES ON

MAIN STREET

JEWISH LITERATURE AND CULTURE
Series Editor, Alvin H. Rosenfeld

Julian Levinson is the Samuel Shetzer Professor of American Jewish Studies and Associate Professor of English Language and Literature at the University of Michigan–Ann Arbor.

EXILES ON MAIN STREET

JEWISH AMERICAN WRITERS AND
AMERICAN LITERARY CULTURE

Julian Levinson

Indiana University Press

BLOOMINGTON AND INDIANAPOLIS

This book is a publication of

Indiana University Press
601 North Morton Street
Bloomington, IN 47404-3797 USA

http://iupress.indiana.edu

Telephone orders	800-842-6796
Fax orders	812-855-7931
Orders by e-mail	iuporder@indiana.edu

MANUFACTURED IN THE UNITED STATES OF AMERICA

Library of Congress Cataloging-in-Publication Data

Levinson, Julian.
Exiles on main street : Jewish American writers and American literary culture / Julian Levinson.
p. cm. — (Jewish literature and culture)
Includes bibliographical references and index.
ISBN-13: 978-0-253-35081-7 (cloth : alk. paper) 1. American literature—Jewish authors—
History and criticism. 2. Jews—United States—Identity. 3. Group identity in literature.
4. Jews in literature. I. Title.
PS153.J4L48 2008
810.9'8924—dc22
2007046930

1 2 3 4 5   13 12 11 10 09 08

To Lisa

CONTENTS

CONTENTS

PART 4
"ORATING IN NEW YORKESE":
THE LANGUAGES OF JEWISHNESS IN POSTWAR
AMERICA 143

Illustrations appear on pages 109–117.

ACKNOWLEDGMENTS

During the many years it took me to write this book, I was blessed with a mighty stream of good council and encouragement from teachers, colleagues, friends, and family. The book began life in the English department at Columbia University, and, though it retains only a few sentences from its original version, I would like to thank those who saw this project through to its first formulation: David Damrosch, Moshe Gold, Jonathan Levin, David Roskies, and Maura Spiegel. Over the past seven years, the University of Michigan has been a wonderful environment in which to grow as a scholar and as a human being, and I am grateful to my colleagues here for their support and insight. Among those whose attention to my work has made a tremendous difference, I include Sara Blair, George Bornstein, Todd Endelman, Jonathan Freedman, Zvi Gitelman, Mikhail Krutikov, Marjorie Levinson, Deborah Dash Moore, Anita Norich, Shachar Pinsker, Sidonie Smith, and Alan Wald. This manuscript also benefited from readers from the broader academic community, and I especially want to thank Jonathan Boyarin and Mark Shechner, who gave generously of their time and expert advice. Among those whose editorial assistance helped—really saved—me at various stages of the production of this book, let me also mention Patrick Barry, Alex Beringer, Olivia Bustion, Elliot Gertel, Joshua Lambert, Daniel Mintz, James Mitchell, and Valerie Moses. For his ready aid in all computing matters, I thank James Sullivan.

I am deeply indebted to a number of individuals and institutions that provided resources and materials for my research. The Mellon Foundation and the Memorial Foundation for Jewish Culture provided grants to support the early stages of my work. I am also grateful to the staffs of the Hatcher Library at the University of Michigan, the Rare Book and Manuscript Library at Columbia University, and the YIVO Institute for Jewish Research, where I performed much of my research. For help tracking down photographs and other documents, I am grateful to Nancy Shawcross from the University of Pennsylvania Rare Book and Manuscript Library and Isaac Gewirtz, curator of the Berg Collection at the New York Public Library. The staff of Indiana University Press has been extremely supportive throughout the process of transforming the manuscript into a book, and I would especially like to thank Janet Rabinowitch and Lee Sandweiss for believing in this project and Joyce Rappaport for editing the manuscript and entering the enormous changes I made at the last minute. I am truly inspired by the Frankel family's commitment to Judaic studies, and I want to thank them for their ongoing support of Judaic Studies at the University of Michigan.

There are many others whom I would like to acknowledge, either for reading and commenting on sections of this book or for contributing in more general ways to its emergence. While this list could be exceedingly long indeed, let me mention Marc Caplan, Josh Cohen, Richard Cook, Benjamin Friedman, Adam Haslett, Rick Hilles, Jonathan Karp, Mark Kuzmack, Benjamin Lee, Ziv Neeman, Martin Scherzinger, Eden Steinberg, Nicolas Sywak, and Ori Weissberg. For her expert advice with my prospectus, I thank Joyce Seltzer. Also, because he promised me a job should all else fail, I would like to thank Massoud Badakhshan from the Haight Ashbury Music Center; and because he welcomed me to his table and taught me how to pray, I thank Rabbi Ahron Hecht from the Richmond Torah Center of San Francisco.

Finally, my family has been an unending source of love and support over the years, and, for their ongoing faith in this project and tolerance of my intermittent self-enclosure within it, I extend my deepest thanks. I would like to thank in particular my parents Carl and Eleanor, my stepfather Stephen, my grandparents Gila and Harry (O"H), my siblings Gordon, Charlotte, Edward, and Rachel, my parents-in-law Marianne and Maynard, and my dog, Wheatie. My daughter, Chava, was born just as I was rethinking the original version of this work, and now, at five and a half, she is one of my most engaging and brilliant interlocutors. My wife, Lisa, has touched me and inspired me in ways I can hardly hope to express. I dedicate this book to her knowing full well that it is hers as much as it is mine. She knows every word of the manuscript, and lobbied nobly to save other bits from the trash. Through your devotion to me and confidence in my work—not to mention the unimaginable hours you have logged reading, commenting, and correcting—I have come to understand something of what the Spanish poet Pedro Salinas meant when he called one of his books *La Voz a Ti Debida* (My Voice Because of You). It is quite simply the fact that I would never have written this book had it not been for you.

EXILES ON

MAIN STREET

INTRODUCTION

America I still haven't told you what you did to Uncle Max after he came over from Russia.

—Allen Ginsberg, "America" (1956)

I

When the Puritan settlers claimed the New World as their "New Jerusalem," they laid the foundation for what would later emerge as the central Idea of America: that this would be a land of new beginnings, where the burdens of the past would be shrugged off and the road to salvation opened wide. How did this radical Idea influence the self-understanding of Jews when they began arriving en masse during the second half of the nineteenth century? Would they too embrace some version of the millennial vision crafted by their Puritan predecessors? Would they dissent from the reigning ideology of their new home in the name of Jewish tradition and cultural memory? Would they rearrange the terms of their tradition in line with the Idea of America? Such questions would not have been especially pressing, of course, for John Winthrop or Samuel Mather or Cotton Mather or any of the other Puritan preachers who sought to bring hope to their constituencies while steeling them for the task of taming the wilderness. Nor would Benjamin Franklin, John Adams, or Thomas Jefferson have given these questions much thought a century later when they proposed as a seal for the newly formed United States the image of the Israelites crossing the Red Sea, with Moses at the helm, his brow illuminated by a pillar of fire. For all of their evocations of the ancient Israelites, the founders' rhetoric remained unmistakably analogical. If the Bible served as their guidebook, there was no confusion about the direction of history: it was moving forward and westward and the Jews were people from another time and place. Nonetheless, people who still considered themselves Jews did exist, and they too came to settle in America. How would they reshape their identities as Jews in the face of the radical newness called America?

This is the central question I address in this book.[1] To be sure, it is not a new question, and it has been asked in one way or another by generations of scholars, writers, demographers, journalists, and Jewish communal organizers. Most commonly the question of Jewish American identity has been addressed as though each term in the amalgam were a relatively stable, fixed entity. The goal, simply put, has been to see how much of the entity we call *Jewishness* has been retained and how much of the entity we call *Americanness* has been absorbed. When framed in this way, the question has often led in one of two directions, either to expressions of celebration and relief (e.g., "You see, they remained Jewish after all"); or to pained admissions of defeat (e.g., "You see, they're not even real Jews anymore"). Recent scholarship has developed much more nuanced approaches to this question, characterizing the dialogue between Jews and American culture as an ongoing, dynamic interaction between two entities that are themselves in a state of flux. Among the scholars who have moved beyond the "either-or" approach and whose work has influenced and inspired my own, I would include Hasia Diner, Arnold Eisen, Norman Finkelstein, Sylvia Barack Fishman, Andrew Heinze, Michael P. Kramer, Eli Lederhendler, Deborah Dash Moore, Jonathan Sarna, Jeffrey Shandler, Donald Weber, Hana Wirth-Nesher, and Stephen Whitfield.[2] Using substantially different vocabularies, methodologies, and types of evidence, these scholars all testify to the ways Jewishness and Americanness have interacted with, overlapped, modified, and sometimes intensified each other—whether in the domain of literature, popular culture, religious practice, or that more nebulous sphere we might call "self-understanding." These scholars have pointed in different ways to the inadequacy of accounts of "vanishing" American Jews and of Jewish American culture as a show of empty signifiers.[3] They have underscored instead the unpredictability and, in different ways, the ongoing vitality of the Jewish encounter with America.

I offer this book as a contribution to this unfolding discussion. Focusing primarily on the realm of literary culture, I explore ways in which the exposure to American culture—in particular the visionary literary tradition identified with figures such as Ralph Waldo Emerson and Walt Whitman—has provided Jews with new ways of understanding themselves *as Jews*. Let me quickly list (in the manner of one of Whitman's poetic catalogues) some of the encounters between Jews and American literary culture I consider in the chapters that follow (take a breath): Emma Lazarus (1849–1887) meets Emerson while she is an adolescent, begins writing poems in an Emersonian vein, and ends up producing poetic allegories about the "soul of Israel"; Mary Antin (1881–1949) internalizes the language of Transcendentalism and ends up bearing witness to the ecstasies known *only* by pious Jews of the shtetl; Ludwig Lewisohn (1882–1955) joins the culture of literary dissenters in pre–World War I Greenwich Village, becomes a close associate of H. L. Mencken, Sinclair Lewis, and Theodore Dreiser, and goes on to become the most outspoken Zionist novelist America has ever produced; Waldo Frank (1889–1964) becomes a key figure in the revaluation of Walt Whitman in the 1910s and goes on to explore strategies for recreating Jewish mysticism in modernist literary forms; Anzia Yezierska (1885–1970) becomes an intimate friend of the iconic American philosopher John Dewey, and weaves the story of their relationship into a series of allegories for the rebirth of the prophetic Jew on the Lower East Side; I. J. Schwartz (1885–1971) translates Whitman into Yiddish and goes on to write *Kentucky* (1925), a Whitmanian epic in Yiddish about the adventures of a Jewish pioneer in the American wilderness; Alfred Kazin (1915–1998) writes *On Native Grounds* (1942), uncovering the rebellious impulse in modern American fiction, and then writes a series of autobiographies about growing up in Brownsville, culminating in a book unapologetically entitled *New York Jew* (1978); Irving Howe (1920–1991) explores strategies of historical representation in the regionalist writings of William Faulkner and Sherwood Anderson and then devotes himself to recovering Yiddish literature in English translation, providing a link for a generation of Jewish writers and readers to the pre-Holocaust Jewish past.[4] In each case, an encounter between a Jewish writer and American literary culture yields an occasion and a set of terms for redefining Jewishness.

That writers revise their precursors is nothing new in this third decade since the publication of Harold Bloom's *The Anxiety of Influence*. But
I am less interested in tracing a Bloomian struggle for the mantle of
"strong poet" than I am in exploring how a language for shaping Jewish
identity is crafted, won, or discovered in the course of an encounter with
American literary culture. I use the metaphor of "shaping" here to underscore the idea that identities are formed out of materials that already exist
and to suggest that the act of fashioning an identity is in many ways
analogous to the work of an artist.[5] While I follow Bloom's lead by closely
attending to the dynamics of revision and intertextuality, I do not abide by
his premise that literary creation must be viewed first and foremost in
terms of the individual's solitary battle against belatedness.[6] I am also
interested in what might be called the *effects* of literary production, the
ways literature provides new resources for imagining oneself and one's
relation to the world.[7] I understand the act of writing not—or not only—in
the Bloomian sense of confronting and battling the precursor, in order to
find one's voice, but also as a quest to refurbish a tradition, to summon the
voices of the past, and to sponsor ethical and political engagements.

In the chapters that follow, I offer a series of portraits of individual
writers whose careers may be charted in one way or another along an
arc of "return." I have chosen writers whose imaginations were initially
sparked by major currents in American literature, by movements such as
Transcendentalism, American modernism, and Southern regionalism. In
many cases, they went on to become some of the most vocal advocates of
American literature, writing critical works that shaped the terms in which
this literature has been read and understood.[8] In one way or another, all of
the writers in this study subsequently found their way to a heightened
form of Jewish identification, although the "Jewishness" they turned
to was uncertain and improvised and, in many cases, something they
had never known. These movements toward Jewish identification were
prompted in each case by a complex set of historical and personal developments. A recurrent theme of this study will be how a turn to Jewishness
has provided a perspective from which to respond to crisis—be it the
pogroms in Russia, the recrudescence of antisemitism in 1920s America,
the Holocaust, or the phenomenon of "deradicalization" in Cold War
America. Still, these writers remained, so to speak, within the orbit of
American literature. The Jewishness they constructed for themselves reveals traces of the vocabulary and conceptual structures of American literary culture. It also shows the contours of fantasies—both positive and
negative—that non-Jewish Americans had about Jews. In short, I forego
the quest for some normative and stable "Jewish sensibility" that can be

either expressed or repressed and explore instead how Jewish writers have drawn on multiple resources to project new models of identity. My hope is to move from the idea that Jewish writers have some inherent or given "Jewish experience" to express and toward the idea that a new version of Jewishness can be formed in dialogue with American literary culture, its vocabularies, conceptual categories, and implicit politics.

One of the reasons American literature has been a fruitful field for Jewish self-imagining is that this tradition has fostered a particular kind of oppositional idiom, rooted in the idea of the outsider as seer and cultural critic. As Sacvan Bercovitch has written, "American writers have tended to see themselves as outcasts and isolates, prophets crying in the wilderness."[9] For Jews in America, this role has often seemed like a natural position to inhabit. Not only does it resonate with their historical memory of oppression and ongoing sense of themselves as an embattled minority, but it also connects with the traditions of socialism and anarchism that are a central chapter in American Jewish history. Moreover, the idea of the inspired American isolate resonates with themes in the prophetic traditions of Judaism, which have continued to function as the Jew's cultural inheritance, even when faith and observance have been abandoned. After all, as Bercovitch and many others have shown, the stance of the American writer can be traced back to Puritan discourse and ultimately to the texts of the biblical prophets. By adopting a "prophetic" stance, then, the Jew becomes typically American while also coming back into contact, at least potentially, with sources that are indigenous to Judaism. Having encountered the idea of the prophetic outsider in its American guise, the Jewish writer can reclaim this figure as particularly *Jewish* and as a precedent for him or herself.

Every book about cultural history may be found guilty of highlighting only those writers or texts that are congenial to the book's overall thesis, and since this charge is no less imaginable here, I should hasten to note that this would have been a very different book indeed had I chosen to concentrate on another group of figures, which might have included names such as Gertrude Stein, Mike Gold, Lillian Hellman, Nathanael West, Muriel Rukeyser, Arthur Miller, J. D. Salinger, Norman Mailer, or Paul Auster. Each of these figures may be and has been called "Jewish" or "half-Jewish," in the case of Salinger, but, to my knowledge at least, none has evinced any particular inclination to "return" to Jewishness. A study focusing on these latter authors might have a great deal to say about the directions taken by *Jews* in American culture, but considerably less to say about the ways in which Judaism and Jewishness have been reimagined and reconfigured. What I look at, then, are figures who have engaged in some kind of sustained and *explicit* meditation on the meaning of being

Jewish. Considered together, these case studies reveal what might be imagined as a "potential energy" inherent within American literary culture that leads some writers to reclaim Jewish traditions at specific moments and in specific ways. Since the impulse to "return" to Jewishness is a pervasive phenomenon in modern Jewish culture in general, this study also suggests ways of linking Jewish American writers to the broader, international context of modern Jewish culture.

As for the fact that I group together writers associated with a wide variety of different genres (from poetry, to autobiography, to the novel, to criticism), I should say that at the back of my mind I have applied to each of these figures the Yiddish phrase *kultur tuer,* which might be translated as "intellectual" or "cultural doer" or, as I have thought of it, "culture maker." I like this phrase for the sense of agency it connotes. If combined with Clifford Geertz's famous definition of cultures as "webs of significance [that man] himself has spun," we gain a picture of Jewish writers actively engaged in the process of recreating the framework through which identity and the world itself is perceived.[10]

II

If these tales of reclamation have seldom figured prominently in earlier accounts of Jewish writing in America, it is because such accounts have more commonly emphasized movements *away* from Jewish distinctiveness. Let me briefly identify a few of these approaches and suggest how and why the one offered in this book differs. The first typifies works such as Robert Alter's *After the Tradition* (1968); Allen Guttmann's *The Jewish Writer in America: Assimilation and the Crisis of Identity* (1971); Leslie Fiedler's essays in *Fiedler on the Roof* (1991); and, more recently, Ruth Wisse's *The Modern Jewish Canon* (2001). In these studies the Jewish experience in America is generally charted as an inexorable process of cultural attenuation, and works of literature are consulted as evidence for this process. A given work of literature, that is, becomes a sort of barometer, measuring the level or extent of Jewishness within the larger Jewish community. For Fiedler, if Jewish American writers evoke the figure of Jesus, it is because the "deep psyches" of American Jews in general have been emptied of traditional Jewish mythology and theology, exposing them to "foreign" influences (not, as I will propose, because these writers are engaged in deliberate acts of repossession).[11] For Wisse, the story of modern Jewish literature begins with the Yiddish writer Sholem Aleichem and ends with Israeli writers like Yaakov Shabtai and Amos Oz. English-language writers in America are marginal to her canon, relegated to a cul-de-sac along a grand thoroughfare connecting Yiddish to modern Hebrew. If Jewish American literature deserves mention, it is because it supplies what Wisse calls "negative evidence of a community that has traduced its values and followed strange gods."[12] Wisse herself plays biblical prophet here, bemoaning a people who have strayed from the true path.

A second tendency draws on psychoanalytic models to explore how Jews have responded to the experience of being cast in the role of social and/or religious "Other." Here a common kind of analysis seeks to illuminate strategies for reducing or neutralizing the perception of Jewish difference in the eyes of non-Jews so as to ease the process of Jewish assimilation into white America. Sander Gilman's voluminous work is representative of this approach.[13] While he focuses on the German rather than the American situation, he offers "Jewish self-hatred" as a lurking, possible condition for all Jews in modern Western societies. Gilman then explains diverse kinds of Jewish creative productions—including both positive and negative portrayals of Jews—as reactions to being exposed to negative stereotypes: a negative portrayal mimetically reproduces what others are saying about Jews, and a positive portrayal is an effort to reconfigure or deflect some stereotype. A variant on this approach, which has been particularly influential in studies of race in America, is Michael Rogin's work on blackface performance, *Blackface, White Noise: Jewish Immigrants in the Hollywood Melting Pot* (1998). In Rogin's formulation, Jewish performers put on blackface as a way of symbolically "washing themselves white,"[14] of convincing their audiences (and perhaps themselves as well) that they belonged on the white side of the color line. From this perspective, Jewish popular culture, epitomized by the film *The Jazz Singer* (1927), functions pragmatically as a stratagem for easing Jews into whiteness. What Rogin and Gilman share is an underlying premise that the basic drama of Jewish life involves a desire to "make it" in the mainstream and to deny or deflect any interpretation of Jews that would pose a barrier. If Jews have been seen as not-quite-white or sickly or grotesque, it has fallen to the producers of Jewish culture to sanitize, purify, or "whiten" Jews.

Yet another approach can be seen in Werner Sollors' *Beyond Ethnicity: Consent and Descent in American Culture* (1986) and Walter Benn Michaels' *Our America: Nativism, Modernism, Pluralism* (1997)—both of them highly influential works in the study of American ethnicity. These studies offer what might be considered structuralist accounts of the formation of ethnic identity. Dispensing with the premise that the "margin" and the "center" really constitute distinct spheres, they seek to understand how these spheres are constructed through a common set of terms and in relation to one another. Michaels explores how the discourse of race stretches across works produced by "ethnic" and "nonethnic" writers. He also contends that the argument for cultural pluralism that emerged in the second and third decades of the twentieth century turns out to share the same structure as the exclusionary nativist argument.[15] Sollors argues that the selves constructed by autobiographies such as Mary Antin's *The Promised Land* (1912) and Ludwig Lewisohn's *Up Stream* (1922) are structurally analogous to what has become a normative version of *American* selfhood, namely that of the American ethnic self, balanced between old and new worlds.[16] Sollors reads evocations of ethnographic details, the translation of selected words from Yiddish, and the rejection (in the case of Lewisohn) of the standardized life of the masses as part of the warp and woof of *American* identity. In both cases, constructions of the Jew in Jewish American texts are seen as reflections of dominant symbolic structures and conceptions of selfhood. To lay claim to a form of Jewishness, for Sollors and Michaels, is to follow a reflex in the culture at large and to reproduce its own pervasive logic. They thus disavow the possibility that a voice constructed through "dominant" categories can meaningfully speak for or in the name of some antithetical set of values or aims (which, I might add, makes one wonder a bit about the status of their own critical discourse).

In response to the first of these groups (Wisse et al.), I tend to be more agnostic about what constitutes a genuinely "Jewish" text. To attempt to measure feats of the Jewish literary imagination using a yardstick that registers only "legitimate" forms of Jewishness seems to me to foreclose the enterprise of criticism from the start. My goal has been to allow the writers to define *Jewishness* in and on their own terms. Of course, the ideal of openness implied here is in some sense illusory, since what one will call Jewish will somehow stand in relation to a relatively fixed set of traditions. But there is still a significant difference between trolling about for legitimate and illegitimate forms of Jewishness on the one hand, and exploring ways in which Jewishness has been reconfigured, on the other. My response to the second and third approaches, similarly, is that they leave little room for the imaginative, inventive, intentional, and dialectical processes of cultural production. In response to the psychoanalytical framework, I would propose that other dynamics might be discerned in the history of Jewish culture than the drive to assimilate. And in response to the construction-of-ethnicity folks, I propose that a construction of Jewishness can have multiple effects—depending on the political and social context, depending on the constituencies to which a text is addressed, and depending finally on the idiosyncratic ultimate recipient of a text or performance: the reader. I am interested in glimpsing some of the unpredictable results that might arise when structures of meaning are combined and rearranged.

Also, when Sollors and Michaels endeavor to demystify ethnicity, they beg the question of the deeper motivations that lead individuals to speak on behalf of larger constituencies in the first place. The work of demystifying, in other words, tends to crowd out any possibility of agency.

To contextualize my own approach, I would point to a tendency that has emerged in Jewish studies over the past fifteen years or so to highlight the *productive* dimension of the interaction between Jewish and non-Jewish cultures. From this standpoint, the walls of the proverbial "ghetto" are always permeable; interaction and not insulation typifies the Jewish relation with the "outside world." An example of this premise in action is Amos Funkenstein's chapter on the interaction between medieval Jewish exegesis and Christian readings of the Bible in *Perceptions of Jewish History* (1993). Funkenstein discovers that Nachmanides is heavily influenced by medieval Christian typology, and that various concepts in his Torah commentary might be read as direct translations into Hebrew of Latin terms such as *typos* and *figura*.[17] As Funkenstein reads him, Nachmanides' hermeneutical approach conjoins Kabbalistic, neo-Platonic, and Christian typological elements. A similar method might be discerned in Ernest Rubinstein's study, *An Episode of Jewish Romanticism: Franz Rosenzweig's "The Star of Redemption"* (1999), which foregrounds the role played by German Romanticism, and particularly the aesthetic philosophy of Friedrich Schelling, in Rosenzweig's "New Thinking."[18] And finally, David Roskies's work on S. Ansky and the "paradigm of return" has proven most useful for my own work. Roskies traces Ansky's life as a three-part journey. Born into a traditional Jewish home in Vitebsk, he subsequently left home and became a passionate defender of the Russian folk, the *narod*, under the influence of Russian populist thought. He then returned to his own people, working as a collector of folklore and writing one of the signature works of modern Yiddish literature, *The Dybbuk*. Roskies interprets this third stage as a direct effect of the second: "the very culture that seduced him away provided him with a rationale for and a means of retrieval."[19] In all three examples, a non-Jewish cultural form—Christian typology, German Romanticism, Russian populism—has proven indispensable to the work of cultural renewal: "strange gods" have enabled the refashioning of Jewish culture. Indeed, one would be hard pressed to imagine any form of Jewish life or culture that did not enter into commerce, dialogue, and psychic battle with neighboring cultures.

What remains to be articulated is the occasion for this work itself, the scene of its writing, which might enable the reader better to grasp some of my own investments. Let me, then, intrude autobiographically and briefly locate the reader at a moment that will serve as the hypothetical point of origin for this project. A little more than ten years ago, I was living in San Francisco, my hometown, having taken time off from graduate studies in English literature at Columbia University. Any lingering desires to write the thesis on Joseph Conrad and Henry James I had been planning were quickly dissolving in the esprit of a city known more for championing the joys of self-expression than for fostering the rigors of scholarship. Yet it was here of all places, home of The Grateful Dead and the Merry Pranksters, where a Human Be-In had once attracted 20,000 people hoping for immediate nirvana, that I found myself irrepressibly drawn to practice Judaism, to study Yiddish, and to pore over the novels, poems, essays, and autobiographies of American Jews. I had found a tiny community of Jews to pray with in a renovated garage at the home of a Lubavitcher Hasid, recently arrived from Crown Heights. I studied Uriel Weinreich's *College Yiddish* in the Jewish library, which was well stocked but always eerily deserted. I discussed Irving Howe and Clement Greenberg with a transplanted New Yorker and emeritus historian from U.C. Berkeley named Samuel Haber. I also befriended an experimental performance poet, Alan Kaufman, who invited me to do a solo act I had worked out—a version of "Hava Nagila" played on a heavily distorted electric guitar—during the "Challapalooza Chanuka" celebration he organized at a local club called Slim's. In addition to all of this, I was working part-time for a tiny Jewish foundation, which meant that I was in regular contact with a number of progressive Jewish organizations ranging from Jews for Racial and Economic Justice in New York to the Shalom Center in Philadelphia to the Israel/Palestine Center for Research and Information in Jerusalem.

It wasn't exactly a "Jewish community" I had found, but something far more improvised, heterogeneous, and wayward than anything Moses Mendelssohn, Samson Raphael Hirsch, Theodor Herzl, Chaim Zhitlovsky, or any other theorist of modern Jewish identity could ever have imagined. And yet my variegated spheres of engagement were held together within the balance of a single, often mysterious impulse to draw upon and "root" myself (the metaphor is strained) in the cultures and traditions of the Jews. I was also aware that my engagements were part of a larger American tradition of self-fashioning, even as I was often brought to reconsider my own relationship to America, and to wonder in what sense I might still be counted as a member of a diaspora community.

What this study attempts, in sum, is to provide a genealogy for at least one version of Jewish American culture. In so doing it broaches larger questions about the relationship between ethnicity, religion, and literary culture in American life in general. The central object of my focus remains literary culture because, for one thing, my training and predilections have led me to search for innovation in verbal art, and, for another, as I hope to demonstrate in the chapters that follow, literature has been one of the chief sites of innovation in Jewish American culture. My principle of organization is chronological, both because chronology reveals the shaping role of history and because I understand criticism as analogous in many ways to storytelling, and stories are easiest to grasp chronologically. Nevertheless, I should reiterate that my broader agenda here involves rethinking the benefits of constructing a master narrative for Jewish American culture. Such narratives, as we have seen, move all too easily from some idea of a substantive Jewishness to assimilation, from street-front shuls to self-erasure. While the conditions under which literature is written change dramatically over time, many of the processes of reclamation and reformulation that I describe recur in successive generations. When one unhinges the work of literature from the master narratives commonly used to chart the "Jewish experience," what emerges is a considerably less deterministic field of cultural production.

PART 1

BREATHING FREE IN
THE NEW WORLD:
TRANSCENDENTALISM
AND THE JEWISH SOUL

No wonder, then, if these waters be so deep, that we hover over them with
a religious regard.

—Ralph Waldo Emerson, "The Poet"

A striking pattern emerges when we survey some of the representative
literary works of American Jews from the late nineteenth and early twentieth centuries: the men tend to be melancholic while the women are
exuberant. Consider the final chapter of Abraham Cahan's *The Rise of
David Levinsky* (1917), where the protagonist, having just narrated his rise
to financial success in the needle trade, comes to brood upon the psychic
losses he has incurred along the way. The price of his American success, it
turns out, is alienation from an inner self whose connections to the Old
World seem as ineradicable as they are inexpressible. Levinsky embodies
the American Jew as split subject, his fate underscoring the existential

implications of a widespread Yiddish proverb from the period, *Amerike iz a gonif* ("America is a thief"). He cannot help but look back in sadness at the pious lad he used to be, as we observe in the novel's final, haunting lines: "David, the poor lad swinging over a Talmud volume at the Preacher's Synagogue, seems to have more to do with my inner identity than David Levinsky, the well-known cloak manufacturer."[1]

Sholem Asch creates a similarly agonized character in his Yiddish-language novel *Onkel Mozes* (Uncle Moses), published serially in Cahan's *Jewish Daily Forward* in 1918. Here the immigrant-cum-tycoon is Moses Melnik, who lords it over a sweatshop filled with his former countrymen from his shtetl, Kusmin. At the lowest point of his moral decline, Moses causes a group of striking workers to be beaten in front of his shop—a scene that dramatically expresses the corrupting effects of the American marketplace. Like Cahan's novel, *Onkel Mozes* builds to a scene of agonized self-reflection. Gazing at the grave of his long-deceased first wife, Moses recognizes that "all his young life, his real life, lay buried there in his wife's grave. And there beside the grave was a vacant space—waiting for his body."[2] His "real life"—the life of his spirit—is already dead and gone. What we learn from these novels is that in America, there is no chance for resuscitation, repentance, or return. And even if this negative view of America is read as a critique of capitalism, an expression of these authors' abiding socialist attitudes, the tone of these final scenes is wistful rather than strident: the task at hand is that of mourning, not rebelling. From the standpoint of Levinsky's and Uncle Moses's Jewish souls, coming to the New World is like walking the plank.[3]

How different is it, then, to turn to the celebrations of the American experiment in the writings of Emma Lazarus and Mary Antin. As different as these writers are from each other—the first an affluent New York–born Sephardic Jew; the second a Yiddish-speaking immigrant from the Pale of Settlement—they share a positive vision of America as a place where the deepest longings and aspirations of Jews might be fulfilled at long last. In numerous poems and essays, Lazarus evokes a "soul of Israel" that can finally emerge from its protective shell and unveil its deep reserves of spiritual power. And in her famous autobiography *The Promised Land* (1912), Antin describes a "golden truth" at the core of Judaism that has survived as an "heirloom" from her past and that continues to feed her spirit in the present. Rather than representing Jewishness and American-ness as distinct and antagonistic spheres, these writers imagine Jewishness as a spiritual essence that has endured.[4] Where Cahan and Asch see a fracturing of the Jewish self in the New World, these women writers affirm underlying continuities with the past. Some vital Jewish core has remained intact, and, in different ways and different genres, they feel themselves called upon to bear witness to its power.

Thus if we are to observe the interaction between Jewishness and Americanness in its most *productive* form, we would do well to begin with these two founding mothers of Jewish American literature. By beginning here, we avoid the pitfall of reading the mournful-Jewish-man narrative as the normative literary mode for American Jews. To account for the role of gender here, we should note that when David Levinsky brings to mind his Jewish past, what he recalls is an image of himself "swaying over the Talmud"—Talmud study being one of the central practices of rabbinic culture, and traditionally reserved for men alone. Whereas Cahan uses a specific, embodied, and male-dominated ritual as a symbol for Judaism, Lazarus and Antin describe more "spiritualized" versions of Judaism, articulated through concepts such as the soul and the deep, private self. Such concepts, often associated in the Victorian imagination with femininity, reveal the powerful influence on their writing of Romanticism—specifically, as I will argue, its American offshoot, Transcendentalism. It may turn out, paradoxically, that Lazarus's and Antin's ability to imagine an enduring Judaism in the New World will depend on their *distance* from the institutions of rabbinic culture and on their access to a rhetoric of spirituality whose provenance is largely Romantic and Victorian.

In the following discussions, we will see how the motif of the Jewish "soul" emerges in Jewish American writing through a dynamic encounter with Transcendentalism. For a lineage of the body of ideas we are considering here, it is useful to recall Perry Miller's description of the New England Transcendentalists as "children of the Puritan past who, having been emancipated by Unitarianism from New England's original Calvinism, found a new religious expression in forms derived from romantic literature and from the philosophical idealism of Germany."[5] Lazarus and Antin are both children of the Jewish past who, having been emancipated by American political culture, find new ways to express their identities as Jews in forms derived from Transcendentalism. The central proposition of part 1, then, is that when Lazarus and Antin reread Judaism through the lens of American Romanticism, they offer ways of inhabiting Jewishness that any continued insistence on the centrality of rabbinic culture, narrowly defined, might ignore.

1

SONGS OF A SEMITE

Emma Lazarus and the Muse of History

> The Jewish Question which I plunged into so wrecklessly & impulsively
> last Spring has gradually absorbed more & more of my mind & heart—it
> opens up such enormous vistas in the Past & Future, & is so palpitatingly
> alive at the moment—being treated with more or less ability and elo-
> quence in almost every newspaper and periodical you pick up—that it
> has about driven out of my thought all other subjects—I have reached the
> point now where I *must* know Hebrew.
>
> —Emma Lazarus, Letter to Rose Hawthorne Lathrop, 1882

When Emma Lazarus wrote "The New Colossus" (1883), her famous homage to the "huddled masses yearning to breathe free,"[1] nobody thought of calling her a "Jewish American writer." That Lazarus herself might be called a Jew—or some other declension of the term that circulated at the time, such as "Israelite," "Hebrew," or "Semite"—was hardly in question. But the idea that American literature might contain a specifically Jewish subtradition, with a particular mode of address and a distinct set of concerns, had hardly been conceived in the America of 1883. While many of Lazarus's lyrics and narrative poems dealt explicitly with episodes from Jewish history, and even though the "wretched refuse" described in "The New Colossus" was clearly meant to include East European Jewish immigrants, the broader culture she inhabited did not possess a clear notion of what it could mean to be an American writer and a Jew at the same time.[2]

According to the nomenclature of her day, Lazarus would have been conceived primarily as a "poetess," a term that in late Victorian culture stood for refinement and sensitivity, as well as sentimentality.[3] It would not have been inconsistent with this role if the writer in question occasionally treated exotic themes—she might even be felt to possess some secret intimacy with darker, foreign peoples—but such themes would have been read as largely symbolic performances, the work of fancy rather than the expression of some deep, abiding loyalty. When in 1850 Elizabeth Barrett Browning gave her collection of love sonnets the title of *Sonnets from the Portuguese,* she was appealing to the notion of the poetess as conduit for the exotic, though nobody doubted that these were Browning's own creations or that their real connection to "the Portuguese" was tenuous at best. Though Lazarus was known to come from a Jewish family, her Jewish poems might have been read in a roughly similar way when they were first published. At times, indeed, Lazarus herself appeared to want to minimize the seriousness of her Jewish allegiances. When her volume of poems, including a verse drama on the martyrdom of a medieval Jewish community and assorted lyrics on Jewish themes, was published in 1881, she struck an apologetic tone in a letter to her friend Rose Hawthorne Lathrop (daughter of Nathaniel): "My little book of 'Semitic' poetry is at last out. . . . It is sombre & tragic, but I hope you will care for it a little for my sake."[4] The volume was entitled *Songs of a Semite,* a bold statement perhaps, but also one that suggests some ambiguity about Lazarus's self-positioning as author, especially in the context of late Victorian poetry, with its predilection for the dramatic monologue form. Were these to be read as dramatic monologues written by a refined poetess from the hypothetical perspective of "the Jew," or was Lazarus herself truly to be seen as the Semite in question and these poems as her true confession?

It seems clear at any rate, that Lazarus's poems on Jewish themes placed considerable pressure on prevailing ideas of authorship in nineteenth-century America. For even if the phrase *Songs of a Semite* may evoke Browning's *Sonnets from the Portuguese,* and even if Lazarus's self-effacing note to Lathrop suggests an impulse to distance herself from these works, the fact remains that in many of Lazarus's works the distinction between writer and Jew begins to collapse. In works such as the poetic cycle *By the Waters of Babylon,* as we will see, she explicitly thematizes the encounter between the modern American Jew and her ancient Jewish legacy. In retrospect, Lazarus heralds the beginning of what we can properly call Jewish American literature—especially if we mean by this a tradition of writers in America of Jewish descent who have grappled explicitly with the meaning of Jewishness.[5] A few generations later, when Karl Shapiro called his 1958 collection *Poems of a Jew,* he may not have been consciously echoing Lazarus's *Songs of a Semite,* but the similarity in title reveals the continuity of its theme—the continuity, more specifically, of the sense of Jewish self-assertion as a bold and possibly subversive act in and of itself. How did Lazarus come to write these poems? How did her "Semitic Songs" rearrange the terms of late nineteenth-century American literary discourse? And how did she position herself as an American Jew in relation to the "Semite" in her works?

An Emersonian Beginning

Lazarus was born in 1849 into a prosperous family with deep roots in America.[6] Her father's family were long-standing members of America's Sephardic elite; her mother's, the Nathans, were Ashkenazic in origin and similarly well-established in New York society (intermarriage between these groups was common throughout the nineteenth century).[7] Both the Lazaruses and the Nathans had been in America since before the revolution; and both were members of the oldest congregation in New York, the Spanish and Portuguese synagogue Shearith Israel. Her paternal grandfather served as synagogue president from 1846 to 1849 and had even co-edited the country's first English–Hebrew Sephardic prayer book. By the time of Lazarus's birth, however, her father had substantially distanced the family from organized Jewish life, devoting his energies to rising in an expanding antebellum economy. He achieved great prosperity as a sugar refiner—the summer house he built in Newport, Rhode Island, was only the most conspicuous sign of his success. As might befit such a family, Moses Lazarus had his daughters educated by private tutors who taught them foreign languages and introduced them to classical and European literature. It was only natural, given this background, that when Emma Lazarus began writing poems in her early adolescence, she emulated the great European tradition stretching from Petrarch through Alfred Lord Tennyson and the Brownings. Impressed with his daughter's talents (and eager, perhaps, to bolster his claims to social legitimacy), Moses Lazarus had a collection of his daughter's juvenilia printed for private circulation in 1867.

In an encounter that would set the course of her early career, the nineteen-year-old Lazarus met Ralph Waldo Emerson, who by the 1860s was the undisputed reigning dean of American letters.[8] During the period just after the Civil War, Emerson was wont to offer his services as literary mentor to aspiring young writers, including a number of women such as Helen Hunt Jackson and Louisa May Alcott. As Anne Boyd shows in *Writing for Immortality: Women and the Emergence of High Literary Culture in America* (2002), Emerson played a key role in enabling many women writers to imagine themselves as artists. His personal mentorship and support of iconoclastic self-expression were instrumental in the development of a new model of female authorship that emerged in the 1860s and 1870s.[9] So it was that when Lazarus followed up the meeting by sending him her poems, he responded with encouragement: "I observe that my poet gains in skill as the poems multiply," he wrote. "I should like to be appointed your professor, you being required to attend the whole term."[10] The avuncular tone here belies the seriousness with which he later read her work. Emerson became Lazarus's mentor, and, inspired by his example, she eagerly enlisted in his program for creating an indigenous and daringly original American literature.

In his letters to Lazarus, Emerson encourages her in terms that recall his signature essays and lectures. Echoing "The Poet," he calls her attention to a greater reality accessible to those who eschew ingrained habits of mind and conventional ways of seeing: "It is sufficient happiness to have the eye opened to the miracle of nature, & the ear to that music which reports it, & which we call poetry" (Rusk 6). The key Emersonian idea here is that of the *sufficiency* of individual consciousness: one's inherent resources require no outside supplement. To goad Lazarus onward in this heroic adventure of consciousness, Emerson lays out a reading curriculum, ranging from Thoreau to the Bhagavad Gita, along with the warning that undue obeisance to past achievements can weigh down the spirit. In response to Lazarus's long poem *Admetus,* Emerson urges her to leave behind motifs from classical literature altogether: "[T]hough you can throw yourself so heartily into the old world of Memory, the high success must ever be to penetrate unto & show the celestial element in the despised Present, & detect the deity that still challenges you under all the gross and vulgar masks" (Rusk 10). Such directives resonate with basic Emersonian doctrine, going back to "Nature" (1837), in which he abjures the building of the "sepulchres of the fathers" and calls for "a poetry and philosophy of insight and not of tradition."[11] History, tradition, and memory all posed a threat to the fundamental task facing all Americans and writers in particular. As he wrote in "Self-Reliance," "The centuries are conspirators against the sanity and authority of the Soul" (Whicher 157). The individual soul was capacious enough to supply the writer with all he or she needed, and nature, not history, was the proper source and target for one's meditations.

Whether Emerson had any awareness that Lazarus was a Jew or what he would have made of this fact are hardly clear. From Emerson's perspective in Concord in the 1860s, the reality of living Jews could hardly have been a matter of any great import. In any case, his prospectus for American culture looked to the creation of a new community of self-reliant individuals; questions of race or creed were irrelevant, at least in theory. It is clear, nevertheless, that insofar as Judaism has any explicit role in Emerson's writing, it is as a foil. When Emerson evokes "Hebraism" in his essays, it is as a limiting principle, as in *Representative Men* (1850), where he writes of the mystic Emanuel Swedenborg that "[h]is perception of nature is not human and universal, but is mystical and Hebraic. . . . The Hebraic muse, which taught the law of right and wrong to men, had an excess of influence for him" (Whicher 212). Anticipating Matthew Arnold's wariness of the moral rigors of Hebraism, Emerson links the "Hebraic" with a binding legalism; "mystical" stands here for dogmatism, an otherworldly focus that blinds one to the immanent splendor of nature.[12] In Emerson's paradigmatic essay "Self Reliance," the figure of the "Israelite" is evoked explicitly as a type of spiritual failure:

> [Followers of creeds] say with those foolish Israelites, "Let not God speak to us, lest we die. Speak thou, speak any man with us, and we will obey." Everywhere I am bereaved of meeting God in my brother, because he has shut his own temple doors, and recites fables merely of his brother's, or his brother's brother's God. (Whicher 163)

Unwilling to activate their own powers of perception, the "foolish Israelites" embody the antithesis of the self-reliant individuality Emerson hopes to foster. Emerson's Israelites recite the fables of others, as if to admit defeat before the challenge of heeding the genius within. The goal Emerson sets for the American of his day, then, is to reclaim precisely the kind of spiritual autonomy surrendered by the Israelites in the wilderness. The temple that once stood in Jerusalem must become a symbol for the temple within.

Emerson's effect on Lazarus at the time was evidently to buoy her up. She eagerly followed his directives and became his acolyte: "I have only been reading Thoreau's Concord River & Letters, & a poem or two of Walt Whitman," she wrote him in June of 1868. "But these writers are so in harmony with Nature that they do not take me away from the scene. I no longer wonder at your admiration of Thoreau . . . for he is now more alive to me than many who are living near me" (SP 312). She too will turn away from the past, from memory, and track her own responses to the world outside. An example of Lazarus's early poetry at its most Emersonian is *Epochs,* a long work that builds upon an epigraph drawn from Emerson's essay "Spiritual Laws": "The epochs of our life are not in the visible facts, but in the silent thought by the wayside as we walk." Lazarus fleshes out Emerson's appeal to interiority in a cycle of sixteen poems, each one devoted to a different internal state. She moves through moments of negativity (e.g., "Regret," "Longing," and "Grief") before arriving at "Patience" and ultimately "Peace." The final four lines of "Peace" envision a soul that has been released from all burdens:

> The mystic-winged and flickering butterfly,
> A human soul, that drifts at liberty,
> Ah! who can tell to what strange paradise,
> To what undreamed-of fields and lofty skies! (SP 49)

The bouncing iambic rhythm recalls the long tradition of English poetry, but the sentiment is Emersonian. Lazarus's cycle underscores the teleological vision of Emerson's "Spiritual Laws," referenced in her epigraph. She too imagines the soul as a vector driven by "spiritual laws" toward a future of boundless promise.

Here in her early works, then, Lazarus writes as a Transcendentalist—a singer of American heroism and a researcher of the unencumbered soul. Nor did she ever lose this early enthusiasm for Emerson and his prospectus for American culture. More than a decade later, after her turn toward Jewishness, she wrote in her essay "American Literature" (1881) that Emerson's essays were the seed-bed from which a distinctly American school had flowered. His influence had penetrated to "the very fiber of our best intellectual life," which she traced through Thoreau, Whitman, Bret Harte, and Harriet Beecher Stowe (SP 164). When Emerson died in 1882, Lazarus published a sonnet in his honor along with a long appreciation for *The Century Magazine,* citing his example as proof that a democratic society can foster moral and aesthetic refinement.[13] But even as Lazarus sustained her enthusiasm for Emerson, her subsequent engagements with Jewish history led her to complicate and transform the poetics of Transcendentalists. As she emended the Emersonian principles that she had absorbed as a young writer to make room for expressions of Jewish loyalty, Lazarus revealed the power of American Romanticism to unleash ambitious creative energies while also demonstrating that Jewishness might very well stand for a different set of priorities—and for a different vision of the past and present—than that which Emerson had proposed for all Americans.

The Theory of the "Two Jews"

Sometime around the mid-1870s, Lazarus began to shift her focus away from the adventures of her own soul, and, as if to countermand Emerson's instructions, borrowed increasingly from European culture. Among her numerous experiments, which included a novel based on an episode from Goethe's life and a cycle of poems inspired by the German Romantic composer Robert Schumann, she increasingly took themes from Jewish history and tradition—a direction she would sustain to the end of her life. Among these "Jewish" works were a parable adapted from the Talmud and transcribed into blank verse ("The Birth of Man"); a long narrative poem based on a fifteenth-century epistle from a loyal Jew to his former master, the latter of whom became a bishop after conversion ("An Epistle from Joshua ibn Vives of Allorqui"); a verse tragedy about the martyrdom of a group of Jews in the medieval town of Nordhausen (*The Dance to Death*); and a host of shorter poems about biblical themes or about the "Jewish soul" as it had sustained itself across the centuries. Beginning in the early 1880s, Lazarus also became deeply involved in philanthropic activity on behalf of the persecuted Jews of Russia, writing strident essays in the popular press decrying antisemitism and joining forces with a group of wealthy Jews in New York to form the Society for the Improvement and Colonization of East European Jewry. They hoped to resolve the crisis facing Russian Jews by purchasing land in Palestine for the purpose of their resettlement.[14]

Most accounts of Lazarus's "Jewish conversion" explain it as a response to the pogroms that swept through Russia in the early 1880s. But while the pogroms undoubtedly summoned her to speak publicly on Jewish issues and no doubt preoccupied her enormously, we must also understand how her representations of Jewishness drew upon ideas and images that prevailed in the America of her day. We might note that the idea that individual Jews can be brought back to their people by witnessing anti-Jewish violence has a long pedigree in myth and history—from the biblical account of Moses witnessing the beating of a Jew by his Egyptian taskmaster to accounts of Theodor Herzl's "conversion" after witnessing the public degradation of Alfred Dreyfus in 1895. And so, in Lazarus's case, commentators look to the pogroms in Russia to play this catalytic role.[15] Still, her new allegiances, not unlike Herzl's a few decades later (or, indeed, those of any Jewish writer who "returns"), were shaped within terms that already existed in the culture she inhabited. Indeed, Lazarus's increasing fascination with things Jewish must be seen in the context of her dialogue with American literary culture. Let us, then, move beyond the idea of some inchoate Jewishness that simply welled up when she learned of the attacks on Russian Jews, and inquire deeper into the ways she constructed her Jewish aesthetic out of prevailing images and ideas.

There are, to begin with, indications that Jews played a more complex symbolic role in the nineteenth-century American literary imagination than Emerson's easy dismissal of the Israelites would suggest. Even while symbolizing spiritual backwardness, Jews were also imagined as representing a direct link to the heroic biblical past—the very past that functioned symbolically as the paradigm for the settlement of America. The figure of the Jew could be seen, therefore, as at once a debased creature and a strangely evocative relic from the ancient past, a duality that we might call the theory of the "two Jews." This dual view comes across in an article Walt Whitman wrote in 1842 for the New York newspaper *Aurora,* "Doings at the Synagogue," in which he describes a chance visit he and his friends paid to the Crosby Street Synagogue in downtown Manhattan. As Whitman describes it, the scene was confounding in its strangeness: "the whole affair had much the aspect of an unintelligible mummery."[16] But, in spite of what he describes as the "uncouth jabber" and "fantastic garb" of the worshipers, Whitman could not divest himself of the thought that he was "amid the people of ancient Jewry; the people who kept themselves apart from the contagion of the world." The sounds of the jabbering modern Jew clash with this solemn image of "ancient Jewry," an image Whitman evokes with considerable respect. When William Dean Howells retraced Whitman's footsteps a half-century later, he similarly imagined that the Jews he encountered had stepped straight out of the Bible, "that old Hebrew world which had the sense if not the knowledge of God when all the rest of us lay sunk in heathen darkness."[17] Howells and Whitman both associate the Jews they encounter with a noble spiritual legacy, documented in the Bible. However uncouth and outlandish contemporary Jews may seem on the outside, these writers remain fascinated by the notion that modern Jews might retain an inner connection to the ancient Hebrews.

This complex reaction to contemporary Jews is also reflected in Henry Wadsworth Longfellow's famous poem "The Jewish Cemetery at Newport" (1858). Here the poet is startled by the prospect of a Jewish cemetery that stands out amid the vital natural world. (Note how the presentiment of Jews in America seems to *startle* these American poets):

How strange it seems! These Hebrews in their graves,
    Close by the street of this fair seaport town,
Silent beside the never-silent waves,
    At rest in all this moving up and down!

  .   .   .   .

Closed are the portals of their Synagogue,
    No Psalms of David now the silence break,
No Rabbi reads the ancient Decalogue
    In the grand dialect the Prophets spake.

Gone are the living, but the dead remain,
    And not neglected; for a hand unseen,
Scattering its bounty, like a summer rain,
    Still keeps their graves and their remembrance green.

How came they here? What burst of Christian hate,
    What persecution, merciless and blind,
Drove o'er the sea—that desert desolate—
    These Ishmaels and Hagars of mankind?[18]

What is "strange" to the poet is not that the Hebrews are dead but that they were so recently alive—and here in the "fair seaport town" of Newport.[19] The poet appears troubled by the disjuncture between these modern Jews and his idealized image of the ancient prophets, and yet the one seems inevitably to point back to the other. What makes the scene all the more arresting is the poet's sense that the Jews buried in Newport must have been fleeing a "burst of Christian hate." The graves of the Jews lead him to reflect on some kind of failure within Christianity. And though Longfellow might have conceivably written these Hebrews into the Puritan story of deliverance in the New World, seeing them also as pilgrims in search of freedom as Mary Antin will later do, his poem describes them as *eternal* outcasts, as "Ishmaels and Hagars." Longfellow cannot imagine the New World as a sanctuary for these Jews, whose foreignness is emphasized in the poem through their conflation with the mythological progenitors of the Arabs, the quintessential "Orientals" from the standpoint of mid-nineteenth-century America.[20]

Such texts by Whitman, Howells, and Longfellow show that a distinct spiritual power was associated with Jews in nineteenth-century America. They also suggest that the Jewish presence in the New World complicated the official mythos of American life. Modern-day Jews embodied a resistance to the "New Jerusalem" narrative, since they retained their sights, at least in theory, on the "Old Jerusalem." (None of these writers, nor their readers, would have realized that leaders of Reform Judaism, such as Isaac

Meyer Wise, were at this very instant dispensing with the traditional no-tion of Jews as an exilic people yearning for a return to Zion.) The idea of "ancient Jews" on American soil challenged the American claim to em-body the future hopes of humankind. And if Emerson called in "Nature" for a turning away from the "sepulchres of the fathers," Longfellow's poem hints at the challenges facing anyone who might engage in this project. At the very moment that Longfellow contemplates the "fair seaport town," he, for one, remains fixated on Jewish sepulchres in the center of Newport, suggesting just how difficult this avoidance of "the fathers" might be. Read in relation to Emerson's declaration of cultural independence from the fathers, Longfellow's poem seems to register something approaching pa-tricidal guilt, as if the slain progenitors of Christianity had returned to haunt the American poet precisely when he would enjoy his independence from the Old World (and his holiday in Newport). The point is that Jews are associated with an uncanny and lingering power ("the dead remain"), complicating Emerson's easy dismissals of the Israelite. Here is the Jew not as legalist nor as a type for spiritual weakness, but as a figure of uncanny persistence, connected to a noble past.

By the 1870s the presence of actual, living Jews became an increas-ingly conspicuous fact of American life. This was the period of the first significant demographic transformation in the American Jewish commu-nity, whose population swelled from 15,000 in 1840 to approximately 250,000 by 1880.[21] The new immigrants were largely poor merchants and tradesmen from German-speaking regions in central Europe, and their sudden presence established for the first time a class hierarchy within the American Jewish community. To understand how these newcomers were viewed by Jews and non-Jews alike, we must recall that this was also the heyday of the field of evolutionary biology. Recent studies by Matthew Frye Jacobson, Noel Ignatiev, Karen Brodkin, and Eric Goldstein have traced the effects of the popularization of racial science in nineteenth-century America. They show that the period of mass European immigra-tion, from the 1840s through the restrictive legislation of 1924, witnessed a reorganization of the social hierarchy in America, "a fracturing of white-ness" into multiple scientifically determined races.[22] Under the spell of racial thinking, Jews and non-Jews alike came to understand Jewishness as a racial as well as a religious category, though the precise relation between the two was seldom worked through in any systematic way.[23]

The difficulty in sorting out these differences can be observed in the language that circulated after a notorious incident in 1877, when the wealthy German-born Jewish banker Joseph Seligman was denied access to the Grand Union Hotel in Saratoga, New York.[24] The grounds for this rejection, as explained by the hotel owner, Judge Henry Hilton, were that "Christians did not like [Jews'] company and for that reason shunned the hotel." In elucidating his charge, Hilton distinguished between socially desirable Jews, whom he called "Hebrews," and a class of objectionable Jews, whom he called "Seligman Jews." As he explained in a front-page interview in the *New York Times*, "[H]ere is the Seligman Jew, who represents nothing that is standard Hebrew; he is to the Hebrew what the shyster is to the law profession—he is the 'Sheeney.' He has made money; he must advertise it in his person. He is of low origin and his instincts are all of the gutter."[25] Hilton's dichotomy reflects a more pronounced (and more derogatory) version of what we saw in Whitman's article and Longfellow's poem. Once again we find a complex interweaving of two versions of the Jew: as "standard Hebrew" (an admired figure), and as "Sheeney" (a debased figure). The acceptable "standard Hebrew" would presumably be closer to the noble religious heritage that Whitman and Longfellow reference in their writings, while the "Seligman Jew" is closer to the racialized and degraded figures in their discourse.

The endurance of these conflicting images suggests why Jews could not be relegated once and for all to the single category of Racial Other, a position that in any case was already taken by enslaved Africans and their descendants. Jews' ambiguous status was reinforced by their symbolic role in the national mythos as prototypes for America's original European settlers. The impulse to distinguish between two kinds of Jews may thus be seen to reflect distinct ideological needs in nineteenth-century American culture: to maintain a positive image of the biblical Israelite on the one hand, while demonizing the interloping and basely capitalistic "dirty Jew" on the other. Lazarus's family, given their deep roots in America, would have been ideal candidates for Hilton's category of the "Hebrew," but given the impossibility of disentangling these figures once and for all, the negative alternative must also have been hovering closely by.

The Faith of Fallen Jews

For someone like Lazarus, who considered herself a Jew but who had little connection to any traditional communal life, this ambiguous identity might have been a source of anxiety, and one might be tempted to read her through the theoretical lens offered by Sander Gilman's theories, namely as a writer concerned with dispelling and "purifying" negative images of Jews.[26] But I will instead suggest how the discourse of race seems also to have generated new kinds of allegiances and alignments. Indeed, Lazarus's response to the new discourse of race reflects what might be considered a *productive* function of racial thinking: the idea of race provides the grounds for her identification with East European Jews and by extension with a form of symbolic power linked back through time to the biblical past. Her connection to the Jews via race might have had advantages from her perspective since it meant that what Longfellow calls the "grand dialect the prophets spake" might be her rightful inheritance as well. At a moment when language, social class, and religious practice set clear boundaries between different kinds of Jews, the idea of race could generate a new basis for solidarity both with contemporary Jews and "ancient Hebrews."

This development was reinforced by Lazarus's discovery in the 1870s of German Jewish historiography, a field that offered new ways of conceptualizing the Jewish experience across time.[27] Especially significant was her study of Heinrich Graetz's multivolume *History of the Jews,* which she began reading under the tutelage of Gustav Gottheil, a newly arrived Reform rabbi from Posen. (Gottheil hoped to spark Lazarus's interest in Judaism so she might contribute to a new hymnal he was editing.) If history had become, in Yosef Hayim Yerushalmi's formulation, "the faith of fallen Jews," we might say that it was precisely this ersatz faith that galvanized Lazarus's imagination.[28] Referring to Graetz, a figure whose influence on modern Jewish culture can hardly be overemphasized, Lazarus later wrote that she was "firmly convinced . . . of the truth of the axiom that a study of Jewish history is all that is necessary to make a patriot of an intelligent Jew."[29] What made Graetz so serviceable for Lazarus was his construing of Judaism through the Romantic vocabulary with which she was already familiar. Following the theorists of the Science of Judaism, the *Wissenschaft des Judentums* movement, Graetz argued that Judaism could be reduced to a single idea, one that in Hegelian fashion is brought to "maturity" and revealed through the processes of history. "If we survey Judaism in its broad outlines," Graetz wrote in 1849, "and if we remove the husk from the grain—the productive ideas from the gross facts—we would come upon the original vital impulses that are implicit in the very idea of Judaism."[30] For Graetz, this idea of Judaism was first expressed as a protest against paganism: "It is precisely to negate [the idea of paganism] . . . that constitutes Judaism's predestined vocation: to show the paucity of truth in paganism and its harmful effects on social morality."[31] Jewish history from Graetz's perspective is a continuous battle between worldviews in which Judaism figures at once as endangered minority and as challenger.[32] The "outer life" of Judaism is a history of suffering at the hands of an intolerant majority (the pagan world slips into Christendom in his narrative), while the "inner history" is a history of scholarship, pious devotion, and the sheer refusal to capitulate. Such a dualism could be readily mapped onto the dichotomy between biblical Jew and hounded victim in the American imagination: what Graetz added was a sustained and impassioned analysis of how the originary "idea of Judaism"—which in the American context is associated solely with the biblical period—had continuously expressed itself across time.

The first works that Lazarus published in a Jewish periodical—a translation and two imitations of Heinrich Heine—reveal her newfound fascination with Jewish history. In 1823, two years before his conversion to Christianity and during a period of heightened antisemitism in Germany, Heine had conceived the idea for a three-part poem dealing with medieval antisemitism. He wrote the first section, "Donna Clara," but soon abandoned the project, having sketched out the unwritten poems in a letter to his friend Moses Moser. Lazarus translated "Donna Clara" into English and used Heine's letter to complete his trilogy for him, in essence "ghost-writing" Heine's unfinished work and entering modern Jewish literature via Heine's abandoned project. The story of this poem's composition is a powerful symbol, underscoring the very different possibilities for a Jew in nineteenth-century Germany and America. Whereas the German Jew converts to Christianity, hoping to gain his "entry ticket" into gentile society and abandoning his projected work on antisemitism, the American Jew completes the poem and launches a career as an unofficial public defender of the Jews.[33]

Heine's poem describes a midnight tryst in medieval Spain in which the world-weary daughter of an "Alcalde" meets her paramour, described simply as a "handsome knightly stranger" ("der *schoene unbekannte Ritter*"). In the moonlight, they exchange "fond endearments," interspersed with the young woman's gratuitous expressions of antisemitism: "I hate these gnats in summer / E'en as though they were a rabble / Of vile Jews with long, hooked noses" (SP 187). Summoned back to her castle, the Alcalde's daughter asks the knight for his "precious name," which he has so closely hidden. The knight lets out a "gentle laugh" and, while kissing her lips and forehead, declares in the poem's final lines, "I, Senora, your beloved, / Am the son of the respected / Worthy, erudite Grand Rabbi, / Israel of Saragossa" (SP 188).[34] The knight imitates the style of the noblewoman's aristocratic discourse in a declaration that makes her confront her worst fears: she has fallen for the dirty Jew who seemed a handsome knight. Heine symbolically exacts revenge on his own society by figuring the Jewish speaker as someone who flawlessly imitates the rules of Spanish decorum (as Heine and Lazarus strictly adhere to the rules of prosody), even despite being labeled as an unassimilable alien.

Heine's "Donna Clara" is a telling example of the kind of poem Graetz had in mind when he nominated Heine as the consummate *Jewish* poet of the nineteenth century. Graetz looks to Heine first and foremost as an opponent of Christendom, as somebody whose veins were "imbued with true Jewish spirit," in spite of his apostasy. Heine's renunciation of Judaism was not true apostasy, Graetz proposes, but rather like the covert acts of "combatants who, appropriating the enemy's uniform and colors, can all the more easily strike and annihilate him."[35] With his portrait of Heine as a combative Jewish poet, "hiding out" in the German language, Graetz anticipates contemporary theories that link minority writing to subversive forms of mimicry and underhanded critique.[36] Lazarus, too, seems drawn to Heine for his rebellious spirit, but, given her Emersonian background, his Jewish rebellion will have a metaphysical as well as a social import. When she adapts Heine's poetics for her own American Jewish project, the Jew will stand for not only a hated Other, as in "Donna Clara," but, as we will see, a figure imbued with prophetic vision.

After completing the remaining poems in Heine's trilogy, Lazarus wrote a series of poems that return to the medieval past to stage the conflict between Jew and Christian. In these poems, Lazarus evokes the Jew as a vulnerable figure whose suffering reveals the depths of Christian hypocrisy. An example is "Raschi in Prague" (1880), based on a legend holding that the renowned medieval exegete was put to death while visiting the Jewish community of Prague. Lazarus's Raschi becomes another eloquent Jewish hero and a tragic figure undone by an intolerant gentile world. Another example is "The Guardian of the Red Disk," a dramatic monologue from the point of view of an evil Christian citizen of Malta in 1300 who is celebrating the decree of the Fourth Lateran council of 1215 requiring Jews to wear identifying badges. The speaker's fears about Jewish contamination ("it sets my flesh a creep to think!" [SP 184]) recall and amplify the association of Jews with the uncanny that permeates Longfellow's poem on the Jewish cemetery ("the dead remain"). Lazarus's most fully developed treatment of Jewish history, and her most extensive work on a Jewish theme, is *The Dance to Death: A Historical Tragedy in Five Acts* (1882). A "closet drama" (meant to be read, not performed), the work deals with the annihilation of the Jewish community of Nordhausen for allegedly poisoning the drinking wells and causing the black plague. It is worthwhile briefly to trace its somewhat byzantine plot since this work clearly reveals how Lazarus weaves biblical images and motifs into an account of antisemitism and spiritual resistance. Seen as a response to the outbreak of the pogroms in Russia, Lazarus's tragedy might be read as a specifically American contribution to the tradition of modern Jewish literature of destruction, a tradition that includes works such as Hayyim Nachman Bialik's "The City of Slaughter."[37]

Lazarus's tragedy begins with the apparition of a prophetic blind man in the medieval town of Nordhausen; the man presents an urgent warning to the Jews: "Everywhere torture, smoking Synagogues, / Carnage and burning flesh. The light shines out / Of Jewish virtue, Jewish truth, to star / the sanguine field with an immortal blazon" (SP 117). Although an angel has revealed to him a mounting threat to the lives of local Jews, they refuse to heed the warning: "But truly we are blessed in Nordhausen / Such terrors seem remote as Egypt's plagues" (SP 114). As it turns out, the Christian establishment does resent the Jews, and a campaign against them takes shape, spearheaded by the Landgrave. In a sub-plot, an illicit affair develops between Prince William, son of the Landgrave, and Liebhaid, daughter of the town's most respected Jewish elder. Lazarus stages here a version of the Book of Esther: Liebhaid's father, Suesskind, blesses the union, encouraging his daughter to exploit her connections to calm the rage of the Landgrave, to "change his scorn / Of the Jew's daughter into pure affection" (SP 127). The Purim-story motif becomes explicit as the Prince recalls learning of a Purim celebration and of that "holy time's bright legend . . . of the queen, / Strong, beautiful, resolute, who denied her race / To save her race." He thus appeals to his beloved, "You are my Esther—but I, no second tyrant" (SP 128). The redemptive conclusion of the Book of Esther is preempted in this narrative, however, as the Landgrave's evil counselor, Schnetzen (a stand-in for Haman), convinces the Landgrave that his son has fallen for a Jewish plot and a specially brewed "love-elixir." The evocation of the Esther story ironically belies the town's Jews' insistence on the remoteness of the biblical world and its hardships: the historical persecution of Jews has continued, but this time without the saving intervention of God.

Just as the Jews' tragic fate is being sealed, Suesskind reveals before a city hall assembly that his alleged daughter, Liebhaid, is no Jewess at all, but the daughter of Schnetzen, the Haman-figure. Suesskind explains that she was saved from a fire when she was a few days old. As the Jews are preparing to be executed, Suesskind urges Liebhaid to acknowledge her Christian birth, marry the prince, and avoid a fate that is not properly her own. Here the Book of Esther subtext transforms into that of the Book of Ruth. Liebhaid responds to her adoptive father: "If I be offspring to that kite / I here deny my race, forsake my father . . . Thy God is mine, / Thy people are my people" (SP 163–164). These lines echo Ruth's speech to her mother-in-law: "Whither thou goest, I shall go . . ." (Ruth 1:16). Where Liebhaid had been preparing to operate as the Jew in the alien Christian camp, she now embraces her role as the born-Christian in the Jewish camp. In the play's dramatic final scene, the Jews (along with Liebhaid) are led into a giant fire, where they accept their martyrdom by dancing in the flames. In a stirring final speech, the Jewish elder, Suesskind, announces that in time their deaths will be avenged. The "lamp" of Jewish truth will be preserved in times to come for the "Jew-priest, Jew-poet, Jew-singer, or Jew-saint" of the future (SP 169). With this speech, Lazarus hints at the function of her own work, which constitutes a response to the injustices suffered by Jews throughout history and at her historical moment as well. She is herself the "Jew-poet" her protagonist prophecies. In "The New Colossus" the image of the lamp will return as the symbol of American freedom ("I lift my lamp beside the Golden door"); here we see it as a specifically Jewish inheritance and Lazarus herself, implicitly, as its bearer in the present.

Lazarus's *The Dance to Death* must be seen in the context of her increasingly prominent role as a public Jew at the height of the pogroms. Indeed, she envisioned the publication of *The Dance to Death* as itself a public act: in a letter to *The American Hebrew* accompanying the play's manuscript, she writes that "it would be highly desirable to publish [the play] now, in order to emphasize the cruelty of the injustice done to our unhappy people."[38] It is illuminating that on the one occasion that Lazarus chose a pen name for herself—when she entered an essay contest sponsored by the Y.M.H.A. in 1884—she invented the name "Esther Sarazal."[39] With the writing of *The Dance to Death,* then, Lazarus has developed a conception of Jewish art as public intervention: Lazarus becomes herself an "Esther" who, like the figure of Liebhand in the play, moves into the gentile world as a loyal Jewish emissary.

The Prophetic Voice

The vision of Jewish history in *The Dance to Death* reflects what Salo Baron has described as the "lachrymose" view of Jewish history typical of German Jewish historiography, namely the view of Jewish history until the Enlightenment as an unremitting tale of humiliations and woe.[40] But, as we have seen, Lazarus also emphasizes that the "lamp" of truth has been passed down through Jewish history, with her own poems providing a new form for its expression. In her works from the mid-1880s onward, Lazarus moves from the Heine-esque ironic mode and from the tragic form of *The Dance to Death* to poems that imagine a spiritual rebirth in contemporary America. The record of violence against Jews has continued to pile up, with the outbreak of the pogroms signifying but the latest in a long, lachrymose history, but in America a new dispensation has dawned. And from the standpoint of America, Lazarus sees herself called, elected, to proclaim a new rising of the Jew.

An example of Lazarus's prophetic mode is "The New Ezekiel," a short poem constructed as a series of questions followed by a series of bold assertions. Like Whitman's article on the Crosby Street Synagogue, the poem begins by expressing wonder at the gulf dividing a debased modern Jewry from their ancient heritage: "Is this the House of Israel, whose pride / Is as a tale that's told, an ancient song? / Are these ignoble relics all that live / Of Psalmist, Priest, and Prophet?" (SP 232). Rather than simply marveling at this gulf, however, Lazarus imagines an ongoing connection to the biblical past, linking the present to an originary revelation. Evoking Ezekiel's vision of the valley of dry bones, she heralds a rebirth of the Jewish spirit, coupled with a return of prophecy to Israel: "The spirit is not dead, proclaim the word / Where lay dead bones, a host of armed men stand! / I ope your graves, my people, saith the Lord / And I shall place you living in your land" (SP 232). The poem's conceit is that God has delivered this message to the poet, who becomes a modern-day Ezekiel beholding a vision of Jewish spiritual rebirth, presumably in their ancestral homeland. Themes such as Israel's abominations and of God's punishments, which are central to the discourse of biblical prophecy, are absent. Instead, the figure of Ezekiel provides an image for the Jewish American poet who has suddenly gained access to the powers of vision and speech. Instructively, Lazarus's evocation of Ezekiel echoes and recasts the opening paragraph of Emerson's "Nature," when he asks rhetorically, "Why should we grope among the dry bones of the past?" (Whicher 23). But whereas Emerson calls upon his readers to turn away from the "dry bones of the past" and enjoy an "original relation to the universe," Lazarus imagines a *repetition* in the present of the very same miracle that Ezekiel witnesses. For the modern Jewish poet, inspiration comes not from turning away from the past, but from reimagining oneself as the inheritor of its power.

In the last work to be published in her lifetime, Lazarus constructs an extended allegory for her assumption of the role of Jewish poet–prophet. *By the Waters of Babylon: Little Poems in Prose* is a cycle of seven poems that projects a view of Jewish history from the expulsion from Spain in 1492 to the pogroms of 1881, to the arrival of masses of Jewish immigrants in America, and finally to the appearance of the Jewish poet in the New World. With these "little poems in prose," divided into numbered passages, she moves away from her more familiar Victorian forms toward an idiom that recalls the King James Bible. These poems are coded as specifically "Jewish" through this evocation of biblical discourse.[41] The language of the Jewish imagination, Lazarus implies, is the language of the Bible (even if hers is a version of biblical discourse linked to the quintessential Protestant translation).

The first poem, "The Exodus," recalls the expulsion from Spain through the template of the biblical Exodus narrative. A bedraggled collection of Jews flees Spain as a hostile local villager "sets on their trail his yelping cur." Just as Lazarus's "despairing exiles" are leaving Spain, the "world-unveiling Genoese" (SP 242–243), Columbus, is also departing for the New World, heralding the future protection of Jewish exiles in the New World.[42] But the image of the Jew as homeless victim is gradually displaced by the image of "Israel" as a heroic principle of endurance. In the second section, "Treasures," the poet directly addresses "Israel," imagined as an entity containing a diamond buried beneath a "coal-black prison."

> 3. Buried in the bowels of earth, rugged and obscure, lies the ingot of gold.
> 4. Long hast thou been buried, O Israel, in the bowels of earth; long hast thou slumbered beneath the overwhelming waves; long hast thou slept in the rayless house of darkness.
> 5. Rejoice and sing, for only thus couldst thou rightly guard the golden knowledge, Truth, the delicate pearl and the adamantine jewel of the Law. (SP 243)

Lazarus's point that the truth of Judaism must be excavated from the "bowels of the earth" reflects the theory of the "two Jews" we have already seen as a prevalent feature in the nineteenth-century American imagination. Here she uses the image of the earth to represent the external, "natural" circumstances of Jewish life, the circumstances that create the debased or racialized Jew. The true Israel—the "Hebrew" or biblical Jew we have seen—remains inchoate, "slumbering." The "jewel of the Law" has been concealed beneath this exterior.

Coupled with this drama of Jewish perseverance, the poem also develops a narrative showing the poet's own coming to awareness. In the fourth section, "The Test," the poet shifts perspective from the migrating Jews to an "I" who belongs to the American present. She calls to mind a parade of noble Jewish types, "a Prophet with four eyes"; "a Poet, who plucked from his bosom the quivering heart"; and "a placid-browed Sage" (SP 245). Her "test" comes when she is confronted by the contemporary descendant of such noble figures: "I beheld the shuffling gait, the ignominious features, the sordid mask of the son of the Ghetto" (SP 245). Can the contemporary poet detect signs of a noble heritage beneath this exterior? Eventually this question gets formulated as a challenge to the reader: "But thou—hast thou faith in the fortune of Israel?" (SP 246). As if to goad the reader onward, the final poem in Lazarus's cycle offers a series of instructions:

> 12. Thou shalt say to the bigot, "My Brother," and to the creature of darkness, "My Friend."

13. And thy heart shall spend itself in fountains of love upon the ignorant, the coarse, and the abject.

14. Then in the obscurity thou shalt hear a rush of wings, thine eyes shall be bitten with a pungent smoke.

15. And close against thy quivering lips shall be pressed the live coal wherewith the Seraphim brand the Prophets. (SP 246–247)

Once again the seemingly debased East European Jew (a figure who seems always to be male) turns out to possess concealed powers, uniquely accessible to the Jewish poet of today. When the addressee of the poem embraces this figure ("Thou shalt say to the bigot, 'My Brother'"), she is suddenly released into the plenitude of speech, a transformation evoked through the scene of Isaiah's theophany, when his lips are purified by a piece of coal.[43] The image from Isaiah works to overcome the division between the grotesque East European Jew and the empathetic American Jew. After all, Isaiah is branded by the Seraphim because *he* feels himself to be impure and dirty. This would suggest an association between Eastern and American Jew, both of whom stand in need of purification. Finally, Lazarus's sequence dramatizes a dual transformation: the American Jew redeems the Eastern Jew by recognizing his inner treasure, and the Eastern Jew redeems the American Jew by reconnecting her to the Jewish past. When the American Jew identifies with the East European Jew, she comes into contact with a deeper spiritual reality ("in the obscurity thou shalt hear a rush of wings")—which is also figured as an encounter with the substratum of her own being.

"By the Waters of Babylon" thus stages Lazarus's return to the Jewish fold, as modern poet and as witness to the endurance of the Jewish soul through history. By invoking in her title the image of the psalmist weeping in Babylon, Lazarus aligns the Jewish American writer with other Jewish singers in exile. Her indebtedness to Emerson is still palpable, but with a crucial, *Jewish* difference. In Emerson's letters to Lazarus, he called upon her to reject inherited ways of seeing and to "detect the deity that still challenges you under all the gross and vulgar masks." Emerson's entire project might be summarized as an effort to name and affirm this "deity," which he sometimes called the "over-soul" and sometimes simply "the self." When Lazarus responded to this Emersonian challenge, she discovered a trope for spiritual power in "Israel," an image for a collectivity that had preserved its truth during the long nightmare of history. Lazarus retains Emerson's faith in the continuing availability of inspiration, while asserting that the source and origin of this inspiration is in history as much, if not more, than in nature.

During the last years of her life, Lazarus dedicated herself to the study of Hebrew, a logical extension of her efforts to craft a "biblical" Jewish poetics. Over the next years, she became sufficiently proficient in Hebrew to translate directly from the original. Just before she died, she completed a translation of a short lyric by al-Harizi entitled "Consolation," which was published in *The American Hebrew*:

> Oh, were my streaming tears to flow,
> According to my grievous woe,
> Then foot of man in all his quest,
> On no dry spot of earth could rest.
> But not to Noah's flood alone,
> The covenant's bright pledge was shown,
> For likewise to my tears and woe,
> Behold once more revealed—the Bow![44]

This brief work attests to a sustaining faith amid exile. Without faith in the covenant, the poet would be in such distress that he would set loose a flood of tears comparable to Noah's flood. The final lines, where Noah's vision of the rainbow is evoked as an answer to the poet's tears, contain an ambiguity in the original. Al-Harizi's text reads: *Ki gam lidmai niratah ha-keshet* (literally: "For also to my tears appeared the rainbow"). This could mean either that the poet has actually *seen* a rainbow or, what is more likely, that he takes consolation from the memory of Noah's having seen it. By rendering the line as a visionary experience in the present ("Behold once more revealed—the Bow!"), Lazarus suggests that the covenant reproduces itself in every generation, as visionary experience. As in her own poems, Lazarus's translation retains Emerson's faith in the continuing availability of inspiration, while also asserting that the source and origin of this inspiration is the old covenant between God and Israel or, indeed, the faith in the covenant expressed by a medieval Hebrew poet.

Lazarus's turn to Hebrew translation and her efforts to sing on behalf of Jewish faith and endurance suggests, finally, that her muse resides neither on Parnassus nor on Sinai, but within Jewish history itself. It is in Jewish history, in the eloquence and piety of historical figures from Rashi to al-Harizi and revealed in collective acts of martyrdom and devotion, that Lazarus discovers a plenitude of meaning and a power that for Emerson exists solely in the present and in nature. Lazarus's turn to Hebrew translation and her efforts to craft a "prophetic" poetics in English express her own version of piety and her conviction that it was possible to resituate herself within the continuity of Jewish history and to speak on behalf of its further unfolding.

On a final note, we might consider that American literature contains something of a precedent for Lazarus's portrayal of the Jew in the character of Hester Prynne, who occupies an analogous symbolic position in Hawthorne's Puritan community in *The Scarlet Letter* as the Jews in the medieval village of Lazarus's *The Dance of Death*. Numerous parallels link Lazarus's medieval Jews with Hester Prynne: both have been condemned for crimes against the Christian order; both are feared as figures of corruption and have been relegated to the margins of established society; both are specifically referred to as "oriental" (recall Hawthorne's description of Prynne as possessing "in her nature a rich, voluptuous, Oriental characteristic,—a taste for the gorgeously beautiful");[45] and both come to possess a heightened insight into the inner lives of their Christian neighbors. Lazarus seems directly to recall Hawthorne's text when she describes the Jews' badge in "The Guardian of the Red Disk" as a "*scarlet* stamp of separateness, of shame" (emphasis added), and when in "Raschi in Prague" she again evokes the badge as a "brand of scarlet degradation." The point here is that the American literary tradition seems already to have marked a space for the heretic/pariah. When Lazarus writes her Jewish figures into this space, she calls forth the range of implications already present in Hawthorne's text. What is most suggestive about this parallel is that Prynne is of course not merely a figure for the shunned outcast; she also embodies the principles of liberation and rehabilitation in Hawthorne's text. Particularly in her speeches to Dimmesdale in the forest, where she exhorts him to "begin all anew!" Prynne represents the voice of the New World in its most antinomian guise: "The world's law was no law for her mind" (267). By the concluding chapter of *The Scarlet Letter,* Hester has become a quasi-prophetic figure, advising those who approach her in need that "a new truth would be revealed" (241). Lazarus's Jewish figures will also be associated with prophetic insight, though their "new truth" is figured as an endurance and revival of an "old truth." Lazarus, the American prophet as Jew, does not finally consign herself to the wilderness, where she might sing a song without precedent. Rather she positions herself within the mainstream of history, as the recipient of an ancient heritage whose truth is unchanging.

2

ECSTASIES OF THE CREDULOUS

Mary Antin and the Spirit of the Shtetl

Prophets, messiahs, miracle workers might have their day, still the Jew was conscious that between him and God no go-between was needed; that he, as well as every one of his million brothers had a portion of God's work to do.

—Mary Antin, *The Promised Land*

In 1898, eleven years after Lazarus's death, a firsthand account appeared in the New York weekly *The American Hebrew* by a sixteen-year-old girl named Mary Antin, in which she described her experiences as an immigrant en route to America. The text, later published in book form under the title *From Plotzk to Boston,* originated as a long letter Antin wrote at the age of eleven, in Yiddish, to her uncle back home.[1] It had been rendered into English and adapted for publication with the help of Boston's most prominent Reform rabbi, Solomon Schindler—a radical social reformer and leading advocate for new immigrants.[2] But even as more acculturated Jews had a hand in shaping the young Antin's language, it was evident that the weight of authority within Jewish American discourse around immigration had begun to shift from the well-established Jewish communities gazing upon the newcomers to the immigrants themselves. Published in the same periodical in which Emma Lazarus's Jewish poems had appeared a little over a decade earlier, Antin's account offered readers a chance to test Lazarus's hypothesis about the spiritual fortitude of those shtetl Jews who were suddenly clamoring at the gates of the New World. Here was the voice of one of the "huddled masses" herself, representing her own experience and uncovering details about Jewish life in the Old World that American-born Jews had only imagined (or read about in the writings of Heinrich Graetz). In short, here was the immigrant Jew not merely as symbol of the Old World, nor as object of charity, but as writer. What Antin presented in *From Plotzk to Boston* and later in her celebrated autobiography, *The Promised Land* (1912),[3] was not only evidence of the courage and tenacity of the immigrants, but also of their fervent patriotism and an almost uncanny ability to internalize and project the mythos of American life only a few years after arriving on American shores.

The most common view of Antin during her lifetime and ever since has been as the paradigmatic exponent of the idea of the melting pot. It seems fitting in retrospect that Israel Zangwill, author of *The Melting Pot* (1908), should have written the introduction to *From Plotzk to Boston*, where he prophesied that Antin would "add to those spiritual and intellectual forces of which bighearted American Judaism stands sorely in need."[4] For Zangwill, Antin was exemplary in her efforts to throw off the negative influences of her past and embrace the blessings of American freedom. Even more telling is the praise Antin received from Theodore Roosevelt, whose "new nationalism" included a categorical rejection of the idea that a true American could have a "hyphenated identity." For Roosevelt, Antin was a veritable poster child for Americanism, so much so that he begged permission to print her photograph in the autobiography he was planning. "You are an American in whom I so deeply believe," he wrote her in 1913, "that I should be sorry if I could not include your photograph."[5] During this same period, Antin was attacked on what are essentially the same grounds by the most prominent critics of melting-pot ideology. In influential essays that gave strength to the movement for "cultural pluralism," Horace Kallen and Randolph Bourne both evoke Antin as an example of the wrong kind of Americanization. Kallen writes in "Democracy Versus the Melting Pot" (1915) that "[Antin's] 'Americanization' appears too much like an achievement, a *tour de force*, too little like a growth."[6]

And Bourne asserts in "Trans-National America" (1916) that Antin "forgets that when [our foreign-born came] it was not aboard other Mayflowers, but upon a 'Maiblume,' a 'Fleur de Mai,' a 'Fior di Maggio,' a 'Majblomst.'"[7] For these champions of cultural diversity, Antin's name became a by-word for the "forgetting" of one's cultural past, which was seen as a capitulation to homogenizing forces.[8]

The past decade has witnessed, however, a renewed interest among literary scholars and historians looking for insights into the experience of immigration. In a key article, Michael P. Kramer has proposed to reclaim *The Promised Land* for Jewish American literary history by seeing in its assimilation narrative a representative American Jewish fantasy and one that turns out to involve a much more complex renegotiation of identity than the term *assimilation* generally allows.[9] Others have sought to identify and describe evidence of lingering Jewish loyalties in Antin's work in spite of her much vaunted Americanism.[10] On the basis of a close reading of Antin's correspondence, for example, Evelyn Salz reveals an Antin who was deeply engaged with the Jewish cultural politics of her day and who herself became an advocate of Zionism after attending the 1914 Conference of American Zionists.[11] In what follows, I will argue that the emphatically American identity Antin created for herself still left room for a "spiritualized" Judaism, which continued to play a central role in her imagination. Given that she grew up in the shtetl, her initial exposure to things Jewish was entirely different than Emma Lazarus's, and yet, having honed her literary powers after coming to the United States, Antin drew on many of the same literary influences as Lazarus and often described Judaism in terms that recall Lazarus's Jewish Transcendentalism. This Jewish dimension of Antin's literary project emerges most clearly when her famous autobiography is read alongside her works of fiction, two of which return to the world of shtetl. These short works, which point toward a larger literary project that never reached fruition, represent an early and specifically American entry in the genre of "shtetl fiction," a genre that has roots in the Jewish Enlightenment, the Haskalah, and has figured centrally in modern Jewish culture ever since.

Antin and the American Jewish Awakening

When Antin fashioned herself as the mouthpiece of the striving immigrant, her adopted country was becoming embroiled in an increasingly fractious debate around the question of immigration. As historian John Higham has shown, what began in the 1890s as an essentially populist reaction against immigrants in a time of economic depression was transformed in the decade from 1905 to 1915 into a systematic ideology, engineered by patrician nativists and bolstered by pseudo-scientific theories of racial difference.[12] This was a period of heightened discrimination against African Americans, increased fear of the "Yellow Peril," and increasingly pervasive antisemitism. Though it would be a few years before the nativist agenda would gain sizable political victories, proponents of immigration were already under significant pressure. When Antin's autobiographical work *The Promised Land* was published in 1912, then, it carried the burden of defending Jews against charges that, as racial others, they were unassimilable into American life. In defiance of nativist suspicions, Antin offered her own life as proof not only that Jewish immigrants "yearn to breathe free" but that, given half an opportunity to do so, they will become exemplary citizens. Such a message harmonized exceptionally well with the pronouncements of Theodore Roosevelt's Progressive Party, which was formed in the same year *The Promised Land* was published. According to the party's platform, one of its central goals was the "assimilation, education, and advancement" of new immigrants. When Antin gained national prominence, she became an advocate of the Progressive Party, celebrating its position on immigration as a necessary antidote to rising nativism. Given her claims to have transcended her past, Antin was in many ways an ideal spokesperson for a party that announced itself as "unburdened by tradition."[13]

But while, as many have noted, Antin was clearly making a direct political intervention with her book, we might also situate *The Promised Land* in the broader context of the history of American Judaism. Here we should bear in mind that Antin was prompted to write *The Promised Land* neither by Israel Zangwill nor Theodore Roosevelt, but by her close friend Josephine Lazarus, sister of Emma, and a prominent Jewish essayist in her own right. When *The Promised Land* was published in 1912, two years after Josephine Lazarus's death, it bore a dedication that read: "To the Memory of Josephine Lazarus Who lives in the fulfillment of her prophecies." So devoted was Antin to this Lazarus that she named her only daughter Josephine. What would it mean to read Antin's autobiography not merely as pro-immigrant propaganda but as a fulfillment of Josephine Lazarus's "prophecies"?

Josephine Lazarus's career may be linked with a development that Jonathan Sarna has termed "the late nineteenth-century American Jewish Awakening." Sarna argues that beginning in the late 1870s, a new ethos began to emerge in American Judaism, reflected by "a return to religion, a heightened sense of Jewish peoplehood and particularism, new opportunities and responsibilities for women, a renewed community-wide emphasis on education and culture, a burst of organizational energy, and, in time, the growth of two new movements in American Jewish life: Conservative Judaism and Zionism."[14] In this context and in the years following her famous sister's death in 1887, Josephine Lazarus became a prominent public figure.[15] Her books *Mystery, Prophecy, Service, Freedom* (1890) and *The Spirit of Judaism* (1895) advocated for a renovation of Judaism to meet the needs of the present. Invited to participate at the World's Parliament of Religions in Chicago in 1893, she gave a speech in which she described the cultural moment as one in which a new mandate for religion had arisen. "Out of the heart of our materialistic civilization has come the cry of the spirit hungering for its food. . . . What the world needs today . . . is a new spirit put into life, which will re-fashion it upon a nobler plan."[16] Liberal Christianity was answering these spiritual needs for its constituents, and now Judaism had to follow suit. Her proposal was a form of Judaism that would bring Jews directly in touch with what she called "the inward living voice, the heaven-sent message" (SJ 23). The trope of an "inward voice" recalls the Quakers' "still small voice," but her suggestion that Jews are bearers of a "message" resonates more with the idea taken from the Prophets, and emphasized by nineteenth-century Reform Judaism, of Israel as a "light unto the nations." Lazarus seeks to affirm interiority and revelation at one and the same time.

The core teaching of Judaism, according to Josephine Lazarus, was embodied in the figure of the prophet who establishes contact with divine truth. In statements such as the following we hear strong echoes of her sister's work:

> Above the inert mass, the dull crowd of Pharisees and Scribes dwelling within the lifeless body of the Law, have arisen the divinely gifted men, the prophets and seers of the world, who saw God and spoke face to face with Him. From Abraham to St. Paul they were men who threw off the idolatries and superstitions of the times, the bondage of the letter and proclaimed the inner, not the outer, law,—the spirit, not the form. (SJ 23)

Reiterating a common trope from Reform theology, Lazarus claims the "inner law" as the central teaching of the true Judaism. When Paul rejected the letter, then, he was truly enacting the ideals of a tradition stretching all the way back to Abraham.[17] But while this may sound like a mere case of Jewish apologetics and an erasure of any kind of Jewish particularity, Lazarus maintains elsewhere that Jews still possess a particular message to deliver to the world *as Jews*. If Christianity bore witness to the necessity of love, Judaism understood the necessity of duty and moral action, and since humanity depended on both, Jews had to recover the wellspring of their own faith for the sake of all.

Josephine Lazarus met the young Mary Antin in Boston in 1899 while preparing to write a review of Antin's first book, *From Plotzk to Boston*. At their very first meeting, Lazarus encouraged Antin to keep a journal, and over the next decade, she became a mentor to Antin, introducing her to important literature, including the essays of Emerson, and repeatedly encouraging Antin to write her autobiography. "For twelve years," Antin later recalled, "from the time she first knew me until her death, she was always reminding me of this thing she wanted done."[18] For someone like Antin, raised in a traditional East European family, Lazarus's notion that Jewish piety meant, above all, adherence to the "inner voice" must have seemed quite novel indeed. And yet, Antin came to see her own Jewishness through Lazarus's categories. "I see Miss Lazarus frequently," Antin wrote a friend in 1905. "She has a wonderful consciousness of race, and she makes me feel that my Jewish descent is something that I must bear about consciously—something that I must account for every day that I live. She stirs me in many ways" (Salz 41). Seeing herself through Lazarus's eyes, Antin came to understand that as somebody raised in the Pale and yet fully conversant in American culture she was in a position to give a firsthand account of a powerful religious tradition, based on the direct apprehension of the divine. The relationship between Josephine Lazarus and Mary Antin suggests that when Antin came to write her autobiography, she was not only addressing debates around immigration; she was also demonstrating that Lazarus's fantasies of her were true, that her Jewish descent had equipped her with a capacious soul.

Conversion Stories

In its opening sentences, *The Promised Land* heralds a story of conversion or, more specifically, rebirth: "I was born, I have lived, and I have been made over. Is it not time to write my life's story? I am just as much out of the way as if I were dead, for I am absolutely other than the person whose story I have to tell" (PL 1). Her ostensible purpose will be to explain how a girl named Mashke from the Pale of Settlement became "Mary Antin," American citizen, writer of polished English, and ardent patriot. Like many conversion stories, from Augustine's *Confessions* to the spiritual autobiographies of the early Puritans, Antin locates agency in an external force. The oddly passive construction in the phrase "I have been made over" positions the nation itself as the prime agent in her transformation. Antin's "rebirth" hinges, it would seem, on the acquisition of *citizenship*, which, much more than any mere legal category, confers a new existential status on the Jew: "I was a Fellow Citizen, and George Washington was another," she writes. "It thrilled me to realize what sudden greatness had fallen on me; and at the same time it sobered me as with a sense of responsibility. I strove to conduct myself as befitted a Fellow Citizen" (PL 177). Her new address, new language, and new name, which now carried the dignified title of a surname, all reflect the pleasures of possessing equal status before the civic law.

Within the symbolic framework of Antin's book, if America stands for the new law, Judaism would stand for the "old law"—a relic from the Old World with no purpose in the New. Her repeated evocations of Jewish practice as a species of "medievalism" confirms this view. "I began life," she says in her introduction, "in the Middle Ages, as I shall prove, and here I am, your contemporary in the twentieth century" (PL 3). In her overview of shtetl life that begins the narrative, she describes rabbinic Judaism as an irrational, bewildering set of rituals and beliefs held in place by the "mountainous volumes of the Talmudists and commentators" and the "mazes of the Cabala" (PL 33–34). Simple laws such as the prohibition to work on the Sabbath day had been "construed by zealous commentators to mean much more" (PL 103). These excesses are reflected in institutions dominating shtetl life, like her brother's heder, where she used to go to bring him food. The heder is portrayed as a dismal place where the rabbi used a ruler for "striking the bad boys on the knuckles, and in a corner of the room leaned a long birch wand for pupils who would not learn their lessons" (PL 29).[19] She is particularly critical of the exclusion of women from the sphere of Jewish learning: "It was not much to be a girl, you see. Girls could not be scholars and rabbonim" (PL 29). Judaism is thus figured along the lines of what Kant—in a very different context—described as heteronomy, a condition of being determined by "other" laws, anathema to one's inner being. Gender divisions come to epitomize this oppressive, arbitrary system. Liberation from the Old World will also mean liberation from the straitjacket of gender norms.

To tell the story of her liberation from this condition, Antin employs a rhetorical strategy common in Puritan discourse, namely the use of scenes or "types" from the Bible to chart her own experiences in the New World. Thus she casts immigration to the New World as a new version of the Israelites' escape from bondage in Egypt with America playing the role of the land of milk and honey. Moreover, particular scenes from the first half of Antin's text are replayed and, as it were, fulfilled in the second half, as though the two halves of the book are themselves reflections of "old" and "new" dispensations (e.g., in the first half she is excluded from her brother's Hebrew school, and in the second half she herself flourishes in her school in Chelsea; in the first half she describes the Russian flags she was forced to display, and in the second she praises the "red, white, and blue"). These tacit evocations of Christian salvation history become explicit in her second book, *They Who Knock at Our Gates: A Complete Gospel of Immigration* (1914). Here Antin vigorously promotes an open-door immigration policy, arguing that all immigrants are (as she herself is) capable of contributing productively to their new nation. Once again, her rhetoric is patently biblical:

> We in America are in a position to hasten the climax of the drama of unification. . . . Once the thunders of God were heard on Mount Sinai, and a certain people heard, and the blackness of idolatry was lifted from the world. Again the voice of God, the Father, shook the air above Bunker Hill, and the grip of despotism was loosened from the throat of panting humanity.[20]

Bunker Hill stands metonymically for the American Revolution and figuratively completes the process of human salvation begun at Sinai. This time it is not just the Israelites, a "certain people," who receive God's voice, but all of "panting humanity." Antin recasts Sinai and, by extension, Judaism itself as an earlier stage in a universal redemption narrative, a "drama of unification." By moving from the revelation for the "chosen few" to the revelation for all, Antin rehearses the familiar Pauline reading of Judaism, with the difference that Bunker Hill has come to replace Calvary as the site of fulfillment. Hence Antin's work is a "Gospel of Immigration": its "good news" is that the kingdom of heaven is nigh, with the American body politic taking the place of the body of Christ as the agent of salvation.

Thus we seem to have traced a conversion narrative that hinges on the acquisition of American citizenship. Antin's story reads like a Puritan spiritual autobiography; the difference, however, is that in place of Christ, the nation itself serves as the agent of redemption. Embedded within this account, though, are the makings of a second story of transformation, one that focuses less on America as a regenerative force than it does on a wholly individualistic process that Antin calls "self-birth." Within the terms of this second account, no external force or agent is responsible for the young Jew's transformation. There is no need for the intercession or "grace" of America, since her inner resources are sufficient to enable her development.

The Promised Land is filled with scenes in which the young Antin gains sudden insight into the heart of things, seeing past the constructs of her time and place. In the opening passage of the book, she describes a trip to Vitebsk where she discovers that the Dvina River she knew from Polotsk flowed there as well. The river teaches her that "[t]he boundary between Polotzk and the rest of the world was not, as I had supposed, a physical barrier" (PL 6). By observing nature, she learns that Polotsk is one point along a grand continuum. In the chapter "The Tree of Knowledge," Antin recalls an "impious" experiment she undertook one Sabbath afternoon. While the rest of her family was napping, Antin endeavored to test God by carrying a handkerchief outside her house, beyond the boundary permitted for carrying on Sabbath. Amazingly, God seemed to find nothing objectionable in the young Antin's transgression: "An age passed in blank expectancy. Nothing happened!" (PL 101). Once again, the focus is on boundaries monitored by human beings—in this case the constructs of Judaism—that turn out to be permeable, at least for the adventurous spiritual seeker. The point is that Antin's "impious experiments" are meant to stand for a deeper sort of piety, an impulse to know God directly.

Another key passage comes from the chapter "I Remember," in which Antin conjures memories of her native Polotsk. While taking a stroll through the countryside one day in early spring, she experienced a sudden, mystical transport:

> In the long black furrows yet unsown a peasant pushed his plow. . . .
> Suddenly he began to sing, a rude plowman's song. Only the melody
> reached me, but the meaning sprang up in my heart to fit it—a song of
> the earth and the hopes of the earth. I sat a long time listening, looking,
> tense with attention. I felt myself discovering things. Something in me
> grasped for life, and lay still. I was but a little body, and Life Universal
> had suddenly burst upon me. . . . For the space of a wild heartbeat *I knew,*
> and then I was again a simple child, looking to my earthly senses for life.
> But the sky had stretched for me, the earth had expanded; a greater life
> had dawned in me. (PL 71; italics in original)

This passage testifies to a wholly private experience of awakening to spiritual knowledge: for the space of a wild heartbeat, Antin and *Antin alone* discovered things. Seen in relation to broader currents in American religious writing, the scene recalls a number of narratives that hinge on similar scenes of spiritual awakening. Indeed what we have here might be considered a type scene common to American spiritual autobiography: a testimony of an experience of divine unity in the presence of nature. Jonathan Edwards' account of his early life contains a nearly identical scene. While walking "abroad alone, in a solitary place in my father's pasture," Edwards suddenly discovers the glory of God as an immediate presence. "As I was walking there, and looking up on the sky and clouds, there came into my mind so sweet a sense of the glorious majesty and grace of God, that I know not how to express. . . . God's excellency, his wisdom, his purity and love, seemed to appear in every thing; in the sun, moon, and stars."[21] Emerson records a similar experience in "Nature" where sudden awareness overcomes him while crossing "a bare common": "the currents of the Universal Being circulate through me; I am part and particle of God" (Whicher 24). We are also reminded of the fifth section of Whitman's "Song of Myself," where the speaker wanders into a "clear summer morning" and experiences a mystical oneness with all things: "Swiftly arose and spread around me the peace and knowledge that pass all the argument of the earth."[22] What Antin performs here, then, is an act of self-inscription into an American tradition of personal testimony; and the spiritual sensibility she describes is itself a version of the "gnostic" sensibility that Harold Bloom calls "the American religion."[23]

But what is surprising about these passages is that they refer to moments *before* Antin ever set foot in America. Citizenship, America, and George Washington are all far in the future and seem beside the point. Looking back on the moment listening to the plowman's song, Antin determines that it was there, in the landscape of Polotsk, and not in her classroom in Boston, that she became aware of "universal truth." Are we witnessing, then, an awakening that occurs under the auspices of American society or a development within the framework of East European Jewish life itself? One response would be to say that Antin was specially marked out to become a "spiritual American," even when surrounded by the "thick" Judaism of Polotsk. But this notion itself puts pressure on her claim about having been "made over" by America. What we begin to see is a cleavage between the idea of American citizenship as the key to salvation and a spiritual sensibility linked to the tradition identified most centrally with Emerson. If a premise of the "American religion" that Antin embraces is that individual consciousness is sufficient for the experience of God—indeed that God can *only* be known by confronting nature in solitude—then Antin's celebration of American civic institutions comes to seem less important than her affirmations of her own inner resources. The Progressivist Antin, who looked to *institutions,* is decidedly different from the Transcendentalist Antin who looks to *intuition* as a transformative force.

But while Antin's text seems to belong to the tradition of American spiritual autobiography, she herself suggests that her spiritual sensibility is in fact a legacy from her Jewish past. There are numerous moments in Antin's text when she discovers a precedent for her spiritual sensibility in her Jewish forebears. In the second chapter, "Children of the Law," she offers a portrait of her great-grandfather Israel Kimanyer, a Hasid whose piety was apparently famous throughout the region. "Israel was poor to the verge of beggary," she writes, "but he prayed more than other people . . . and sat up nights to commune with God" (PL 33). When Antin elaborates on her great-grandfather's piety, she describes a sort of Transcendentalism avant la lettre:

> Stripped of its grotesque mask of forms, rites, and mediaeval superstitions, the religion of these fanatics was simply the belief that God was, had been, and ever would be, and that they, the children of Jacob, were His chosen messengers to carry His Law to all the nations. . . . Out of the mazes of the Cabala *the pure doctrine of ancient Judaism* found its way to the hearts of the faithful. Sects and schools might rise and fall, deafening the ears of the simple with the clamor of their disputes, still the Jew, retiring within his own soul, heard the voice of the God of Abraham. Prophets, messiahs, miracle workers might have their day, still the Jew was conscious that between himself and God no go-between was needed. (PL 33–34; emphasis added)

The language of this passage recalls Josephine Lazarus's theological writings, with their emphasis on Abraham's original contact with God and their invention of a Judaism based on the "inward voice; the heaven-sent message." In Antin's text, similarly, the "true" Judaism is not some arbitrary set of laws, threatening to rob the individual of her autonomy, but rather an inspiring metaphysical doctrine, stressing the individual's ability to gain access to God. Traditional Jews hear the "voice of God" in the depths of their souls; no "go-between" is needed. Institutions, conventions, and even rituals all become secondary to the underlying relationship between the individual Jew and God. This is, then, the "pure doctrine of ancient Judaism" that is expressed in her great-grandfather's idealism and which is Antin's inheritance as a Jew born in Polotsk. Referring precisely to her great-grandfather's "pure" faith, she writes, "[t]his is the living seed which I found among my heirlooms, when I learned how to strip from them the prickly husk in which they were passed down to me" (PL 35). The organic metaphors of seed and husk suggest that Antin's capacity to respond with wonder and piety to the world around her is a product of her lineage, a kind of "natural" Judaism passed down through the generations.

These positive views of Judaism shift our perception of Antin from the image of a convert to Americanism to that of a modern Jew suddenly aware of a spiritual core beneath the accretions of rabbinic Judaism. Indeed, her descriptions of East European Judaism often recall the discourse of Jewish reformers, from the *maskilim* (advocates for secular education), to champions of Reform Judaism, to early Zionists. Like such figures, Antin criticizes the forms of East European Jewish life but exculpates Jews themselves on the grounds of historical exigency. If Jews have turned inward with ever greater fervor, it is because they have been "trained by the cruel centuries of [their] outcast existence" (PL 211). Their elaborate rituals are a response to oppression, a "fortress" built by prisoners of the Pale "in defiance of their jailers" (PL 26). This explanation hardly redeems the rituals and trappings of rabbinic Judaism, of course, which, one presumes, would be readily dispensed with by any Jew given a chance to breathe freely. But neither does it mean that Jews in America will or should cease being Jews. Antin demonstrates this by pointing to her mother, whom she holds up as an exemplary modern Jew. Having undergone what Antin calls a "process of emancipation," her mother conforms outwardly to the standards set for her by gentile America, but on the High Holidays, "her soul is stirred as of old, and she needs must join in the ancient service." Antin interprets this as an indication that her mother has "dropped the husk and retained the kernel of Judaism" (PL 192). This is, as it were, Antin's own formulation of J. L. Gordon's famous ideal, the de facto anthem of the Haskalah: "to be a Jew at home and a man in the street." To read Antin thus as a *maskil* in the American context is to see in her reformulation of Judaism an example of broader developments in modern Jewish culture, specifically the effort to make sense of Judaism in the face of the unprecedented freedoms (and conflicts) of modernity. It also shows where she parts company with Emerson and Whitman: as much as she describes her apprehension of "Life Universal" as a private experience, she also associates it with "ancient Judaism," a tradition handed down through time. This is a version of the "American religion" that still leaves room for collective memory.

Fiction and the Recreation of the Shtetl

But as much as Antin seems eager to endorse this spiritualized version of Judaism, she also seems unsure at times about whether the "kernel" of Judaism *can* be so easily separated from the specific traditions of East European Jewish life. The intense nostalgia that arises within *The Promised Land* suggests an abiding sense that something crucial may indeed be lost in steerage. At times, the text gets overwhelmed by a nostalgia so forceful that it threatens to overwhelm the forward movement of the coming-of-age narrative, as if Mary were inclined to remain Mashke. When Antin describes experiences involving scents or foods, *The Promised Land* virtually bristles with yearning for Polotsk: "I can dream away a half-hour on the immortal flavor of those thick cheese cakes we used to have on Saturday night" (PL 74). Elsewhere, she recalls the joy of the yearly festivals: "Passover was beautiful with shining new things all through the house; *Purim* was gay with feasting and presents and the jolly mummers; *Succoth* was a poem lived in a green arbor" (PL 61). In the passage about her Hasidic great-grandfather, she describes with astonishment a little cabin that his friends built for him: "That little cabin was fit to be preserved as the monument to a species of idealism that has *rarely been known outside the Pale*" (PL 33; emphasis added). For Antin, the sheer power to believe exhibited by her great-grandfather survives as a singular triumph in human history. Such a view challenges the notion that Judaism might flourish in America separated from the specific conditions and arrangements of shtetl life. A gap seems to open up between her goal of reaffirming a "purified" Judaism in America and her impulse to celebrate the uniqueness of the spirit of the shtetl, epitomized by her great-grandfather's faith and piety.

It is within the space of this gap, I would suggest, that there emerges a mandate for Antin's fiction. During the same years that she was working on *The Promised Land*, Antin published three short stories in the *Atlantic Monthly*, two of which return the reader to the traditional community of Polotsk. Antin is not commonly discussed as a fiction writer, but I would propose that she came to see the writing of fiction as a forum for paying homage to the spiritual life of the shtetl, without necessarily endorsing its manifold rules and regulations. Fiction afforded her an opportunity to recreate the *experience* of Old World faith, precisely when her patriotism and her politics pulled her to deny its hold on her. In turning back to the shtetl in her fiction, Antin reveals another similarity she shares with the East European *maskilic* tradition. As in the early stories of S. Y. Abramovitsh, the "*zayde*" or grandfather of Yiddish literature, Antin also writes texts that present a complex mixture of critique and celebration.[24]

Antin's "Malinke's Atonement" (1911) tells the story of an impoverished family in Polotsk who come into possession of a hen, a rare luxury for the Sabbath table and a cause for rejoicing. Just as they are reveling in their future culinary pleasures, a metal wire is discovered in the bird's intestine, indicating that it may not be kosher. The young daughter, Malinke, is sent to the rabbi, who promptly informs her that, no, the hen may not be eaten. Malinke, a "bold" child known for rushing through her prayers, weighs her options on her way home: "[Her] thoughts climbed from the plaintive to the curious, from the curious to the rebellious, from the rebellious to the defiant."[25] She resolves to lie to her mother for the sake of their repast, assuring herself that only she will suffer the consequences should God become angry. To this point, the narrative resembles moments in *The Promised Land* when the young Mashke willfully defies the strictures of Jewish Law, as in the scene where she carries a handkerchief across the permitted boundary on the Sabbath. But whereas in *The Promised Land* these scenes offer proof of the writer's freedom from superstition, here the point seems just the reverse: Malinke violently chokes on a bone during dinner, which she interprets as a sure sign that her sin has called down the wrath of God. In an effort to atone for her sin, she sacrifices her most prized possession—patent leather shoes she uses only on Sabbath—by casting them into the river, after the style of the New Year's ritual of *tashlich*. If her sin has been a willful displacement of God's will by her own, she must repent by relinquishing the symbol of her vanity.

Unlike *The Promised Land*, then, where the river symbolizes the unity of nature, in "Malinke's Atonement" it is charged with ritual significance, a place for the cleansing of sin. The problem facing this protagonist is not how to shrug off arbitrary influences (as in *The Promised Land*), but how to atone and return to God. And, as it turns out, for Malinke, the act of doing penance will have immediate results. When the rabbi learns of Malinke's exertions, he has pity on her, explains that his decision was made in haste, and that the chicken may be eaten. He then takes her on as his first female student, revealing that in fiction, at least, the culture of the shtetl is capable of reforming itself. The story ends with Malinke reflecting on divine forbearance: "She who had sinned the most was the most blessed of all little girls in Polotzk. The Lord had accepted her atonement" (MA 319). This affirmation of God's powers, of course, is framed as the naïve understanding of a child. Readers are expected to recognize this as an instance of dramatic irony: we know that the rabbi's sympathy, and not any sort divine force, has intervened. Malinke's restored faith in God is reserved for her alone, with her readers left to imagine and admire it.

A nearly identical narrative strategy is employed in "The Amulet" (1913). A childless couple is in despair over their chances of being fruitful and multiplying. The husband, Yankel, procures an amulet crafted by the mystical Rebbe of Kadino, which he gives his wife, Sorke, confident that it will cure her barrenness. An editorial interjection assures the reader that amulets and such are, of course, but the "parasite superstition which had overgrown the noble tree of the faith of the Ghetto";[26] and yet, in the course of the story, Sorke manages to get pregnant, to her immense delight. When Yankel seeks out the old woman who gave him the amulet to thank her, she remembers that the amulet carries a warning: if twins are born, one will die; if it is a girl, the mother will die; but if it is a boy, all will go smoothly. Her advice is simple: "You must have faith, Master Jew."

Yankel redoubles his acts of piety and worship, chanting Psalms with the abandon of one possessed. Finally, in the very last words of the story, Sorke delivers a boy and survives. From the perspective of the modern American reader of the story, the birth of the son may appear to be sheer coincidence; but from the perspective of Yankel within the story, it represents a confirmation of his faith. As an effect of dramatic irony, Yankel gains a renewed confidence in God, while the reader is invited to marvel at his idealism.

"The Amulet" makes explicit at one point an idea that surfaces in both of these stories, namely that "there is a form of ecstasy that only the credulous can know" (A 36). The text can point to this "ecstasy" and even try to recreate it through Antin's suspenseful plotting, but finally the implied reader is not enjoined to embrace the literal views of "the credulous." We no longer believe in amulets, Antin realizes, but she offers a vicarious form of faith to readers who are willing momentarily to suspend their disbelief. This is fiction as thought experiment, a transitory inhabiting of alien premises (both conceptual and geographical). Antin's stories construct the shtetl as a counterworld to the American present, and through the resources of narrative art—dramatic irony, in particular—this world is animated and sustained. In her fiction, Mary remains Mashke (or, at least Malinke); God forgives her for denying Him; and an amulet works its magic for a childless couple. In the face of a tradition she could neither wholly endorse nor wholly reject, Antin turns to fiction to distill and preserve its essence.

By reading Antin's fiction alongside *The Promised Land*, we recognize the divergent roles played by different genres in Antin's writing: if her autobiography proposes that the spirit of the shtetl can be readily adapted to the American present, her short stories bear witness to the singularity of East European Judaism. They suggest that the most potent expressions of faith may belong on the other side of the Atlantic. These stories thus point to something more broadly about the role of literature in modern Jewish culture. If fiction permits a temporary suspension of disbelief, it might provide a vicarious experience of Jewish faith, even when the traditional expressions of that faith seem outmoded.

To conclude, and to revisit the role of gender here, we might read Emma Lazarus and Mary Antin in light of what Paula Hyman calls the "paradoxes of assimilation" in nineteenth-century Jewish life.[27] Hyman contends that as Jews became more assimilated into Western societies, absorbing the behavior patterns and gender norms of middle-class gentile life, Jewish women tended to become *more* identified with things religious, while men seemed readier to relinquish any ties to Judaism that might hinder their success in the public sphere. Under the terms of the prevailing bourgeois model of female domesticity (the "cult of domesticity"), religion fell within the women's domain since it "drew upon emotion to disseminate morality and fortify social order" (25). The Jewish woman was called upon to become what Reform rabbi Emil Hirsch, writing in 1895, described as a "Priestess of the Jewish ideal, Prophetess of Purity and Refinement."[28] From this perspective, it makes sense that a figure such as Lazarus or even Antin, once she became more Americanized, might feel empowered to speak on behalf of Judaism, and it also makes sense that their rhetoric would trade in concepts such as *purification*. But Hyman's insistence on reading this development under the sign of assimilation obscures the dynamic potential offered by this new role. When Lazarus takes over the role of "prophetess," it will not merely be in the guise of the "angel in the house" that Hirsch describes, but as a visionary literary artist who sets a new agenda for Jewish culture in America. And when Antin sets out to affirm the prophetic ideal set up by Josephine Lazarus, she finds herself returning in her imagination to Polotsk, recapturing in fiction the *experience* of Old World Judaism. In both cases, the "spirituality" of the Jewish woman expresses itself not in prostrations to the "cult of domesticity" but in the writing of literature.

And as much as their work is inspired and informed by ideas taken directly from Transcendentalism, Lazarus and Antin also come to distance themselves from some of its tenets, particularly from the radical dismissal of history we see in Emerson. Lazarus and Antin both turn back to Jewish history to find images for idealism, perseverance, and courage. What both Emma Lazarus and Mary Antin show, then, is the particular tenacity of fantasies of the Old World in modern American Jewish culture. Even as they celebrate their freedom from rabbinic law and from centuries of persecution, they invoke images from the Jewish past as metaphors and tropes for spiritual power. Their impulse to turn toward this past suggests a critique of the antinomian strain in Emersonian Transcendentalism and, more broadly, of American individualism itself. A Jewish Transcendentalism, as constructed by their writing, keeps alive not only faith in the individual's access to divinity, but also an understanding of the present as an outgrowth of the past. It is the burden of this kind of Jewish American writer to attempt to capture—in forms and in a language utterly alien to the Jewish past—its quintessential gestures.

PART 2

BATTLING THE NATIVISTS: MYSTICS, PROPHETS, AND REBELS IN INTERWAR AMERICA

Jewish thought has always been crisis thought.
—Waldo Frank, from *Bridgehead: The Drama of Israel,* 1957

The history of American Jews from World War I through the 1920s is riven by two contrasting motifs: an increased movement into the middle classes and a pervasive new sense of unease. On the one hand, the children and grandchildren of immigrants were moving away from the congested streets where their "greenhorn" forebears had once lived; they were entering white-collar professions from law to pharmacy to social work; and they were beginning overall to enjoy the entitlements that went along with being "American." But at the same time, a new mood of reaction had overtaken the country, and the welcome extended to Jews and other "Others" was offset by increasingly visible signs of xenophobia. As one foreign visitor observed in 1927: "The essential characteristic of the post-war period in the United States is the nervous reaction of the original American stock against an insidious subjugation by foreign blood. . . . They have a vague, uneasy fear of being overwhelmed from within."[1] The most notorious expression of such fears was found in Henry Ford's *Dearborn Independent*, which printed countless "revelations" of Jewish conspiracies to take over the world, as well as a 1920 collection entitled *The International Jew: The World's Foremost Problem*. Such fears fed the rising campaign against European immigration, which culminated in the passing of the Johnson-Reed Act, known also as the National Origins Immigration Act of 1924. Under the terms of this legislation, the annual total number of new immigrants from each country could not exceed 2 percent of its contribution to the 1890 population of the United States.[2] This quota effectively set an end to the period of mass migration of Jews from Eastern Europe. Even as Jews were making it in America, the image of the Jew as a potentially subversive un-American had been ratified by congressional decree.[3]

In this reactionary political climate, new imperatives arose for Jewish writers in America. In the work of Ludwig Lewisohn, Waldo Frank, and Anzia Yezierska in particular, a new discourse began to take shape in which America figures as a land of *broken promises* and the Jew symbolizes a voice of critique and moral conscience. The figure of the Jew functions variously in their work as hounded victim, rebel, or sage (and sometimes all three simultaneously). Also, and most interesting for us, these writers often connect the figure of the Jewish outsider with the "true" mission and purpose of America, what Frank calls the "secret" or "mystic" America. If America was out of joint, it had fallen to the Jew (along with various allies) to set things aright. Lewisohn, Frank, and Yezierska have never been considered as forming a group, but they are linked by striking similarities: they each found a voice during the postwar backlash against foreigners (they all published important works in 1919); they each aligned themselves with subversive cultural and political movements, including aesthetic modernism, psychoanalysis, socialism, and feminism; and they each associated Jewishness with energies of social and political dissent and spiritual renewal. Seen in relation to the Jewish dialogue with Transcendentalism we saw in the previous chapter, we might say that this highly polarized political climate called forth a role for the Jewish American writer that was already imagined, though not yet fully embodied, by Emma Lazarus and Mary Antin: the Jew as truest believer in American ideals and as dissenter from the American status quo. This dissonance leads, in the case of these three writers, to an impulse to reclaim Jewishness, as if to recover a language for idealism. A common motif in the texts we will consider is that of the Jew who returns to his or her people, recovering psychic and spiritual strength.

We should note that, as Walter Benn Michaels has argued, for Jews and members of other groups to valorize the "ethnic" outsider in post–World War I America was in some ways to reiterate the very argument that defenders of the "native stock" were insisting upon.[4] Just as nativists were charging that Jews and other Others were unassimilable foreigners, many ethnic writers were portraying members of their groups as somehow inherently marked out for a special destiny, different in kind than that of their Anglo-Saxon neighbors. Indeed, the very same racialist terminology that nativists used to justify their distaste for Jews often cropped up in texts by Jews themselves. And yet to read Lewisohn, Frank, and Yezierska merely as upholders of a static system of racial difference would obscure the *critical* impulse in their writing. I will propose that the language of race should not obscure the ways that Jewishness functions for these writers as *ethos* (a guiding set of beliefs) just as much as *ethnicity* (the empirical fact of belonging to a lineage group). The act of returning that they represent may be considered not simply some affirmation of racial or ethnic continuity, but an allegory for the amelioration of injustice. We must also bear in mind that these figures are neither racial scientists nor sociologists but writers who constructed narratives about individuals engaged in the project of self-formation. In the novels we will explore in the following chapters—particularly Lewisohn's *The Island Within,* Frank's *Rahab,* and Yezierska's *Bread Givers*—Jewishness appears not so much as a stable or given identity but as a body of accumulated wisdom that must be perennially recovered, reclaimed, and reapplied.

3

"PILGRIM TO A FORGOTTEN SHRINE"

Ludwig Lewisohn and the Recovery of the Inner Jew

> In those somber forests of his striving his own soul rose before him, and
> he saw himself,—darkly as through a veil; and yet he saw in himself some
> faint revelation of his power, of his mission.
> —W. E. B. Du Bois, from *The Souls of Black Folk*

Few writers in Jewish American history have labored as hard during their
lifetimes for so little posthumous fame as Ludwig Lewisohn (1881–1954).
From the 1920s through the early 1950s, he devoted himself tirelessly to
the task of bringing American Jews back into the fold—not necessarily to
the synagogue, but rather to what he called their abiding "Jewish consciousness." In his voluminous output, including autobiographical writings, novels, stories, essays, journalism, and criticism, Lewisohn decried
assimilation as a plague that had left generations of modern Jews stranded
in a shadowy no-man's land, distant from the underlying currents of their
own psychic lives. The costs were nervous symptoms, confusion, and

moral degradation. But it was still possible, he insisted, even for Jews in modern America to reabsorb the psychic and spiritual heritage that was rightly their own and to regain dignity and a moral compass. What was required was a dramatic reorientation of one's life, a "resurrection" of the concealed Jew out of the inner self.[1] Never before had a Jewish writer in America asserted with such vehemence, such assurance, and in so many different genres, that to be Jewish was to belong to a separate current of human life, no matter how acculturated one believed oneself to be.

During his lifetime, Lewisohn's message was one that many estimable figures, both Jewish and non-Jewish, found trenchant and timely. He received high praise from Carl Van Doren, H. L. Mencken, Thomas Mann, and Sigmund Freud.[2] When Harold Ribalow edited *A Treasury of American Jewish Stories* in 1950 (the first anthology of its kind), he included an entire novella by Lewisohn, explaining that the latter had "contributed more richly than any other writer to Anglo-Jewish literature in this country."[3] Today, half a century since his death, all but one of Lewisohn's nearly thirty novels are out of print. The index for the *Cambridge Companion of Jewish American Literature* (2004) makes two incidental references to his career. One of my colleagues vaguely recalls him as somebody who once occupied center space on his parents' bookshelf. On the other hand, a massive two-volume biography was recently published by Ralph Melnick, as if in an attempt to set the record straight in one fell swoop.[4] Jewish historian Steven Zipperstein has also proposed that, in his efforts to think through the meaning of ethnicity in America, Lewisohn may be closer to our concerns today than a writer like Lionel Trilling, who has received considerably more press.[5] Here I will similarly argue for Lewisohn's significance. The positions he staked out in the 1920s set a benchmark for self-assertiveness in Jewish American literature, and while few have matched the dogmatism that characterizes his work, many subsequent writers have continued to grapple with the very same questions about assimilation and return that were Lewisohn's abiding concerns.

From Berlin to Greenwich Village

Lewisohn spent his first seven years of life in the charmed world of late nineteenth-century Berlin, where his family led a comfortable existence punctuated by strolls through the Tiergarten and summers in a rented house by a lake in Straussberg.[6] Though his grandfather had served as a rabbi to scattered congregations in East Prussia, all the members of Lewisohn's family considered themselves "Germans first and Jews afterwards" (US 17). In this they were like many of Berlin's Jews, who had thoroughly internalized the ideals of mainstream German society and even enacted many of its basic rituals, from reading the Brothers Grimm to singing Christmas carols.[7] Lewisohn's childhood as an acculturated German Jew was cut short, however, marking him for a rather different destiny than his peers. When in the early 1890s his father's failed business scheme to import Italian fruit sent the family spiraling into insolvency, they immigrated to America, settling at the suggestion of relatives in Charleston, South Carolina. Charleston possessed a rich Jewish past and several flourishing Jewish institutions, but the young Lewisohn grew up far outside the organized Jewish community. Interestingly, as he writes in his autobiography *Up Stream,* the fact that the Lewisohns were nominal Jews and yet stayed away from the synagogue made them something of a mystery to the local gentiles, who eyed them with more suspicion than they did the town's religiously affiliated Jews. To follow a non-Christian religion was still to be identifiable according to prevailing identity categories; to be a non-practicing Jew was to occupy a nebulous position, with no real precedent. Perhaps for this reason neither his mother, a "spiritual child of the German folk" (US 21), nor his father, "an agnostic reared on Huxley and Haeckel" (US 49), had any complaints when Lewisohn augmented his studies at a Baptist-run school with Sunday School lessons at a local church. By the time of his adolescence, Lewisohn considered himself a Southern gentleman in-the-making and, by his own later admission, a believing Christian. "I accepted," he later wrote, "the Gospel story and the obvious implications of Pauline Christianity. . . . I accepted Jesus as my personal savior and cultivated, with vivid faith, the habit of prayer in which I persisted for many years" (US 50–51). Lewisohn, the future scourge of assimilation, started out as a virtual Christian.

After a successful stint at the University of Charleston, where he gained the support of a patrician faculty more wary of Negroes than of Jews, Lewisohn enrolled at Columbia University. He hoped to earn a Ph.D. in English literature and to launch himself on an academic career. One of the primary, if unstated, mandates of American academia during this period (Lewisohn began to attend Columbia in 1902) was to shape a national elite class by providing moral and cultural training. Ivy League English departments, in particular, were outposts of gentility, where gentleman scholars defended civilization by safeguarding linguistic purity. Lewisohn's attempt to enter these elite precincts was premised on the hope that literary talent could compensate for, or even masquerade as, breeding. His proposed dissertation topic was a history of the literature of South Carolina, a topic he had already treated in depth in a series of articles in the Charleston *News and Courier.* In these pieces, printed under the somewhat presumptuous title *Books We Have Made*, Lewisohn extolled "our" Carolinian literary tradition while bemoaning its demise during the period of Reconstruction.[8]

Lewisohn's burgeoning self-image as a Southern man of letters was reinforced when two years into graduate school he was selected by his mentor, Professor William Peterfield Trent, scion of Virginian aristocrats and a founding editor of the *Sewanee Review*, to edit and introduce a new edition of J. Hector St. John de Crevecoeur's classic book, *Letters from an American Farmer*. In this work, Crevecoeur had famously celebrated America for offering an entirely new mode of life in which "individuals of all nations are melted into a new race of men."[9] In his introduction, Lewisohn emphasizes the aesthetic beauty of the book, suggesting also that its patriotic message may have a "tonic quality" at a time when national pride seemed to him to be ebbing.[10] But Lewisohn's own efforts to fashion himself as a European-born spokesman for America soon lost momentum. In an episode that he would later make much of (and to which we will soon return), he was informed by the chairman of Columbia's English department, George Carpenter, that his prospects in academia were in reality quite slim. As somebody of "Jewish extraction," he would find many doors closed, a fact the chairman lamented but hardly protested. Though Lewisohn hung on for a few more years at Columbia, he increasingly felt himself to be neglected by the faculty, and, after struggling with various dissertation projects (the last one on Shelley), he ultimately left in 1907, discouraged and distracted and without a Ph.D.

Lewisohn next found his niche in the bohemian cultural vanguard that was just beginning to take shape in and around Greenwich Village.[11] This was a period Alfred Kazin has described as a "joyous season" when the first great literary society in America since Concord was being formed: "The rents were low, prices generally modest, ideas abundant, and the heady wind of the New Freedom a stimulus."[12] In particular, this new culture set itself in opposition to an old guard, rooted in the academy and associated with critics such as Irving Babbitt, Paul Elmer More, and Stuart Sherman. These latter figures, who came to be known as the New Humanists, emphasized the virtues of self-restraint in the moral life and classicism in aesthetics.[13] They staunchly opposed Romanticism, which they associated with a vague mysticism and moral anarchy. (Among those who responded positively to Babbitt during these years was the young T. S. Eliot, one of his protegeés at Harvard.)[14] Opposed to this tendency, the insurgent new group—including figures such as Van Wyck Brooks, Randolph Bourne, Waldo Frank, and Lewis Mumford—spoke for a liberatory agenda, premised on broadly Romantic values such as organicism, authenticity, and self-expression.[15] These critics and writers, sometimes referred to today as the "Young Americans," established what Alan Trachtenberg has described as a new social formation in American cultural life. They embodied "an American 'intelligentsia' based upon the central figure of the nonacademic generalist literary critic."[16] Ideologically, they flirted with varieties of socialism and strongly supported cultural pluralism. In the second decade of the century, when Lewisohn was finding his bearings, they provided a model for the outsider intellectual, immune to the corruptions of American institutions.

The Young Americans saw American culture as a battleground between the forces of liberation and an older genteel culture they associated with Puritanism. *Puritanism* was their catchword for the collective forces in the culture responsible for squelching vitality and the free play of the mind.[17] In works such as *The Wine of the Puritans* (1908) and *The Malady of the Ideal* (1913), Van Wyck Brooks described a cultural impasse in which the "national mind . . . has been sealed against that experience from which literature derives all its values."[18] In his more caustic, epigrammatic style, Mencken dubbed Puritanism "the haunting fear that someone, somewhere, may be happy."[19] These writers sought to resuscitate what they saw as the indigenous tradition of radical innovation in American letters. America required the stimulus of new energies, and many of these young critics and writers turned back to Emerson and Whitman for inspiration. Picking up on the precedent set by *The Dial* (the tiny New England journal in which many of the Transcendentalists were published), the Young Americans made the small magazine their characteristic venue. Among the cultural and political magazines they were associated with were *Liberator, The Smart Set, Others, The Seven Arts, The Nation,* and *The New Republic.*

Lewisohn found in this cultural ferment a group of allies and a critical style he could embrace. He became staff theater critic for *The Nation,* and he edited an important anthology, *The Modern Book of Criticism* (1919), which contained writings by Americans such as Bourne, Brooks, and Mencken alongside those of Europeans such as George Bernard Shaw and Anatole France. As the nation was gearing up for war, and just as anti-German sentiment was powerfully on the rise, he brought forth his own aesthetic views in a short provocative work called *The Spirit of Modern German Literature* (1916). As if aiming deliberately to shock his readers, Lewisohn declares that the most powerful defense of human freedom is to be found not in mainstream American culture but in a new generation of German writers (his key figures include Thomas Mann, Richard Dehmel, and Rainer Maria Rilke). In the new German writers, Lewisohn discerns a heroic quest for "more soul in life, more inward joy."[20] He claims that they offer a saving alternative to the life-denying austerity of the Puritans, whose legacy Lewisohn perceived in social trends ranging from the rise of xenophobia to the Prohibition movement. The hero of Lewisohn's book is Friedrich Nietzsche, the scandalous thinker who had already been introduced to American readers a few years earlier by Mencken. According to Lewisohn, Nietzsche stands above all for "greatness in the personal life"; Nietzsche's work stands as a powerful antidote to social conformism: "We Americans should feel closest to him," Lewisohn declares, "for we need him most."[21] Thus by the dawn of the 1920s, Lewisohn had made a decisive and dramatic about-face in his career: having started out as a Southern man of letters and a Christian in all but name, he had become a cultural rebel, joining his voice to an assertive new chorus of "Young America." His particular contribution was his deep familiarity with European culture and his confidence that America might prove to be fertile ground for Europe's boldest imaginings.

Jews and the American Avant-Garde

What was the attitude toward Jews among the figures Lewisohn now saw as his allies? We should note that Jews were prominent fixtures in the new artistic and literary culture, especially in the world of publishing, which was revolutionized during this period by Jews such as Horace Liveright, Alfred Knopf, and B. W. Huebsch.[22] The publishing house Boni and Liveright, which established the Modern Library series, performed indispensable cultural work, laying the foundation for the rise of an indigenous American modernist culture. They provided channels for younger writers and made available the work of European thinkers such as Sigmund Freud and Bertrand Russell. The creation of a new cultural sensibility in America was in this sense partly dependent, as it was in Europe, on the patronage and editorial work of Jews. This is not to say that writers like Mencken and others were immune to antisemitism. The recrudescence of antisemitism, notable in the nation at large, was palpable on the cultural vanguard as well. The vicious references to Jews sprinkled through the novels of Ernest Hemingway and F. Scott Fitzgerald and the poetry of T. S. Eliot and Ezra Pound were already standard fare in the slightly earlier work of Mencken and Dreiser.[23] Examples include Dreiser's play *The Hand of the Potter* (1918) with its nefarious, Shylock-type Jewish landlord, or Mencken's innumerable shocking comments such as "[t]he case against the Jews is long and damning; it would justify ten thousand times as many pogroms as now go on in the world."[24]

But such derogatory views of Jews were often offset by positive evocations, even by the very same writers. While there are passages in Mencken's work where he derides Jews as cultural parasites, he praises them in other passages for their ability to shake up the dominant order: "Whenever you find a *Davidsbuendlerschaft* making practice on the Philistines," he writes in the introduction to his translation of Nietzsche's *Antichrist*, "there you will find a Jew laying on."[25] Jews have also been counted among the ranks, that is, of those who would wage a campaign against ignorance or bigotry. For several years running, the *Jewish Who's Who* mistakenly identified Mencken as a Jew, and, when asked why he did not correct the error, Mencken replied "What's wrong about it? Perhaps I am a Jew. Besides it's kind of nice being known as a Jew. A lot of people might give me credit for more brains than I have."[26] In Lewis's *Main Street* (1920), a key text for the new generation, Jews were associated with bohemia, a form of existence that the doomed heroine Carol Kennicott briefly samples, but cannot make her own: "[Carol] was taken to a certified Studio Party, with beer, cigarettes, bobbed hair, and a Russian Jewess who sang the Internationale."[27] The "Russian Jewess" who makes this brief appearance in *Main Street* stands for a kind of freedom that Carol can only dream of in Gopher Prairie, where she is doomed to live out her days as a doctor's wife.[28] And Hemingway, whose vicious portrayal of Robert Cohn in *The Sun Also Rises* (1926) would seem the work of a dyed-in-the-wool antisemite, liked to imagine an alter ego for himself as a Viennese Jewish psychoanalyst named Dr. Hemingstein. In *Death in the Afternoon* (1932), when he criticizes other Americans who have written about Spanish culture, he proposes that abstraction in writing is a symptom of repressed sexuality, adding "this is Dr. Hemingstein the great psychiatrist deducing."[29] In these examples, Jews are imagined as figures endowed with vitality, insight, and a talent for social critique.

The point here is that "the Jew" had emerged as a key symbolic figure in the modernist imagination in post–World War I America, linked with forces of corruption and contamination as well as with occult powers, capable of reshaping and renewing the culture. That such contradictory ideas get attached to Jews during periods of cultural upheaval, particularly when some new version of nationalism is on the rise, is hardly a new story.[30] What I want to emphasize is how the powerful fantasies associated with Jews at such periods can also be *productive* for Jewish writers: the symbolic meanings that get attached to specific groups can be claimed and marshaled by members of these groups toward new creative work. The innovative culture legible in the pages of the new journals thus provided a space in which the Jewish writer could develop a new role. To be sure, some Jewish contemporaries of Lewisohn sought to avoid this ambiguous positioning altogether. George Jean Nathan, an associate of Lewisohn and the co-editor of *The Smart Set* and *The American Mercury,* harbored what his biographer Thomas Connolly has described as a lifelong dread that his family's Jewish origin would be exposed.[31] Nathan went as far as to invent a story that his mother had attended a convent school (the same school, in fact, that Eugene O'Neill's mother had attended). But Lewisohn responded to this period of flux by embracing a form of Jewishness defined first and foremost as an oppositional identity.

Thus, just as Lewisohn linked himself with the American avant-garde, he also came to broadcast his Jewishness. The work in which he explicitly links his role as cultural critic to his Jewish identity is *Up Stream: An American Chronicle* (1922). At first blush, this would appear to be yet another entry in the genre of immigrant autobiography, a genre that included not only Antin's *The Promised Land* but also such patriotic works as Jacob Riis's *The Making of an American* (1901), Horace Bridge's *On Becoming an American* (1919), and Edward Bok's *The Americanization of Edward Bok: The Autobiography of a Dutch Boy Fifty Years After* (1921). Lewisohn's tale is similarly one of immigration and acculturation. But unlike these optimistic immigrant fables, Lewisohn's story is somber and cautionary, reflecting the mood of revolt expressed by his cohorts, and attesting to deep conflicts in American culture. This is clear in his prologue, in which he forewarns the reader of his mission to lay bare "the quite naked and, if need be, the devastating truth" (US 9). He will "drop the mask" and offer his life as a living symbol for others for whom "this moment of history has burned away delusions to the last shred" (US 10). Such an opening gambit, positing the author as an apprentice to a Nietzschean hermeneutics of suspicion, suggests the very opposite of Antin's introduction to *The Promised Land,* with its promise to heal "the bitter sea of racial differences and misunderstandings" (PL 2). Writing after the targeting of Jews during the Red Scare of 1919–1920, Henry Ford's Jew-baiting, and the rise of the Ku Klux Klan, Lewisohn has no simple ecumenical vision to offer. His purpose is to write an exposé of American society, to castigate Americans for their failure to live up to their alleged ideals.

A fruitful analogy might be drawn at this point between Lewisohn's revision of Antin's patriotism and W. E. B. Du Bois's revision of Booker T. Washington's "uplift" message. Du Bois anticipates Lewisohn's image of tearing off the mask when he describes his goal of raising "the Veil" to reveal the experience of the other side of the color line.[32] Both figures declare themselves as enemies of social propriety, particularly of the myths that obscure America's actual treatment of its minorities. Moreover, both Du Bois and Lewisohn may be read as figures who return to their people after an initial distance: Lewisohn will eventually describe his reintegration into "authentic" Jewish life analogous to Du Bois's description in chapter 4 of *The Souls of Black Folk* of encountering the rural black South after growing up in a predominantly white community in Massachusetts.[33] Most notable, perhaps, is their common conception of the "soul," read at once through the discourse of romanticism, biblical prophecy, and race. This analogy suggests common ways in which Jewish and African American identities could be imagined as furnishing a "mission." What is crucial to this analogy is not only that both African Americans and Jews were targeted at this time as racial aliens, but that they could both draw upon the same biblical texts from which American mainstream culture claimed to derive its mandate. If Lewisohn and Du Bois share certain modes of critique, these common approaches have much to do with their similar ways of absorbing and recasting these biblical vocabularies.

In *Up Stream,* Lewisohn describes himself during his youth as a naïve dreamer fired by the ideals of his adopted country. Looking back from the vantage point of a pariah in the 1920s, he recognizes that there were already signs of danger that he should have heeded: he had been taunted in high school for being a foreigner and a Jew; he had been excluded from a fraternity at college; he was ignored as a graduate student. But his faith in America made him overlook these signs: "I was, in brief, a citizen passionately and fruitfully concerned for the welfare of a society which had always received him grudgingly and half-heartedly" (US 175). The turning point in this narrative of disillusionment is the letter Lewisohn receives from George Carpenter, the chairman of Columbia's English department, just as Lewisohn was hoping to establish himself as an academic. Lewisohn reproduces the letter in his text, as if delivering hard evidence for crimes committed against him. These are the chairman's words:

> A recent experience has shown me how terribly hard it is for a man of Jewish birth to get a good position. I had always suspected that it was a matter worth considering, but I had not known how wide-spread and strong it was. While we shall be glad to do anything we can for you, therefore, I cannot help feeling that the chances are going to be greatly against you. (122)

Of the two paradigms of Jewish return that David Roskies identifies—one that turns on a *spiritual conversion,* the other on a *rude awakening*—Lewisohn's autobiography fits squarely into the latter.[34] (In the next chapter we will consider Waldo Frank as more of a "spiritual convert.") Coming midway through the narrative, this letter marks the rude awakening that sets Lewisohn on his new mission. He concludes that as a Jew, he is and will always be perceived as a threat, an "implacable foe" (US 120).[35] At this moment he suddenly considers, as if for the very first time, his underlying relationship to other Jews suffering exclusion from various regimes.[36] If *Up Stream* follows the trajectory of the bildungsroman up to Lewisohn's receipt of the chairman's letter, the conclusion it leads to is hardly some accommodation to reality, but rather a relentless opposition to the status quo, a movement "up stream." As it turns out, the guardians of the national culture have good reason to fear him: from his position outside the mainstream, he can retrieve a vision of true life in all its deformity, undermining the national fantasy of life as a "kindly affair, all pleasantly prearranged" (US 149). His final chapter, "The World in Chaos," presents a counterattack upon the "uproar of reaction and nationalism" (US 231) surrounding him. Lewisohn calls Americans to task for their bigotry, their belligerence, and their willingness to subordinate vital human impulses to the normalizing regimen he calls the "Main Street mentality." The episode of being cast out of Columbia is thus retrospectively figured as an initial parting of the veil, an initiation into the role of marginalized seer.

Lewisohn's emergence as a critic of America may itself be read as the culmination of a certain kind of Americanization story. The subtitle "An American Chronicle" is not so much cynical, then, but affirmative, for when Lewisohn finds a vocation, it will be as an *American* isolate, crying in the wilderness. As he writes, "A writer named, let us say, Stuart Sherman, declares that I pervert the national genius. But suppose *I am the national genius*—Dreiser and Mencken and Francis Hackett and I—rather than Stuart Sherman?" (237, emphasis added). Here Lewisohn is attacking Sherman, the New Humanist, for his harsh review of Lewisohn's anthology, *The Modern Book of Criticism* (1919). Sherman had written that critics of alien birth could not be expected to hear any "profound murmuring of ancestral voices or to experience any mysterious inflowing of national experience in meditating on the names of Mark Twain, Whitman, Thoreau, Lincoln, Emerson, Franklin, and Bradford."[37] In response, Lewisohn attacks Sherman for his bigotry and proposes, moreover, that the truest version of America is *only* alive in the minds of the insurgent critics of the prevailing system. These critics and not the academic elite are the true embodiment of the "national experience."

In framing his critique of antisemitism as part of an effort to reassert America's true mission, Lewisohn recalls the rhetorical strategy that Louis Marshall had used two years previously, in 1920, in his efforts to combat Ford and the *Dearborn Independent*. Marshall, a prominent attorney and

Jewish civic leader who was also president of the American Jewish Committee, launched an interfaith campaign for tolerance, culminating in a public denunciation of Ford in the name of democracy. Among the signatories were 121 prominent Americans, including all living former presidents. As Henry L. Feingold notes, "Marshall rarely mentioned Jews directly. Rather, Ford was pictured as posing a threat to the American values that Jews cherished."[38] This approach (which proved forceful enough to induce Ford to recant his antisemitic views) exemplifies one aspect of what Sarna calls "the cult of synthesis of American Jewish culture," a tendency to align the aspirations of Jews with fundamental American values.[39] But Lewisohn goes farther than this, suggesting at one point that it is *only* in the mind of the immigrant in general and the Jew in particular that the genuine America endures. Lewisohn's prototype for the true American turns out to be, paradoxically, the unassimilated foreigner: "The notion of liberty on which the Republic was founded, the spirit of America that animated Emerson and Whitman, is vividly alive today only in the unassimilated foreigner, in that pathetic pilgrim to a forgotten shrine" (US 236). To be "unassimilated" is to retain the idealism contained in America's founding principles, though the principles are betrayed in actuality. For those who are already immersed in America, the only hope lies in de-assimilating, which Lewisohn describes as a movement from bondage to freedom. In his epilogue he sends out a call to all who would join him: "Somehow we must break these shackles and flee and emerge into some beyond of sanity, of a closer contact with reality, of nature and truth" (US 247). The movement from bondage to freedom, so palpable a feature of American public rhetoric is recapitulated, but this time within the geographical space of America itself. America depends on the emergence of bold individuals continuously rejecting the false America in the name of its deeper promise.

The Souls of Jewish Folk

During the same years in which Lewisohn was representing himself as a radical liberationist in the American vein, he found himself increasingly drawn to understand the place and position of Jews in modern society. By the middle of the 1920s, Lewisohn had absorbed the vocabularies of two emergent ideologies—Zionism and psychoanalysis—in developing an analysis of the modern Jewish situation. Antisemitism, he now saw, was not some invention of post–World War I America; it was deeply interwoven in the fabric of Christendom. Hence the granting of civil rights to Jews had merely created the illusion of "emancipation." Having internalized the universalist ideals proclaimed by liberal society, Jews had sought to convince their neighbors of their underlying humanity. To do so, they had slavishly imitated the styles and attitudes of their gentile host cultures, inflicting upon themselves an inner self-mutilation. The result was the contemporary generation of Jews he described as "sick . . . divided souls" (a version, perhaps, of Du Bois's "double-consciousness").[40] The more he meditated on this predicament, the less he imagined that America could become a "home" for the Jew—no matter to what extent Jews might possess some deeper understanding of America's mission to the world.

There was a way out of this impasse, however. A solution had arisen—most powerfully in the minds of certain Viennese Jews who had diagnosed the self-defeating folly of their fellow Jews: "[It is not] without its special and high significance," he wrote during a sojourn in Europe in the mid-1920s, "that Vienna, where Jewish assimilation has produced its richest fruits, is also the city whence arose with Theodor Herzl the movement of political Zionism and with Sigmund Freud that science of analytical psychology which, though applicable to all men, is first of all an effort on the part of the Jewish people to heal itself of the maladies of the soul contracted in the assimilatory process."[41] For Lewisohn, psychoanalysis is indeed the "Jewish science," closely allied to Zionism as a method for returning assimilated Jews to their abiding true selves. The language of psychoanalysis is everywhere present in Lewisohn's writing, particularly after his time in Vienna, when he came to know Freud and was even briefly analyzed by him. Lewisohn's is a version of psychoanalysis heavily mediated by the discourse of Romanticism: what gets repressed by the assimilated Jew and what Zionism promises to release is not some reserve of sexual energy, so much as Jewishness itself.

Lewisohn attributes his Zionist conversion to the influence of the German Zionist leader Kurt Blumenfeld, who was impressed enough with a speech Lewisohn delivered to the Menorah society in 1923 to enlist him to join forces with the nascent American Zionist movement.[42] (Blumenfeld was a talented propagandist who enlisted Albert Einstein and even Hannah Arendt into the Zionist cause.) After a subsequent meeting with Chaim Weizmann, then head of the World Zionist Organization, Lewisohn traveled to Palestine and published a series of articles in *The Nation* covering the developments in the *yishuv,* the Jewish community in Palestine. These articles, collected in a single volume, *Israel* (1925), called upon Jews of the Diaspora to abandon what he called "the indignity of assimilation" and to learn once more to be "calmly and serenely themselves."[43] Interestingly, this vision of serene authenticity reflects Lewisohn's growing impatience with insurgent writers of the 1920s, such as Mencken and Sinclair Lewis, who had formed his initial set of allies. Gradually he had come to fault them for voicing dissent without offering any kind of alternate vision of human community or solidarity. "The great game of Puritan-bashing and Babbitt-jeering was [ultimately] not for me" (MC 18). In Lewisohn's movement from Greenwich Village bohemian to Zionist, he discovered something to *affirm*. The keynote of his writing then shifted from relentless critique to the motif of return.

Lewisohn's Zionism, a therapeutic program for lost Jews, represented what was and has remained a minority view within the discourse of American Zionism. Most typically, American Zionism has appealed to American Jews as full and legitimate Americans with a vested interest in assisting their suffering coreligionists in other lands. The process that Naomi W. Cohen has called the "Americanization of Zionism" involved articulating the project of building up a Jewish state within the fundamental terms of American citizenship.[44] Nowhere is this approach more evident than in Louis D. Brandeis's famous dictum that "[e]very American Jew who aids in advancing the Jewish settlement in Palestine, though he feels that neither he nor his descendents will ever live there, will likewise be a better man and a better American for doing so."[45] Lewisohn, by contrast, presented a view that veered closer to the German Zionists of the second two decades of the twentieth century, who, as Stephen Poppel has argued, saw Zionism as a process of shaping a new harmonious identity.[46] Their Zionism was not some pragmatic program to defend fellow Jews; it was romantic nationalism, holding out a promise of self-realization. What remains typically American in Lewisohn's writing, I suggest, is his emphasis on the process of getting free itself, on the movement away from the false self and the impulse to begin again. If a recurrent figure in American literature is the fugitive from society, Lewisohn reinvents this figure as the Jew steering clear of the organized pressures of Christendom.[47]

The work that most clearly describes Lewisohn's vision of Jewish liberation is *The Island Within* (1928), a novel he called a "preliminary study toward the ultimately Jewish 'matter' " (MC 179). This is Lewisohn's most significant contribution to Jewish American fiction. A strident and didactic work, it addresses the problem of American Jewish identity in the context of the broader panorama of Jewish modernity. Its ongoing interest lies in its attempt to find a language and a set of images to make plausible the theme of Jewish rebirth in the context of a novel. *The Island Within* takes as its starting point the year 1840 in Vilna, when Mendel, the head of a pious Jewish family, is lured by the early stirrings of the Jewish Enlightenment, the Haskalah. He reads the writings of Isaac-Ber Levinsohn, a critic of traditional Jewish life, and quickly relinquishes his post as a

Hebrew school teacher, a *melamed,* to work for a brandy distiller. In the next generation, Mendel's son Efraim takes a further step, moving with his wife to the Prussian city of Insterburg to seek his fortune in business. Lewisohn makes his novel a study in ethnic semiotics, linking each stage of decline to the disappearance of outward signs of Jewishness: "Efraim had trimmed his beard neatly; the bride was wearing a dress that had been copied from a Warsaw copy of a Parisian model" (IW 29). Efraim's son, Jacob, makes what appears to be the final gesture of assimilation: he immigrates to America, where he finally hopes to "expel from his mind the fear and the shame" that had hounded him as a Jew in Europe. He prospers as the owner of a department store and establishes a fully Americanized family: "Lokshen and gefüllte Milz was all that was left them of the traditions of their race" (IW 72). But Lewisohn's narrative of Jewish loss is suddenly reversed in the fourth generation, in the person of Arthur Levy, Lewisohn's new Jewish hero.

Levy grows up with no knowledge of things Jewish whatsoever, but he cannot shake an intangible sense of difference amid his gentile playmates: "When a teacher or a fellow pupil said 'Levy,' something within him contracted, grew tense, was ready for resistance" (IW 87). In the laboratory of his novel, Lewisohn has stripped the modern American Jew of any external Jewish influences, and discovers not a tabula rasa but an inchoate and barely articulated Jewish identity, initially experienced only as a response to the gaze of the other. To explain this inchoate Jewishness, Lewisohn draws heavily on the language of race. Sometimes we find evocations of Lamarckian evolutionary biology: we read of Levy's "ancestral memories . . . instinct . . . voice of the blood" (IW 79) and "inconceivably mighty and dolorous ancestral resonances" (IW 80). Alternately, we read of outer physiological traces: "his blond hair had a peculiar reddish tinge and a tendency to curl tightly" (IW 97). At other moments the legacy comes through in habits of speech: "that indefinable Jewish undertone—the speech rhythm of Yiddish" (IW 96). At still other moments, Lewisohn seems divided between nature and nurture: "an elemental or, at least, an historic instinct" (IW 169).

This vocabulary suggests that Lewisohn has come to embrace the very terms the critic Stuart Sherman had used to discredit American literature ("Aliens of birth cannot be expected to hear any profound murmuring of ancestral voices . . . in meditating on the names of Mark Twain, Whitman, etc."). Lewisohn's Jew is indeed a racial outsider; and yet *The Island Within* is less concerned with reestablishing some static taxonomy, divided by race, than with the Nietzschean problem of becoming who one is. Lewisohn is less interested in science than in narrative. If the aim Lewisohn sets for his protagonist is to get clear of a false identity, the language of race provides a series of metaphors for the abiding true self that he is seeking to recover. It might also be recalled that there are multiple other sources besides nineteenth-century racial thinking behind the concept of a tacit, enduring Jewish identity. This notion is inscribed, for example, in the biblical trope of the prophet who tries to elude his destiny to deliver a message on behalf of God. Race provides Lewisohn a secularized language for articulating the notion of the Jew as reluctant emissary, as a figure called, in spite of himself, to fulfill a mission.

After receiving his training at Columbia University, Levy, still alienated from his Jewish core, launches out on a career as a psychologist. He meets and marries Elizabeth Knight, a "new woman," a novelist, a suffragette, and a gentile. She offers the distraction of sex: "He was amazed and thrilled and infinitely flattered at the intensity of her response. . . . He needed forgetfulness and ecstasy" (IW 159, 166). Women's liberation is linked here with sexual promiscuity, and is ultimately represented as a threat to the ordered ego. As if to combat these disruptive forces, Levy gravitates toward the new field of psychoanalysis, roundly dismissed by his "WASPy" colleagues as "degenerate, dirty Freudian stuff" (IW 140). In a moment of insight, Levy discovers the key to the psychic maladies of his Jewish patients in their desperate efforts to hide from the fact of their Jewishness: "Flight from experience. . . . Yes, the mechanism of the Jewish anti-Jewish complex was precisely analogous to the mechanism of insanity. . . . He felt this urge toward flight himself" (IW 141).[48] Psychoanalysis is represented here in its most Romantic guise. The point is not to be "cured" and returned to normal life, but to be remade through immersion in the deep soul. This will steel Levy against the allure of the outside world, embodied in the available sexuality of the gentile woman. Becoming a psychoanalyst thus represents for Levy the first step in reorienting his life according to an inner compass.

The turning point comes when he meets an East European Jew, Reb Moshe Hacohen, who is seeking a psychiatrist for an American commission to investigate anti-Jewish violence in Romania. The rabbi, dressed in "an elegant silk caftan with a velvet collar," serves as the novel's deus (*iudaeus?*) ex machina: the sudden apparition that sets Levy straight. He recognizes Levy as a member of his own family: "There is something in your face; I believe we are *mishpoche*—kinfolk; do you know the expression?" (IW 232). Lewisohn brings together the Cohen and the Levy, as if the two priestly tribes have been reunited in America, though only one of the tribes has retained glimmers of its past glory. Hacohen gives Levy an ancient scroll, written by one of their mutual ancestors, and preserved in an old carved wooden chest, which was first mentioned in the opening scenes of the novel as one of the most cherished possessions of Levy's ancestors before they left Eastern Europe. Its reappearance functions symbolically as the return of Levy's intact Jewish soul. The scroll contains a description of the self-martyrdom of the Jewish community of Worms during the Crusades (a story every bit as gruesome as those that form the basis for Lazarus's *The Dance to Death*). When he has finished reading the account, Levy's rebirth is completed: "How still it was about him! Still as the beginning of things" (IW 261). Levy is reborn at the moment he lays claim to the history of Jewish martyrdom as *his* history. At this moment he gains an influx of spiritual power. Like Antin, who discovers a powerful spiritual legacy among her "heirlooms," Levy regains contact with a tradition that seemed lost to history. He has returned to "the beginning of things," before the failure of nerve that afflicted the generations of assimilating Jews immediately preceding him. And the effect of this return is to restore moral agency.

Just after reading the scroll given to him by Hacohen, Levy departs on a mission to Romania to use his psychoanalytic powers to heal the Jewish communities ravaged by antisemitic attacks. As he leaves, he tells his wife that even if she wanted to, she could never remake herself as a convincing "Jewess": "No. Things like that can't be learned. I suppose they have to be resurrected out of one's inner self" (IW 263). In the novel's final passage, we read of Levy's newfound certainty, as he heads off to Europe: "the sky curved over him like a tent against the outer darkness and . . . the earth which his foot trod was his natural habitation and his home" (IW 266). He has begun undoing the turmoil of psychic alienation, having found temporary refuge, like the Israelites in the desert, in the security of a "tent." The paradox of this final image is that it is precisely when he is on the move—on his pilgrimage toward the Old World—that he is in his "natural home." What we have, then, is a Jewish version of the great American narrative of self-liberation. In place of the fantasy of moving westward or "lighting out for the territories," Lewisohn's hero sets out for the Old World.

By staging a transformative encounter between an East European Jew and an assimilated American Jew, Lewisohn anticipates a motif that will resurface in a number of Jewish American texts written after World War II, most dramatically Philip Roth's "Eli, the Fanatic" (1959), Bernard Malamud's "The Last Mohican" (1958), and Cynthia Ozick's "Bloodshed" (1976).[49] In all of these stories, an American Jew confronts a Jew from the Old World who embodies some lost or repressed aspect of the American Jew. In Roth's and Ozick's texts, these Old World figures stand for religious faith; in Malamud's, he symbolizes the wily adaptability and moral seriousness of the Diaspora Jew. As in Lewisohn's novel, these Old World characters all make some kind of demand on the American Jew, and the denouement of each of the narratives depends on the willingness of the American Jew to allow himself (the protagonist is always male in these texts) to be transformed in the process of meeting the demand. The American Jew is called upon, in short, to reintegrate himself into the collective Jewish experience.

Where these postwar narratives differ from Lewisohn's 1928 novel, however, is in the fact that their Old World Jews are all Holocaust survivors. And this may help to explain why these latter narratives all end on considerably darker notes than Lewisohn's. Malamud's story ends with the American Jew locked in hot pursuit of the Old World Jew; Ozick's ends with a scene of moral condemnation; and Roth's with the American Jew transformed into a raving lunatic. These postwar stories are more pessimistic, it would seem, because the Holocaust has opened up an unbridgeable gap between the American and European Jew. Even Roth's protagonist, who takes on the identity of the Holocaust survivor, seems to go mad precisely because he has laid claim to much more than he can properly call his own.[50] Another reason these latter texts seem frustrated in their efforts to imagine a return to Jewishness, perhaps, is that they do not embrace the language of race that helps to account for the reconciliation in Lewisohn's text. Lewisohn's hero is able to reclaim his Jewishness because it already exists inside him as an ancestral inheritance, an "island within." Whereas subsequent Jewish American writers will grapple with the problem of representing solidarity among New and Old World Jews, Lewisohn finds a ready solution in the discourse of race.

A Clash of Civilizations

What, then, defines "Jewish identity" for Lewisohn? The figure for the archetypal Jew in *The Island Within*, Reb Moses Hacohen, reflects the romance with the East European Jew, which has been a hallmark of modern Jewish culture. Martin Buber's reclamation of Hasidism in turn-of-the-century Germany and Franz Kafka's discovery of Yiddish theater a few years later in Prague reflect this impulse to look eastward for more authentic versions of Jewishness.[51] However, Lewisohn discovers the essence of Judaism not in the figure of the Hasid, as Buber does, but in the biblical prophets. Indeed, he reads Buber and all important modern Jewish thinkers as exponents of a perpetually reemerging prophetic tradition. "Read the classics and the records of our people," he writes in the collection *Rebirth*, "[a]nd you will see that the pacifist and spiritual nationalism and self-integration which we achieved in the age of the prophets . . . has been continually reborn in all the luminous minds and characters of the exile from Jehuda Halevi and Martin Buber."[52] For Lewisohn, the prophet becomes a metaphor for the integrated Jew, who remains faithful to his "calling" in defiance of the conformist pressures of the world. This figure enables Lewisohn to merge his ideal of resistance with his definition of Jewishness: "The Prophets," he declares, "were the conscious destroyers of their national state whenever that state became tyrannous" (Israel 221). It is axiomatic for Lewisohn that the prophet and hence the Jew opposes the arbitrary use of force.

For Lewisohn, the figure of the prophet also significantly becomes the archetypal autobiographer. In his essay "Cities and Men" (1927), Lewisohn celebrates the autobiographical impulse as the antidote to neoclassicism, and he looks to Amos, the earliest of the classical prophets, as the first autobiographer. Lewisohn writes that in Amos "the confessing individual had arisen in literature."[53] Elsewhere, in his lengthy study of American literature, Lewisohn locates the biblical prophetic ethos at the center of the American literary sensibility. "Emerson was a moralist and like all important men of letters something of a prophet in the original Hebrew sense of a critic and a judge of his civilization and his age."[54] Thus, if Lewisohn's original approach to Judaism was mediated by his identification with 1920s American rebels like H. L. Mencken and Sinclair Lewis, he now understands this broader American tradition as an expression of Judaism. As a Jew, Lewisohn himself becomes not an epigone or fellow traveler, but origin and prototype for the quintessential American. It also means that as a Jew he can nominate himself to the role of one who calls America back to its own mission. As he writes at the end of his second autobiography, *Mid-Channel* (1929):

> I speak of myself. But what, beyond myself, I am thinking of is what Whitman called, "the good old cause, the great idea, the progress and freedom of the race."
> That is Jewish. It is American too. It was, at least, American once.
> (MC 302)

Whitman's "great idea" has been betrayed by a belligerent and racist America; yet, since America's "great idea" is, according to Lewisohn, originally Jewish, it can be retrieved by the Jew who "returns" to Judaism. The Jew becomes the exemplary American, but only by keeping a distance from what America has actually become. In Lewisohn's scheme, "confession" and "prophecy" are united: the moment individual Jews speak their deepest, personal truth, they have also spoken for a trans-historical principle.

Thus, despite his focus on the problem of the individual Jew's soul, there remains a sense in Lewisohn's writing that the "prophetic ethos" might infuse the culture at large and America in particular. Lewisohn ultimately moves toward what might be called a clash of civilizations model, with the two opposing forces being an oppressive force he names "Christendom" and a redemptive force rooted in the Hebrew prophets. Christendom proper begins for Lewisohn with Paul's codification of a new system of ethics tending toward aesceticism and based upon faith in the afterlife. Its members consist essentially of pagans who were converted to Christianity when the Roman Empire spread throughout Europe. Their inner pagan nature can never be fully eradicated, Lewisohn maintains, and thus political power disguised as ethics must intervene and continuously resubjugate its members: "All Christian ethics are directed toward keeping the original heathen quiet at the heart and powerless beyond the gate . . . The heathen has to be converted again and again" (Rebirth 63). From time to time, the pagans burst through their gates, venting their merciless, warlike natures.

This is precisely how Lewisohn explained the triumph of Nazism and the impending world conflict, which became an increasingly obsessive focus of his writing throughout the 1930s. In reading Lewisohn from the mid-1930s, one is struck with his prescience, as by 1935, his writing had already reached a pitch of apocalypticism. Here is a typically breathless passage from this period:

> The pagan . . . is a convert, and converts, alas! have a habit of relapsing, and today, in this year 1935, two-thirds of the Western World has re-lapsed into pagan barbarism and only, or almost only, in France and Britain and America are there left any profoundly sincere Christians and liberals, any men and women who have put aside the old pagan Adam of their ancestors and accepted the ethos first proclaimed by the teachers and prophets of Israel. (Rebirth xxvii)

Lewisohn envisions the pagan impulse rebelling against the constraints of Pauline Christianity, releasing pent-up rage and dragging the world into barbarism. Fascism, from this perspective, is an apocalyptic unleashing of Nietzschean *resentiment*. The allied powers might still mount an opposition to this pagan–fascist rebellion, but only if they heed the "ethos first proclaimed by the teachers and prophets of Israel." What is central to this ethos, as we have seen, is its equation of moral virtue with "self-integration," and its principled refusal to submit to demagoguery or any system that demands a repudiation of the inner self.

For Lewisohn, the movement of return is an abiding possibility for the modern Jew because Jewishness is rooted in the deep soul. So confident was Lewisohn's belief in the deep soul that he was hardly troubled by the problem of the specific form that modern Jewish culture should take. A true Jew could speak any language, practice Judaism or not, and even live anywhere—in the Diaspora or the "homeland." As Stanley Chyett, one of Lewisohn's students at Brandeis, expressed it, "[h]is salvation was Zionism, not Zion."[55] The one imperative was to reorient oneself according to the compass of the soul, and to accept the mandate to speak on its behalf. Insofar as modern Jews managed to do this, they could provide an exemplary model for others. These premises may make Lewisohn sound willful or naïve to our ears, attuned as they are to more pragmatic ideas about selves as shaped by multiple traditions (and by a complex of individual experiences and biochemical determinants). My proposal here is to read Lewisohn above all as a literary artist occupied with the problem of shaping a language of aspiration. Drawing on biblical, Freudian, Romantic, biological, and American literary traditions, he created an image of the Jew—and of the human soul more generally—as a saving force at a moment when the horizon of history was growing dark. In the next section, we shall see how one of Lewisohn's contemporaries, Waldo Frank, responded to a similar set of social and political pressures and also found his way "back" to Jewishness in the course of a sustained dialogue with American literary culture.

4

MODERNIST FLASKS, JEWISH WINE

Waldo Frank and the Immanence of God

I discovered the Jewish Word; or rather, in a profound crisis of my life, that Word came to me straight as an answer, palpable as the flesh of my body. It is not too much, therefore, to say that I am a convert to Judaism; and as such, I humbly claim the indulgence of my betters.

—Waldo Frank, from "That Israel May Live"

Waldo Frank (1889–1967) has seldom been included in the history of Jewish American literature. Few critics discuss his works; anthologies omit him altogether. This is not entirely surprising, perhaps, since Frank's explicitly Jewish writings are relatively few. Among his nonfictional works, he wrote a chapter on American Jews in *Our America* (1919); scattered essays on Jewish philosophy, Zionism, and antisemitism in the *Menorah Journal* and *Contemporary Jewish Record* (later collected in his book *The Jew in Our Day* [1944]); and a book-length account of his travels in Israel, entitled *Bridgehead: The Drama of Israel* (1957). Of his twelve novels, the only one that involves a sustained and explicit meditation on Jewishness is *Rahab* (1922)—a novel that recasts an episode from Joshua in modern-day New York City. Frank is more commonly known for the influential role he played as a critic and novelist in the American cultural avant-garde in the years immediately following World War I. He was one of the founding editors of the journal *The Seven Arts,* and, in addition to his own experimental "lyrical novels" from this period, he wrote forceful essays touting the aesthetic achievements of writers such as Sherwood Anderson, Jean Toomer, and Hart Crane and of the photographer Alfred Stieglitz. In the 1930s Frank became an important figure on the radical cultural left, becoming the first director of the League of American Writers, a revolutionary organization aimed at galvanizing a proletarian movement in literature.[1] Today he is perhaps best known in the Spanish-speaking world, where his writings on the folk cultures of Spain and Latin America are considered classics.

It is possible, nevertheless, to see in Frank's Jewish writings much more than a mere ancillary concern. He once wrote that "the Jewish Word" came to him "as an answer" in the midst of a personal crisis during the 1920s, and it can indeed be argued that Judaism—or what Frank understood Judaism to mean—provided a linchpin for his variegated aesthetic and political engagements.[2] What he ultimately discovered in Judaism was nothing less than a spiritual language for elucidating, legitimating, and augmenting the project of the avant-garde. As with the other writers we have discussed thus far, Frank described Judaism in essentially Romantic terms, focusing on the drama of the individual striving to make contact with the source of meaning. Frank's language was considerably more "mystical" in emphasis, however. His concerns are less with Jewish history or memory or with the experience of assimilation per se than with the nature of absolute reality, what he called "the Whole." When seen alongside Lewisohn's Zionism, Frank's ongoing commitment to the avant-garde suggests other ways Jewishness could be imagined in relation to American society during the interwar period.

Unearthing the Secret America

Frank grew up in the twilight of the nineteenth century in a bourgeois family on New York's Upper West Side. His father, Julius, was the son of German Jewish immigrants and a successful attorney whose work led him each day to an office near Wall Street.[3] Frank's mother, Helene, came from a wealthy Southern Jewish family, her father having been a blockade runner during the Civil War who later established himself in business in New

York. The home was suffused with the combined ideals of German *Bildung* (Helene, a "radiant soprano," studied with the celebrated, Frankfurt-born conductor Leopold Damrosch) and a strain of nineteenth-century liberal thought rooted in the ideals of Frank's father's hero, Thomas Jefferson. In an act both prescient of his son's vocation and expressive of his own literary proclivities, Julius Frank named his son Waldo David, combining Emerson's and Thoreau's middle names.

As for religion, the Franks had exchanged any sort of synagogue affiliation for membership in the Society for Ethical Culture, the nonsectarian movement that arose out of Reform Judaism. Conceived in 1876 when Felix Adler, son of a prominent American Reform rabbi, returned from Germany armed with Kantian philosophy and Higher Biblical Criticism, Ethical Culture rejected all identifiably Jewish theological categories. In place of a personal God, Adler projected a "Moral Order," rooted in rationality and expressed in clear precepts; in place of ritual, he advocated self-improvement; in place of the covenant, he looked to the dictates of personal conscience.[4] Frank's father was among Adler's greatest advocates; he joined the steering committee of the Ethical Culture Society and spread its gospel at home.

When he later discovered his own path back to Judaism, Frank would assail Ethical Culture as a "degenerate Judaism."[5] He argued that it served mainly as a way-station for middle-class aspirants who preferred not to be troubled by larger questions: "[A]ll the mystery of life, all the harmony of sense, all the immanence of God were deleted from it," he wrote in *Our America* (1919). "And in their place [was] a quiet, moral code destined to make good citizens of eager pioneers" (OA 87). In his memoir, he describes his youth as a period of spiritual deprivation. Friday night dinners were a remnant of traditional Judaism: "Not a word, not a ritual act ever reminded anyone that this was the Sabbath meal" (M 15). When he set off for Yale in 1907, he was by his own later admission "a Jew without Judaism," one who knew nothing of Hebrew and who had never even set foot in a synagogue. He describes two sets of friends at school, a pair of secular Jews from Cincinnati and a pair of New England Protestants. With the latter he urgently debated the role of religion in the modern world; with the Jews, he discussed everything *except* religion. There was a famous old synagogue in New Haven, but, as he recalls, "[i]t never occurred to me in my four New Haven years to enter it. The paradox of all this—the paradox of the paradox, was that its strangeness never occurred to me" (M 39). "Religion" itself seemed a concern of Christians, not Jews; the old synagogue had less reality for him than the Newport Jewish cemetery had had for Longfellow.

After graduating from Yale and sojourning briefly in Paris, Frank was swept up by the cultural and political movements of Greenwich Village in the period around World War I, precisely as Lewisohn had been. The literary scene in which Frank found himself was divided between two trends: on the one hand, an emerging high modernist movement—centered around magazines including *Poetry* and *The Little Review* and associated with cosmopolitan figures such as Ezra Pound and T. S. Eliot; and on the other, the "Young Americans," committed to fostering an indigenous visionary tradition linked with American Romanticism. Frank found a set of allies in the second of these groups. In figures such as Randolph Bourne, Lewis Mumford, and Van Wyck Brooks, he discovered a community of like-minded young writers who shared his dismay at the materialistic and militaristic turn in the country, and who drew a sense of hope from new movements in American literary culture.

A rallying point for their work was *The Seven Arts,* an influential though short-lived magazine that Frank founded and edited along with poet James Oppenheim and critic Van Wyck Brooks in 1916. "We are living in the first days of a renascent period," the editors announced in the inaugural issue, "a time which means for America the coming of that national self-consciousness which is the beginning of greatness."[6] *The Seven Arts* proved instrumental in shaping a modern literary culture linked back to the vision of American Romanticism. While the journal lasted (patrons withdrew support after a year because of the avowedly pacifist views of the editors), it provided a key forum for American writers such as Sherwood Anderson, Robert Frost, Amy Lowell, and Hart Crane. The patron saint of the journal was Walt Whitman, evoked in nearly every article of the first issue as a voice of true freedom and as an indispensable guide for the present age. From Whitman's critique of industrial society in the name of organicism and solidarity—typified by his essay "Democratic Vistas" (1867)—they derived a sense of their own mission and direction. Though Whitman was widely recognized as a kindred spirit by advocates for artistic, political, and sexual freedom, from Oscar Wilde to Emma Goldman to Jose Marti (as well as to several Yiddish poets, as we see in chapter 7), he held an uncertain position in a mainstream American literary culture in which Longfellow and James Lowell were still considered exemplary poets.[7] Nor did the modernist sophisticates set much store by him. Ezra Pound spoke for them when he referred to Whitman as a "pig-headed father" with whom he had reluctantly made a truce.[8] So when Frank and his cohorts sought consciously to follow Whitman's lead, it was in defiance of the conventionalism of the established order as well as the anti-Romantic sophistication of the new modernists.

It was also while editing *The Seven Arts* that Frank began rethinking the place of Jews in modern culture. He articulated his new understanding of Judaism in *Our America* (1919), a manifesto-like work that called for a revolution in the arts to save America's ailing democracy. Framed at one end by an epigraph from Whitman's "Starting at Paumanok" and by a concluding chapter called "The Multitudes in Whitman" at the other, Frank seeks in this work to recover Whitman's radical democratic vision in the context of post–World War I America. The premise of Frank's argument is that the spiritual anemia that has come to typify the national character is a direct result of the process of setting the New World. He discovers that the need to tame the wilderness turned early settlers into paragons of self-discipline—and victims of self-repression. The most successful settlers turned out to be Puritans, who had already internalized the stern work ethic of the rising middle classes in sixteenth-century England. "The Puritan's nature fitted him superbly to be a pioneer," Frank argues, and "the pioneer existence made permanent the Puritan's nature" (OA 63). Puritanism represents, in a word, self-negation: "Whole departments of his psychic life [were] repressed. Categories of desire [were] inhibited. Reaches of consciousness [were] lopped off" (OA 19). Frank discovers traces of this Puritan legacy everywhere from the self-discipline of the businessman, who knows no truth beside lucre, and the philosophy of Pragmatism, with its preference for utility over value. In both cases, spiritual awareness and depth had been sacrificed for efficiency, leaving the nation defenseless against the "sweep of material aggrandizement" (OA 92). The destruction of Indian culture, which Frank discusses in the most plaintive chapter of the book, is a result and haunting symbol of this spiritually deprived American character.

Frank's critique of the pioneer ethos suggests a sharp revision of what was then a more standard account of American settlement. In "The Significance of the Frontier in American History" (1894), historian Frederick Jackson Turner celebrated the frontier as the cauldron for all that was praiseworthy in the American character.[9] The repeated return to primitive conditions along the frontier line, Turner explained, had forced pioneers to develop the individualism, inventiveness, and impatience with European forms and traditions for which Americans have become famous. For Frank, by contrast, the individualist pioneer is only one feature of the American scene, and hardly the more salutary. For him the truly exemplary American is neither the pioneer, the Puritan, nor the self-made man, but the spiritually awakened believer in democracy and human solidarity. And the place where Frank expects to find this believer is not the frontier, but the city, particularly in the new cultural movements in New

York and Chicago, each of which is the subject of a separate chapter in *Our America*.

Among the heroes of *Our America* who embody this positive vision are figures such as Whitman, John Brown, and Abraham Lincoln, all of them linked to a subtradition Frank calls "mystic America." Frank describes these figures as inheritors of a spiritual vision, a rhetorical style, and a political mission that can be traced to the Hebrew Bible: "No external or intellectual reason can explain why we turn instinctively from the divine words of [Lincoln] to the divine words of David or Isaiah. . . . Words came pure from [Lincoln's] prophetic faith as light comes up from fire" (OA 53). Whitman is linked to Moses: "[Whitman] talked with God, standing upon America as Moses upon Sinai. He talked with God, speaking our tongue" (OA 204). Thus the contending symbolic figures in American history are the Puritan (linked to the pioneer and the capitalist) and the prophet (rooted in biblical tradition and linked with political idealists, writers, and artists). Frank's purpose is to recuperate the democratic faith of the latter, which he sees as having gone underground: "The qualities in America I loved were secret," he explains in the preface; "[I was faced with] the whole vast problem of reaching down to the hidden vitals, and of bringing these up—their energy and truth—into the play of articulate life" (OA 3–4). The "secret America" still existed; the problem was finding forms in which to express it.

Frank devotes a chapter of *Our America* to fitting American Jews into this drama of repression and release. He argues that, on the one hand, American Jews recapitulate the negative movement of the pioneers: they too have become immersed in the material life of the country, betraying their spiritual heritage. But, on the other hand, if this has led to a generation of "anaesthetic Jews" (typified for Frank by Ethical Culture Jews like his parents), it has not managed to sever Jews completely from their tradition: "The mystical Jew survived," Frank writes. "But he slept" (OA 84). Jews can still tap into the key "prophetic" insight, which Frank glosses as the "lifting of individual consciousness to the sphere of the universal" (OA 81). What the prophets understood was the true relationship between the finite and the infinite: "If man, who is finite, knows an infinite world, he is infinite as well. He loses his identity, disappears from the snug center of the universe he had so long occupied. But he reappears in a far more powerful modification: as an inclusive attribute of the universal" (OA 81–82). What Frank calls "the Jewish genius" is this dialectical understanding of the universal and the particular. All individuals are "modifications"— the phrase comes from Spinoza—of a divine oneness.

In the emerging cultural revolution in modern America, Frank perceives signs of a "new rising of the Jew," a renaissance among Jewish artists and thinkers energized by this very understanding. He identifies Jewish innovators in a variety of media: in the music of Leo Ornstein, the art criticism of Paul Rosenfeld, the poetry of James Oppenheim, and the photography of Alfred Stieglitz. Ornstein's music becomes "clashing paeans of release" (OA 188), Oppenheim's theme the "[r]evolution of self in a new-won consciousness" (OA 191). Stieglitz becomes for Frank a prototype for the modern visionary who is simultaneously the true Jew: "[Stieglitz] takes up the ancient destiny where the degenerate Jew . . . let it fall. He is the prophet. And his ways are near to the old ways of his people. He has been the true Apostle of self-liberation in a destructive land" (OA 186). To link the quintessential urban artist whose life's work involved the legitimation of photography with "the old ways of his people" reveals Frank's confidence that modern forms can carry and revitalize "ancient" traditions. This will be the key to Frank's modernism: the search for new flasks to hold the old wine of the biblical prophetic tradition.

Frank's *Our America* thus envisions an American avant-garde dependent upon spiritually awakened Jewish artists in its ranks. There are, to be sure, key figures in this movement who are not Jews (e.g., Sherwood Anderson, Dreiser, Mencken, and Bourne), but the point is that for Frank the deeper vision he looks for among America's progressive artists is essentially analogous to what he values in Judaism. For one thing, since Frank is imagining a counter-hegemonic movement from within a Christian society, the insurgent artist must needs resemble the Jewish infidel as a holdout for the real redemption. The figure of the Jew represents the possibility of recovering the utopian *desire* within biblical prophecy without the alleged fulfillment (in Christ). More broadly speaking, Frank imagines the Jew as a direct link to a biblical view of faith, which he sees as a necessary corrective to the "idolatry of the machine" that has overtaken the land. As he announces epigrammatically: "Hebrew the seed; America the fruit" (OA 188). The boldest and most promising aspects of the American experiment are directly fed by the "Hebrew" vision. And if Americans had an innate tendency to become a people "centrifugal, nervous, impatient" (OA 231), the "Hebrew" vision, sustained by modern artists, could still root them, unify them, and remind them that human creation is connected to a transcendent purpose.

The Problem of Form

Just after completing *Our America*, Frank began a period of travel that brought him to the South and the Midwest. Having written about Whitman's "open road" of freedom in *Our America*, he now set out to find it himself. Among his experiences was a stint working in Ellsworth, Kansas, writing editorials on the conditions of farm laborers and working as an organizer for Arthur Townley's Non-Partisan League, a socialist-front attempt to revive the Populist vote. Frank also took a trip through the South with the Harlem Renaissance writer Jean Toomer, who proposed to show him Negro life from the inside. Frank records in his memoirs that he lived "among Negroes as if I were a Negro. . . . It [was] quietly assumed that if I came with Toomer I must be a Negro" (M 103–104). He traveled in Jim Crow cars, stayed with Toomer's friends, and spoke in Negro churches on the continuing relevance of religion in the scientific age—all the while introduced simply as a "professor from the North" (M 105). What he saw affected him profoundly—not only the indignities blacks were forced to endure but also their tenacity and creativity: "This I saw was the meaning of their dance and music. They crooned, they twisted, they slid sideways in escape from a cold world—and they survived!" (M 105). The Negro is a powerful inspiration for Frank, but he remains convinced that as a Jew he has his own traditions to mine.

Frank's private notebooks are a useful guide to his developing ideas about religion during these years. These notebooks contain a series of meditations whose aphoristic format recalls Pascal's *Pensées;* in fact, many passages are set down under the heading "Thoughts" and sometimes "Pensées." As Frank's religious sensibility developed, Pascal was indeed an important influence, providing a model for the solitary religious seeker. While traveling in Richmond, Virginia, Frank recorded a series of experiences that he described in these terms:

> Scattered Notes of Thought and Vision Placed here at random for my own Guidance at such Time . . . when I feel readier to write The Jewish Word—my Own Confession of Jewish Consciousness which came to me in the year 1920: Making me Know Myself at last Part of a Vast Human Drama, a Transcendent Mystery—the Contemporary in a Way Terribly Intense of Spinoza, Philo, Jesus, Jeremiah.[10]

Frank appears to have had a series of religious experiences that he took to be the realization of his own "Jewish Consciousness." The figures he mentions—Spinoza, Philo, Jesus, Jeremiah—became his own personal visionary company, a group of metaphysical thinkers whom he claimed as essentially Jewish, and as his predecessors. Jesus and Spinoza were often evoked as heroes in the discourse of modern Jewish culture—both being heterodox Jewish figures who could be claimed as a part of a usable past for modern Jews. Frank further explicates his notion of Jewish consciousness in these terms:

> We behold in our straitened mind-cell, separate strands of the Whole. And we attempt to bring these strands together within the moment of our consciousness. But they reach forth into dimensions vastly beyond us: where indeed they conjoin into a unitary resolution. It is futile to try and force them into their almighty unity, within our petty fragment of a mind: and it is futile to deplore our failure. Better to watch, in the very insoluble apartness of the strands of Life within our minds, a gorgeous proof of how vastly Life looms beyond us.[11]

Frank reveals here his growing interest in the concept of "the Whole"—a central theme in his work from the 1920s through *The Rediscovery of Man: A Memoir and Methodology for Modern Life* (1958). For Frank, we belong to "the Whole," but our minds can only gain a fragmentary perception of it. Our challenge is to satisfy ourselves with our dim and shifting perception of infinitude. We must be content with partial vision, understanding ourselves as part of "the Whole" while withstanding the temptation to force some false unity.

In the years following these transformative experiences, Frank set himself the challenge of developing a means of bearing witness to this "Jewish" view of the absolute in modern forms. His descriptions in his memoirs of his travels through Eastern Europe reveal how he formulated this challenge. In 1927, on his way to Palestine at the behest of Chaim Weitzmann, who hoped to inspire him to become a spokesman for Zionism, Frank traveled throughout Galicia and Lithuania. Yiddish novelist Sholem Asch served as his guide through Warsaw. In his account of this trip, Frank writes that he felt "separation from these Jews and did not want to be separate." He also calls it a "healing" experience, in which he and the Yiddish-speaking Jews were ultimately able to exchange "tears of empathy" (M 175). He describes the East European Jews as inhabiting a previous moment in history: "These Polish and Galician Jews were, for the most part, ignorant of what had happened in the world since the eighteenth century. In time they were laggards; and under the squalor and the fetor of their filth-cursed homes, they touched eternity and were aware of it" (M 175). Frank interprets the observance of Jewish Law as an effort to make "flesh and bone of their vision of the divine and the eternal."[12] To enact the commandments is to give symbolic expression to an awareness of eternity within temporality. For the modern, Western Jew, the commandments could not and should not be revived or retained: "[The commandments] had come forth from an agrarian, intuitive culture. For our civilization of science, their *equivalents* must be created: commandments (of course, under another name) to rediscover the whole society, the whole man" (M 175; emphasis in original). The organic community had fallen apart, and its cultural forms no longer applied. New forms were required to express the central teaching of Judaism, the doctrine of immanence and the imperative to seek wholeness.

Frank saw the novel as one form that might enable the recovery of spiritual knowledge by bearing witness to the "whole man." In his fictional works from this period, including *Rahab* (1922), *City Block* (1922), and *Holiday* (1923), Frank sought ways to represent the internal states of characters as they engaged in the essentially religious quest to understand their place in the universe. Since the goal was to explore shifts in awareness, he rejected linear form along with any omniscient or otherwise removed perspective. What he developed was an approach he termed the "lyrical novel," which works by shuttling back and forth between objective events and the subjective movements of consciousness, including sense perceptions, memories, and fantasies. These are frequently related by first-person internal monologues, which themselves often break into verse. The closest analogue to Frank's lyrical novels is perhaps Virginia Woolf's *The Waves* (1931), with its use of poetic language punctuated by recurrent images and rhythmic repetitions to represent characters' internal states. In Frank's novels, the internal monologues of different characters are transcribed in a nearly identical lyrical voice, as if to demonstrate the underlying unity that connects individuals across divisions of class, race, and gender.

The work that reveals how Judaism fits in with this project is *Rahab* (1922), published the same year (and by the same publisher, Boni and Liveright) as Lewisohn's *Up Stream*. *Rahab* evokes in its title the Canaanite prostitute who provides lodging to the spies sent by Joshua to stake out enemy territory in Jericho. In the biblical passage, Rahab is ordered to deliver them up to the king, but hides them away, having recognized that the God of the Israelites is "the only God in heaven above" (Joshua 2:11) and that the land is destined for them. When the Israelites return and conquer Canaan, Rahab is spared and, as the text relates, "she dwelt among the Israelites—as is still the case" (Joshua 6:25). Frank's Rahab, by contrast, is a New York City madam named Fanny Luve. Like her biblical counterpart, she is a non-Jew who comes to identify with the Jews for whom she provides shelter. Frank's interest in the biblical figure of Rahab is linked to her status as prostitute (and hence as a figure for the marginal and the "immoral," from the standpoint of Christianity) and also as a convert to Judaism, someone who transforms through the agency of Jews.

Frank also may very well have been aware of the tradition recounted in Louis Ginzberg's *Legends of the Jews*, translated into English in 1909, which claims Rahab as an ancestor of eight prophets and priests, including Jeremiah.[13] In his reworking of the biblical story of Rahab, Frank attempts to speak on behalf of this prophetic tradition in the modernist form of the "lyrical novel."

The novel is framed by a visit from a young Jew named Samson Brenner to Fanny's brothel. A law student who aspires to be a poet, he is, like the biblical Samson, a Jew with depleted strength. When Samson enters the antechamber to the brothel and glimpses the Bible that Fanny holds dear, he confesses that he can't read the original: "If there's any soul in me worth speaking of, it's in that book. Yet I can't read a word of it, except in English . . . I'm ashamed of that."[14] Frank uses this opening, a restaging of the encounter between the Israelite spies and Rahab, to recast the biblical tale of physical danger in enemy territory as an allegory for spiritual crisis. The modern Jew is not in danger from the Canaanites: he is at risk of losing his soul.

For her part, Fanny sees the young Jew as someone who might save *her*, as we learn through the transcription of her internal speech: "Will you at least, after these years, these years, such years, be my healer?" (R 24–25). And indeed, we learn that Samson's powers have remained intact, as if his ancient inheritance were lodged within a deeper layer of his consciousness that he cannot quite access. As Samson recites a poem for Fanny, Frank transcribes her response:

> He spoke his poem through soft hands. The poem was a stiff, an alien thing: but her words she had not spoken in the glow of his face were his and came back to her, a poem.
> —I become myself. . . . He has young eyes—the shadows that rim them are marked by a thousand years . . . (R 42)

Though his poem remains "alien" on his tongue, it gains vitality in the crucible of *her* mind. In this way, the young Jew becomes a catalyst for Fanny's self-knowledge ("I become myself") even though he remains unconscious of his power: the "shadows that rim his eyes" bespeak ancient knowledge. Frank's Jewish visitor to the brothel is thus a kind of "inchoate Jew," one who carries a secret knowledge that he cannot understand himself.

The novel focuses on the transformation of the gentile, who recognizes in the Jewish characters the embodiment of spiritual principles. Through a series of flashbacks, Frank recounts the tumultuous life of his female, gentile protagonist. In her youth, she is seduced by a gallant southerner who turns to alcohol, women, and gambling just as their daughter is born. In her loneliness and abjection, she takes a lover, a Jew named Leon Dannenberg, who becomes the embodiment of insight and holiness in the text, the fully realized Jew who represents the counterpoint to the young lawyer who visits Fanny's brothel. While Fanny is off with her Jewish lover, her husband falls under the influence of an evangelical minister and embraces the church and the habit of proselytizing. When Fanny confesses her unfaithfulness, he sanctimoniously sends her forth from their home *"for the cause of fornication."* His violent rejection of sexuality reveals Frank's polemic against Christianity as reinforcing an artificial dualism. Fanny's Jewish lover now becomes her guide; she must leave her husband and move out into the world. He assures her that she will unearth her "inviolable self" when she encounters the reality of life: "You were muddied and thick. . . . Look down, now through the clearness of yourself, to the dirt base" (R 39). The Jew represents the negation of the pious abstractions of Christianity; his wisdom lies in pointing toward direct experience, the only ground for spiritual knowledge: "We are no longer prophets," he tells her, "save in our lives. Live" (R 77). One gains "prophetic" knowledge by becoming immersed in the "dirt base" of experience. Fanny moves alone to New York City, considering her life now a quest for spiritual knowledge.

Central to Fanny's quest is her effort to rethink the Christian dogmas in which she has been ensnared. As she does this, she dwells incessantly on the enigma of Judaism. Passages in stream of consciousness show her grappling with the theological possibilities bodied forth by living Jews: "The Jews saw God. . . . Why do they leave you, Christ, you and your words in silence? Are they so close to you they do not hear you? Are they so close to you that they are you?" (R 134). Finally the enigma of the Jewish denial of Christ is resolved by her realization that Christ's essence endures within the Jews. But what does Christ signify in the context of Frank's novel? The primacy awarded to unmediated experience in *Rahab* suggests that Jesus cannot stand for an agent of salvation, a healing imposed from without. Rather, as Fanny comes to see, "life is a wound that only life can heal" (R 168): any meaningful solution to the agonies of living must somehow emerge out of actual experience. In later writings, Frank will write of "the Jewish method of confronting the dark terror of human existence," which leads to "the revelation that each man has God within him." He then adds that "this [is] the alpha and omega of the message of Jesus."[15] Jesus is a symbol or a "type" for the immanence of God, not the agent of salvation. In *Rahab,* this notion is encapsulated at a climactic moment of the novel, in a vision Fanny has of Christ:

> She saw him clear upon the long black earth. . . . A tree, blasted by
> lightning, thrust its ruin against a purple sky. . . . Christ raised his arms,
> but his eyes looked down upon the barren earth. He was changed. He
> was twisted like the tree. He was shaped like the tree. . . . He had lost his
> hands even as the tree its leaves. His feet were buried underneath the
> ground. (R 185)

In Fanny's vision, Christ has become indistinguishable from the mate-
riality of the cross itself; he is "twisted like the tree." Jesus is linked to the
depths of existence, not the heights of the heavens. When Fanny has this
"vision," she does not join some hypothetical community of the saved;
rather, she gains renewed conviction in her Jewish lover's teaching about
this world as infused with holiness. At the end of *Rahab*, Frank's heroine is
represented as having reached an initial stage of enlightenment by relinquishing the desire to be healed, by refusing, like the Jews, to look for an
outside agent of salvation. In the final image of the novel, Frank presents
Fanny on her way to rebirth: "From the wreckage of her features there was
born a smile making them clear and sharp, making them fair and high. A
light shone in them" (R 250). According to the logic of the novel, she has
shifted allegiance, like the biblical Rahab, becoming a metaphoric Jew.
Fanny remains within the precincts of the brothel, which stands allegorically for embodied experience, for resistance to pious abstraction, and
for an improvised community of seekers.

Frank's dialogue with Christianity in *Rahab* stands near the beginning of
a long tradition of texts by Jewish Americans that engage with the figure of
Jesus. Among many examples, we might consider Henry Roth's *Call It Sleep*,
which constructs its climactic scene as a symbolic crucifixion and rebirth;
Nathanael West's "Miss Lonelyhearts," which introduces its Christlike protagonist in a tiny chamber whose only decoration is a crucifix; and Arthur
Miller's *After the Fall*, which concludes with the protagonist standing center-
stage, arms stretched out, in yet another impersonation of the Christ figure.
Leslie Fiedler discusses these works in his essay "The Christian-ness of the
Jewish-American Writer" (1983), and calls them examples of "Jewish Chris-
tolatry": they have an obsession with the motif of salvation rooted in a single
suffering individual. For Fiedler, the prevalence of this motif and the accompanying assemblage of Christian symbols that animate these authors' works
prove that their psyches have been hollowed out of any traditional Jewish
mythology and theology. In the vacuum opened up by the departure of
specifically Jewish teachings, the symbols of Christianity come rushing in.
But the reading of *Rahab* I have outlined suggests another conclusion,
pointing to the limits of Fiedler's undialectical archetypal method. What is

crucial in Frank's writing is not the sheer presence of the "Christ motif," but the reclamation of Jesus as the embodiment of Frank's theology of immanence, which he nominates as a specifically *Jewish* doctrine. Frank exemplifies here a broader pattern in modern Jewish culture. "Modern Jewish thought," Susannah Heschel has written, "has been formed not simply by creating a Jewish historical narrative but by attempting a rebirth of the Christian mythic potential under Jewish auspices."[16] When Frank appropriates the figure of Jesus for his lyrical novel, he critiques Christian otherworldliness, offering a (Jewish) argument that if salvation is to be found it must be within embodied experience.

Frank's evocation of the biblical account of Rahab suggests an approach to the novel similar to what T. S. Eliot, in his essay on *Ulysses*, famously called "the mythical method." Eliot understood Joyce to be using the Homeric plot as a way of "controlling, of ordering, of giving a shape and a significance to the immense panorama of futility and anarchy which is contemporary history."[17] Frank is similarly preoccupied with the problem of "significance" in "contemporary history," but, unlike Eliot in this passage, Frank views loss as illusory, as an effect of mistaken consciousness, not of what Eliot called "anarchy which is contemporary history." Frank's faith in "the Whole" immunizes him from Eliot's desperation. He uses the story of Rahab, then, not so much as an ordering principle, superimposed upon chaos, but as a model for the contemporary individual striving toward wholeness.[18]

Belonging and Not-Belonging

To grasp the significance of Frank's fascination with Judaism in the years during and after World War I, we might consider him in relation to the generation of innovative Jewish intellectuals who emerged in Germany during this same period. Indeed, Frank's German cultural background, his parents' commitment to liberalism and rationalism, and his deep estrangement from institutional Judaism all point to the common ground he shared with Jews coming of age during the same years in Germany. Frank's subsequent turn toward modernist aesthetics, radical politics, psychoanalysis, and various forms of mysticism suggest parallels between his intellectual development and that of numerous German Jewish figures of this period, including Walter Benjamin, Martin Buber, Franz Rosenzweig, Gershom Scholem, and Else Lasker-Schueler.[19] Benjamin, in particular, was deeply engaged at different points in his life with each of the ideologies that attracted Frank.

In many ways, the comparison between Frank and these other figures is apt. All tended to conceive of their efforts to reinvigorate Judaism as part of a generational struggle against acculturating parents. Frank's singling out of his father's Society for Ethical Culture as the symbol of American Jewry's failings recalls the Oedipal battles staged in German-language Jewish texts such as Kafka's *Letter to His Father* (1919) or Scholem's autobiographical *From Berlin to Jerusalem* (1980). In all these instances, the fathers are linked with a weakened or depleted tradition. Kafka complains that his father's Judaism "dribbled away" while he was passing it along; Scholem faults his father for making a "deliberate mockery" of Judaism.[20] The sons seek out alternate Jewish traditions that they identify with true spiritual power: Kafka turns to the Yiddish theater, Scholem to Kabbalah and messianism, Buber to Hasidism, and Frank to the tradition of "prophetic" Judaism moving from Jeremiah to Jesus to Spinoza. But a crucial difference may be seen between Frank and his German contemporaries, which may be attributed to his *Americanness.* Unlike Benjamin and these others, Frank was able to imagine a deep and abiding linkage between Judaism and the mythos of his own country. He conceived of Jews as bearers and sustainers of the spiritual vision that nourished America in the first place; hence, they had an integral role to play in America's further unfolding. Frank's turn toward Judaism, which reinforced his sense of himself as a cultural rebel, also reinforced his commitment to what he considered the true destiny of America. In short, from Frank's perspective, the Jew *as Jew* could be woven into the narrative of America's coming-into-fulfillment; Jewishness and Americanness could complement one another for Frank in ways that Jewishness and Germanness could not for somebody like Benjamin.[21] We might say that while the category of Germanness came increasingly to be conceived in static, racial terms, the category of Americanness—in spite of the nativist challenge—could still be embraced by the avant-garde as a progressive idea.

Nevertheless, for all his efforts to link the destiny of Jews with America, Frank maintained that Jews must cling to the notion of exile. Jews could think of themselves as the truest of "spiritual Americans" but only, paradoxically, if they clung to a sense of the uniqueness of their past and ultimate destiny. This becomes a central theme in a number of his later nonfictional writings, where he speculates on the fate of the "Jewish genius" in a world that had suddenly turned unthinkably hostile toward living Jews. These works include a group of essays published in the volume *The Jew in Our Time* (1944), and the book *Bridgehead: The Drama of Israel* (1957), an account of Frank's travels in Israel in the mid-1950s. In these works, Frank insists again and again on what he calls the immutable fact of Jewish *difference*—owing to Jews' spiritual legacy and role as messengers to the greater world. In the same breath that he denounces Hitler's satanic effort to annihilate the Jewish people, for example, Frank warns against the tendency to defend Jews merely by asserting their underlying similarity with all peoples. Antisemitism exists in part, he suggests, because of the unique challenge Jews have posed to incorporate into one's daily conduct the "counterpoint of immanence and transcendence" (B 211), the idea that human life is infused with and structured by a relation to the absolute.

Frank's understanding of Jewish difference made him particularly wary of what he understood as the Zionist aim of achieving Jewish "normalization." After traveling through Israel in the mid-1950s, Frank writes admiringly in *Bridgehead* of the courage and energy of Israelis while expressing dismay over what he calls their "quest for the normal": "Out of the centuries in which the Jews accepted their destiny as apart, and were crucified for it, has come this thirst of the Israelis to be not saviors, not world-leaders, certainly not the Lord's sacrifice, but normal people. . . . But heroes and martyrs are not normal people. And to be a Jew, whether one likes or dislikes it, is no normal destiny" (B 131). Israelis hardly think of themselves as "Jews," he asserts, since the word is "eloquent of all the *abnormalities* of twenty centuries of exile" (B 119). And with the constant threat of Arab invasion, he explains, Israelis have had to pay excessive attention to the problem of self-defense. The problems of practical existence have made them ignore the traditional Jewish concern with eternity.[22] *Bridgehead* concludes with Frank's own midrash on the biblical story of Jacob's dream. Jacob's vision of angels ascending and descending a ladder, Frank proposes, is "a succinct symbol of the nature of Judaism" (B 210). The ladder, he suggests, is an allegory for prayer. "Prayer is a two-way conduit. Man aspires, but also heaven inspires. . . . Here, in a metaphor, we have the immanence of God on earth and in man, and contrapuntally the transcendence of man toward God" (B 210–211). This reading of Jacob's ladder—which recalls Buber's I-and-Thou philosophy or Abraham Joshua Heschel's understanding of God and man in search of each other—follows from the privileging of direct experience over doctrine that we saw in *Rahab:* the divine exists neither as a source of precepts nor as some guarantor of our salvation, but rather as a grounding for human existence that must be encountered and reencountered ever anew.

Having started out after 1910 in the same cultural circles as Ludwig Lewisohn, Frank thus arrived at different conclusions. Both grew up in homes where Judaism was a dead letter, and both found their way to a renewed sense of themselves as Jews in the wake of World War I, after periods of involvement with the same New York bohemian circles. Their understanding of Judaism was shaped within the terms of an American literary culture fired by a self-assumed mandate to topple the moribund genteel tradition. Their differences might be summarized by saying that Lewisohn argued that Jewishness marked out a separate current of human life while Frank emphasized the inherent connection between the Jew and the experimental culture of the avant-garde. Since Lewisohn thought the inner Jew, once liberated, would proceed to speak its own truth, he was uninterested in the problem of literary form. Moreover, he was convinced that since pacifism was a central axiom of the prophets, any Jewish State would necessarily be free of the dangers of militarism. Frank, by contrast, was forever concerned that the constructs of the human mind might obscure the divine, and thus the problem was to find new forms that might keep perception fresh. As for a Jewish state, this too seemed like a traditional "form" that might burden the Jewish genius, which, like the avant-garde, required conditions of "abnormality" to express itself. Thus whereas Lewisohn ultimately became a Zionist, maintaining that at least in principle there could be a true home for the Jew, Frank insisted that the Jew's destiny was to dwell within the broader world and participate creatively in its unfolding. "This is the paradox of Israel: their belonging within their not-belonging," he wrote in 1957. "[And this] applies as intensely (although the terms have changed) to their presence in Tel Aviv as to their presence in New York or Moscow" (B xi). The task of the Jewish writer, as Frank understood it, was to inhabit and bear witness to multiple dimensions: the finite and the infinite, the concrete reality of the here-and-now, and the divine oneness that enfolds all. What Lewisohn and Frank share—and what makes them both representative figures in the encounter between Jewish American writers and American literary culture—is their construction of the "Jewish genius" as a principle of personal and political transformation.

5

CINDERELLA'S DYBBUK

Anzia Yezierska as the Voice of Generations

Take me, cowl'd forms, and fence me round,
Till I possess my soul again.
—Matthew Arnold,
"Stanzas from the Grande Chartreuse"

In the early 1920s, Anzia Yezierska was a newly risen star in the firmament of American literature, having been dubbed the "sweatshop Cinderella" by the popular press upon the success of *Hungry Hearts* (1919), her first collection of short stories. These stories offered American readers a glimpse into the world of the Jewish immigrant, a world Yezierska decorated with a colorful cast of characters: the passionate immigrant girl striving for love and acceptance; the long-suffering Old World mother, tirelessly devoted to her children; the hoary patriarch, steeped in a rigid Orthodoxy; and the gallant gentile man, reaching out to the downtrodden. As Mary Dearborn has proposed, Yezierska was herself one of her most compelling creations.[1] In interviews and magazine articles, she related her life-story as a dramatic rise from the squalor of tenement life to the heights of literary success. She reinforced the fairy-tale-like quality of her life by embellishing certain details, including her age (she tended to make herself younger) and the role played by German Jewish benefactors (they tended to disappear in her telling). Her very name was in many ways an invention, or at least an act of strategic self-positioning: given the name "Hattie Meyer" upon arrival in the New World at about the age of ten, she reclaimed her original, more foreign-sounding name just in time for her appearance in the public eye.[2]

My aim here is to explore her work in relation to the dynamics of Jewish American literary culture in the 1920s that we have identified in the work of Lewisohn and Frank. This may not necessarily seem the most obvious context in which to place Yezierska, since unlike Lewisohn and Frank, she was born in Eastern Europe and grew up as a Yiddish-speaking immigrant on the Lower East Side. Biographically, she shares more with Mary Antin, her exact contemporary. Like Antin, Yezierska arrived in the New World on the verge of adolescence, so that her immersion in American life coincided with her own coming-of-age. She grew up poised between an immigrant community and a greater American society infused with Progressive-Era idealism, and the drama of her early life centered around her family's efforts to combat crushing poverty and privation. At times, her writing recalls Antin's exuberant faith in American civic institutions and in the social agenda of "up lift." Nevertheless, as I will argue, Yezierska ultimately shares more with the rebellious, experimental, and utopian avant-garde of the 1920s than she does with the pre–World War I Progressive moment I associate with Antin. Indeed, in what follows, I will suggest that Yezierska's fiction might be read as a direct reworking of Antin's optimistic immigration narrative in *The Promised Land*. From her perspective as an East European immigrant, Yezierska offers another version of the politically subversive, prophetic Jew.

The Breakdown of Progressivism

Two contexts might be noted for the differences between Antin and Yezierska, one geographical, the other historical. The first forces us to consider the cultural divide separating Antin's Boston from Yezierska's New York. Antin's autobiography traces her American education from a public school in Chelsea to the prestigious Girls' Latin School in Boston and finally to the Hale House Settlement, where she learned the wonders of natural history. The key venue for Antin's writing was *The Atlantic Monthly,* another

Boston institution, which was intent on creating an American literary culture defined by an elegant high literary style. By contrast, Yezierska shaped her outlook amidst the radical political ferment of New York's Lower East Side. She boarded for a time at the dormitory of the Rand School for Social Science, a pioneering workers' education school sponsored by the American Socialist Society. Modeled after the Socialist People's Houses in Europe, it became one of the centers of cultural and educational activity for the radical left in New York. Yezierska read Emma Goldman and Havelock Ellis alongside Emerson and Whitman and became immersed in debates around women's suffrage, sexual morality, and birth control.

We might also consider that Antin and Yezierska shaped their literary projects on opposite sides of World War I, at different moments in the national debate around immigration. Antin published all of her significant works around 1912, during the heyday of the Progressive Party's struggle for immigrant rights. When she wrote *The Promised Land*, she was making a concrete political argument, one that was still relatively mainstream and that still stood a chance of gaining broad support. By contrast, Yezierska came into her own as a writer just after World War I when the nativist backlash against foreigners had become a major political force and the Progressive, integrationist ethos that inspired Antin was already past its pinnacle of public support. Representatives of philanthropic and educational institutions, who in Antin's *The Promised Land* are always heroes, are generally suspicious characters in Yezierska's writing, as in the cynical settlement-house teachers in *Arrogant Beggar* (1927) or the visitors from the "Social Betterment Society" who seek to control their "charges" in her short stories.[3] Yezierska was more inspired by an insurgent movement for cultural pluralism, which looked beyond the Progressive "up lift" message, advocating a new vision of American society as a haven for ethnic particularity. These different attitudes toward Americanization are legible in the names these writers chose to use: whereas the girl who was born "Mashke" will embrace her new name, Mary, the other, born "Anzia," will become Anzia once again.

The immediate context for Yezierska's emergence as a writer was her relationship with Pragmatist philosopher and educational theorist John Dewey.[4] In some ways, this relation was a reprise of the Lazarus–Emerson relationship: once again, a Jewish woman writer meets a towering presence in American letters, and once again this writer stages a confrontation in her own texts with the ideas these men stand for. As the story goes, Yezierska approached Dewey in his office at Columbia University in 1917, hoping he might look over a few stories she had written and help her launch a teaching career. Dewey was impressed enough by the stories to invite her to participate in a seminar he was giving at Columbia and later to join a research project on the Polish immigrant community of Philadelphia. Dewey evidently looked to Yezierska as a "native informant" who might help him understand the inner life of the immigrants targeted by his educational reforms. From Yezierska's side, Dewey functioned as a mentor just as she was developing her voice as a writer. As nearly every commentator on her work has observed, she dwelt recurrently, even obsessively, on this relationship in her novels and stories, playing out multiple scenarios involving a fiery, immigrant "Jewess" and a staid, well-established Anglo-Saxon man. Dewey moved, that is, from being a supporter of her work to being the substance of that work, and in thematizing their relationship she staged the debate between assimilation and cultural particularism.

Dewey's own attitudes about cultural pluralism and the role of immigrants in American life are by no means simple. Some scholars have argued that Dewey ultimately supported a version of cultural pluralism, seeing toleration of cultural and ethnic difference as one of the primary educational goals in a democracy.[5] Dewey was, indeed, a supporter of Horace Kallen's writings on cultural pluralism when they first appeared in 1915, and he decried the rise in xenophobia in American society. On the other hand, revisionist scholars have argued that Dewey's educational theories ultimately envisioned homogenization as a social ideal. In support of this latter view, Clarence Karier has written that "Dewey viewed ethnic and religious differences as a threat to the survival of society, to be overcome through assimilation. Dewey, as well as other liberal reformers, was committed to a flexible, experimentally managed, orderly social change that included a high degree of manipulation."[6] What seems clear is that Dewey's views about cultural difference cannot be easily pinned down as either "pro" or "con," and that, in any case, it is dangerous to use our current thinking about "diversity" as an index for his theories. What is striking, nevertheless, is that he appears to have seen in Yezierska somebody who might help him broaden his own vision.

Yezierska's role in Dewey's imagination may be understood by considering a poem he sent her soon after their first meeting. The poem, which Dewey never published himself, later surfaced verbatim in Yezierska's final novel *All I Could Never Be* (1932), which retells the story of their relationship in greater detail than her other works. A copy of the poem was also discovered among Dewey's papers in the mid-1970s by the scholar Jo Ann Boydston. Its significance to Yezierska is borne out by her proposal to her editor at Houghton Mifflin, Horace Greenslet, to have it printed on the frontispiece of her first collection of stories. The final stanzas read as follows:

Generations as yet unuttered, dumb, smothered,
    Inchoate, Unutterable by me and mine
In you I see them coming to be,
    Luminous slow-moving, ordered in rhythm.
You shall not utter them; you shall be them.
    And from out thy pain
A song shall fill the world.

And I, from afar shall see
    As one watching sees the star
Rise in the waiting heavens,
    And from the distance my hand shall clasp yours,
And an old world be content to go,
    Beholding the horizon
Tremulous with the generation of the dawn.[7]

Written soon after their first meeting, this poem has often been read as Dewey's candid confession of powerful romantic feelings for Yezierska, an episode that in itself reveals a much more complex figure than Dewey's stoical public persona would have implied.[8] I would also suggest that the poem—and the Dewey–Yezierska relationship more broadly—reveals something about the status of the Progressive project itself by 1917. In the poem, Dewey seems to surrender some measure of authority to Yezierska, the immigrant writer, on the grounds that she possesses insight and authority barred to him, the American-born philosopher. Dewey seems directly to evoke Whitman's idea of an inclusive democratic community, but with the crucial difference that Dewey does not possess Whitman's confidence that he himself participates in this new dispensation, that *his* self is wide enough to encompass the multitudes. Compare Dewey's lines, "Generations as yet unuttered, dumb, smothered, / Unutterable by me and mine" with Whitman's lines, "Through me many long, dumb voices, / Voices of interminable generations of prisoners and slaves."[9] Both Dewey and Whitman imagine America as a place where historical injustices will be overcome through *representation,* where the despised "generations" will be given a voice through a representative speaker. But in Dewey's post-Whitmanian poem, the "I" has become a mere spectator; he embodies "an old world, content to go." The voice of the generations is "*Unutterable* by me and mine" (italics added). By emphasizing this gap between an old "me and mine" and a new "you," Dewey seems to register a division between himself and the wider democratic populous, which he associates with Yezierska. Dewey's poem, then, suggests that from his perspective, Whitman's lofty democratic vision—predicated on the idea that the human soul can be crossed by multiple voices—might be sustained by the immigrant, who is uniquely capable of being "in touch" with the people. If Dewey's new "dawn" of social harmony is to be reached, it is Yezierska, the immigrant Jew, who must lead the way.

But if Dewey looked to Yezierska to compensate for his own lack of "vision," how did this transfer of cultural authority affect Yezierska? It would seem, indeed, that she at once embraced her role as conduit for the "generations" and found herself caught up in the unavoidable paradoxes of this situation. On the one hand, she was being entrusted with the lofty task of bringing the social and political mission of the New World itself to its fruition. On the other, these were manifestly *Dewey's* terms and *Dewey's* fantasy of her. In the poem, Yezierska is commanded to become the "generations" incarnate: "You shall not utter them; you shall *be* them" (emphasis added). One version of this paradox is evoked in *All I Could Never Be,* when the Yezierska figure, Fanya Ivanova, brings the Dewey figure, Henry Scott, to the Lower East Side (replicating an actual visit that took place in 1917). Having initially felt ashamed of her people, Fanya now suddenly feels pride when she observes them through his eyes: "He had made her see through the dirt and the poverty into their hearts, until the ghetto rose before her, a city set on a high hill whose light could not be hid."[10] The ghetto, and Jewishness itself, becomes beautiful to her because it is beautiful to him. As if to emphasize that these are his terms, Yezierska borrows John Winthrop's "city on the hill" speech, addressed to the Puritan founders of the Massachusetts Bay Colony, to describe her return to the Lower East Side. She becomes the Jew as Puritan settler, arriving in a Jewish colony in the New World. But how will Yezierska take this role and make it her own? How will she tell her "own" story, and what model of Jewish identity will she articulate as she does so?

Yezierska as Ethnic Modernist

An illuminating text about these dynamics is "My Own People" (1919), written just in the aftermath of her relationship with Dewey and concerned, as the title indicates, with the relationship between individual Jew and the Jewish collectivity. The first image in the story is that of an aspiring writer, Sophie Sapinsky, moving through the East Side ghetto, searching for a room in which to write. Cheap rooms recur in Yezierska's work as transition points, liminal zones where the self can be rearranged in solitude. A room of one's own, however, is never a sufficient end in itself. Isolation exposes Yezierska's heroines to the risk of existential dissolution:

"Was it worth while," Sophie worries, "to give up the peace of home, the security of a regular job—suffer hunger, loneliness and want—for what? . . . Would her writing ever amount to enough to vindicate the uprooting from her past?" (HH 139). Sophie's initial attempts at literary creation fall flat: "[m]eaningless tracings on the paper, her words seemed to her now— a restless spirit pawing at the air." Yezierska transcribes Sophie's inner monologue as an effort to respond not to Dewey, but to another authority, Ralph Waldo Emerson: "Should I call my essay 'Believe in Yourself,' " she asks herself, "or would n't it be stronger to say, 'Trust Yourself'? But if I say, 'Trust Yourself,' would n't they think I got the words from Emerson?" (HH 141). This sequence evokes the feeling of capture we considered in relation to Dewey, laying bare the paradoxical nature of Emerson's efforts to *teach* self-reliance: his presence insinuates itself precisely when Sophie tries to follow the injunction to "trust herself." Sophie gets lost in his platitudes precisely when she would use her own voice.

But this turns out to be merely a transitional moment of loss that precedes insight. Into Sophie's crisis steps her landlady Hanneh Breineh, symbol of exuberance and irrepressible speech. As if in accord with Walter Pater's formula for the aesthetic life (i.e., to "burn always with this hard, gem-like flame"), Yezierska describes Hanneh Breineh as a figure who "burned through the depths of every experience. . . . How every tiny spark of pleasure blazed into joy!" (HH 147).[11] As this Paterian Jewish matriarch recounts tales of her life, her children begin crowding into Sophie's room, filling its previous silence with voices. These figures allegorize the return of Sophie's voice, which draws strength from her restored connection with the Jewish past:

> The crying waste of Hanneh Breineh's life lay open before [Sophie's] eyes like pictures in a book. She saw her own life in Hanneh Breineh's life. Her efforts to write were like Hanneh Breineh's efforts to feed her children. Behind her life and Hanneh Breineh's life she saw massed ghosts of thousands upon thousands beating—beating out their hearts against rock barriers. (HH 143–144)

Like the climactic scene in Lewisohn's *The Island Within,* where Levi opens the scroll that contains the key to his familial past, Sophie suddenly re-claims her place in the continuity of Jewish life. What defines Jewishness here is chiefly a series of subjective qualities—passion, exuberance, expres-siveness, and perseverance (e.g., "thousands beating out their hearts")—under the sign of Jewishness. Jewishness becomes a *mode of being,* linked above all to striving. Seen in this light, Sophie's devotion to writing represents another example of this *Jewish* mode of engagement, essentially analogous to Hanneh Breineh's devotion to her children. In this passage and throughout much of Yezierska's writing, there is also an implicit connection between the historical strivings of the Jews and those of the working class. Sophie's recognition of herself in the "crying waste" of Hanneh Breineh's life thus marks an embrace at once of ethnic and class identity.

Like Waldo Frank, Yezierska is aware that the modern Jew who would speak for this collective Jewish spirit must find the right form. Sophie's task becomes that of finding a written equivalent to this verbal spontaneity. " 'If I could only write like Hanneh Breineh talks!' " she thinks. "Her words dance with a thousand colors. Like a rainbow it flows from her lips" (HH 147). Jewish speech is represented through a quintessentially Romantic image (Wordsworth: "My heart leaps up. . . ."); the rainbow is also the biblical image of God's renewal of the covenant. In this case, it is the Jewish matriarch who stands in for God as the provider of hope for Sophie. And when Sophie glimpses the rainbow in the darkness of her rented room, she experiences an influx of power: "At last it writes itself in me!" Sophie bursts out, "It's their cries—my own people—crying in me!" (HH 151). Yezierska's phrase, "it writes itself in me," displaces agency onto the Jewish experience itself, which apparently has come to radiate through Sophie. This image of the immigrant writer as a conduit for the voices of "her people" can be traced directly back to Dewey's poem to her ("Generations as yet unuttered. . . . In you I see them coming to be"). But Yezierska also insists that her protagonist has had to undergo a trial before emerging as a spokesperson for the Jewish experience. In this story, then, Sophie responds to the Emersonian call to self-reliance only to lose her voice. She finds it again only when she discovers bonds of empathy linking her to Hanneh Breineh, the Jewish matriarch and oral storyteller. More than a simple rejection of Emerson, this might be read as an amendment: here, genuine speech cannot emerge from isolation but must finally be rooted in community and in collective memory.

As she was finding her own voice as a writer in the years after World War I, Yezierska aligned herself with the very same cultural formation we saw in our discussions of Lewisohn and Frank. Significantly, H. L. Mencken was one of the five people to whom she asked her publisher to send a copy of her first book, *Hungry Hearts,* when it appeared in 1919. She felt that he of all people would appreciate the critical impulse behind her work. Also, she publicly aligned herself with Lewisohn when he came under attack for his autobiography *Up Stream* in a review by genteel critic Brander Matthews, one of Lewisohn's former professors at Columbia. Yezierska's defense of Lewisohn, published as a letter to the *New York*

Times, illuminates the political stakes underlying her literary project. In his review of *Up Stream,* Matthews conceded that the text showed "the mental alertness of his race," but his verdict was that Lewisohn's book amounted to an almost libelous charge against America. As such, Lewisohn's book testified to the dangers of granting a full hearing to those who have "failed to take root in the soil." For Matthews, the biggest problem in America was that a new cadre of foreign-born interlopers was suddenly proposing to speak on behalf of the national culture: "No alien of birth can expound the spirit of this literature as the natives of that speech want to have it expounded."[12] Yezierska's defense of Lewisohn appealed to the cultural pluralist idea of America as a composite of peoples, each with its own outlook and talents and each offering resources for cultural renewal: "Foreigners bring new color, new music, new beauty of expression to worn-out words. The foreign mind works on an old language like the surging leaven of youth."[13] Over the course of her letter, Yezierska links the figure of the new immigrant with that of the radical artist, as if the two were necessarily spiritual brethren. She praises newcomers and creative thinkers alike for their "passion for growth, [their] drive for new experience, [their] thirst for wider vision, for deeper realization."[14] This is in effect the same symbolic move we traced in Lewisohn's writing: immigrants, and Jews in particular, stand not merely for the *unassimilated,* but for the *unassimilable,* driven by a persistent impulse to realize their vision.

It is instructive that Yezierska also evokes Waldo Frank as one of her guiding lights. In the climactic scene of her short story "How I Found America," the concluding story in *Hungry Hearts,* a young Jewish immigrant turns in desperation to her teacher, explaining that after years of struggling to find a place for herself in her new environment, her "dream America" seems even farther now than it had been in the old country. "I'm lost in this each-for-himself world. I feel shut out from everything that's going on. . . . I'm always fighting, fighting with myself and everything around me" (HH 178). The teacher, an idealistic American of Mayflower stock, explains that the girl's frustrations are but the sign of misdirected "divine fire" (HH 178). Rather than seeking to adjust herself to the staid conventions that surround her, she should find a means of translating her passion into "expression." To clarify her point and to inspire her young charge, the teacher proceeds to read aloud a passage from Frank's *Our America*—an unlikely choice for a public-school teacher, perhaps, but a way for Yezierska to express her allegiances unambiguously. The immigrant joyously repeats to herself the passage all the way home: "We go forth all to seek America. And in the seeking we create her. In the quality of our search shall be the nature of the America that we create" (HH 180).

These words punctuate the final passage in the story and in the collection as a whole, heralding the possibility of further literary creation. Yezierska's evocation of Frank and her defense of Lewisohn in the *Times* provide a lens for reading her own work as Romantic, subversive, and "visionary" rather than "ethnic," documentary, and realist—terms that are frequently associated with her.[15] The America Yezierska's heroine has "found" at the end of this story is an ideal more than any actual place; the immigrant Jew is poised to reinvent her nation rather than merely settle into it.

One of Yezierska's strategies for inscribing this visionary, "Jewish" perspective in her work is to craft a specifically *ethnic voice,* using Yiddish syntax to defamiliarize standard English. In *Bread Givers* (1925), the narrating voice itself speaks nonstandard English, evoking a shadow Yiddish behind the English of the text. On the very first page, we read, "[F]rom always it was heavy on my heart the worries for the house as if I was mother"; which might be translated more or less word-for-word into Yiddish to get a standard idiomatic sentence (e.g., *Fun tomid on iz mir geven shver afn hartsn di zorgn vegn hoyz elehey ikh volt geven di mame*).[16] The use of nonstandard English to represent immigrant speech was hardly uncommon practice among writers who addressed the Jewish immigrant experience. Israel Zangwill and Abraham Cahan are the best known writers to do this, but examples abound in popular writing of the early twentieth century. What is new in *Bread Givers,* as far as Jewish American literature is concerned, is Yezierska's use of dialect as the *framing* or narrating discourse of the novel itself. Like other writers associated with dialect writing, such as Mark Twain and Charles Chestnut, Yezierska refuses to frame the nonstandard by the standard; nonstandard English becomes the normative language of the novel, tacitly legitimating the unassimilated self.

This Yiddish-inflected English recurrently gives way to a rather different form of discourse in the novel, the elevated English of the King James Bible, which comes through the voice of the heroine's father. Scenes of the father reading evoke another register of Jewish speech. Instructively, the text he cites is the Book of Isaiah, and the passages underscore the messianic impulse ("I will make darkness light before them, and crooked things straight"; BG 16). Once again, we find the prophets used as an emblem for the essence of Judaism. These two linguistic registers might be mapped onto the dual conception of the Jew we considered in chapter 1—the Yiddish-inflected English linked to the immigrant girl, the biblical cadences linked to the patriarchal tradition. Unlike Lazarus, who privileges the biblical as the subterranean "true" speech of the Jew, Yezierska will construct a model of Jewish identity that values both registers.

The narrative of *Bread Givers* describes a movement from rebellion to return, a narrative of repentance that characterizes a number of Jewish American works, including Antin's "Malinke's Atonement" (1911) and Samson Raphaelson's "The Day of Atonement" (1922, which provided the basis for the film *The Jazz Singer;* 1927). The narrative begins with the heroine's rejection of an authoritarian, patriarchal Judaism in the name of American freedom. Over and over the text emphasizes the rigid gender hierarchy in the Orthodox Jewish family, with the father functioning as an intransigent force of oppression. There are alternate, positive qualities linked to him—his alignment with the Jewish working class, his tireless devotion to study—but these will need to be liberated from his authoritarianism. The father keeps the prophetic tradition alive, as it were, but holds it captive. Though three of his daughters succumb to his pressures, ending up confined by disastrous marriages, the youngest, Sara, achieves a fairy-tale-like escape, sallying forth into the broader American public sphere. The narrative can move forward, then, thanks to the recognition that in the New World the power of the Jewish patriarch is limited. Sara's departure from home symbolically recapitulates the great American story of self-liberation: "I felt like the pilgrim fathers," she remarks, "who had left their homeland and all their kin behind them and trailed out in search of the New World" (BG 209).

This pilgrim narrative breaks down, however, when Sara manages to work her way to college where she meets "real Americans" (BG 210) who have never suffered want or had to struggle. There, she finds herself marked as an Other, in terms of both class and race: "How quickly [my fellow students'] eyes sized me up! . . . It said more plainly than words, 'From where did you come? How did you get in here?'" (BG 214). This scene evokes a nearly analogous scene in Mary Antin's *The Promised Land,* in which Antin describes her fellow students at the Latin School, noting that some looked at her askance—"to some, of course, I was 'impossible'" (PL 231)—but she refuses to grant this any special significance: "So my companions and I parted on the steps of the school-house, in mutual respect; they guiltless of snobbishness, I innocent of envy" (PL 232). Yezierska, writing in the mid-twenties, seems intent on bringing out the divisions that are repressed in Antin's text: her heroine *is* wounded by snobbishness and she *does* burn with envy. *Bread Givers* might, in this way, be read as a deliberate and pointed revision of *The Promised Land.* Antin's exuberant "up-lift" narrative of 1912 is no longer compelling for Yezierska, writing in 1925, in the wake of the nativist victories in their campaign against immigrants.

The answer to Sara's experience of exclusion is to return to the Lower East Side and, in effect, to Jewishness. What prompts her return is an assignment for which Sara and her classmates are called upon by their psychology professor (another Dewey stand-in) to recall a time that "anger or any strong emotion" interfered with their thinking. Sara suddenly grasps that her experiences growing up have provided her with "treasure chests of insight" unavailable to her fellow classmates, in spite of their material wealth (BG 223). The experiences on Hester Street she took to be privations and losses are suddenly revealed as the essence of human striving, and Sara becomes the authority on "reality" in her class. Importantly, it is this third section of *Bread Givers,* when Sara returns to Hester Street, that Yezierska calls "The New World": the pilgrim's journey in this text involves a rejection of the hostile environment of the "real Americans" and a return to the Lower East Side. The final stage in the novel, like a third stage tacked on to the two-part structure of *The Promised Land,* involves a reconciliation with her father, who ultimately comes to live with Sara and her newfound soulmate Hugo Seelig (from the identical town in the old country).

Sara's restored Jewish identity is figured as substantively equivalent to her father's: "After all, I was the only daughter of his faith . . . I had it from Father, this ingrained something in me that would not let me take the mess of pottage" (BG 202). Judaism is epitomized here by Jacob's refusal to be Esau, an act of resistance before the allure of the outside world. This identification with the father provides the basis for her repentant return: "Who gave me the fire, the passion, to push myself up from the dirt? If I grow, if I rise, if I ever amount to something, is it not his spirit burning in me?" (BG 286). Yezierska has rewritten Judaism as the quality of *intensity,* linked to the prophetic speech of Isaiah and here rendered through the metaphor of fire. The text transforms Judaism from a patriarchal religion of law into a mode of being, and at this point Sara's subjugation to her father can be overcome. The gender divisions that threaten Sara's autonomy in the first part of the novel are overcome by the excavation of a deep Jewishness, in which father and daughter become indistinguishable and the tradition that seemed to end with him becomes hers as well.

But although this final section is called "The New World," the novel's ending defers any absolute sense of closure. In the final image of *Bread Givers,* Sara is listening to the "fading chant" of her father in the other room, and she feels "a shadow still there, over me. It wasn't just my father, but the generations who made my father whose weight was still upon me" (BG 297). Once again, Dewey's language returns ("generations"), here as a complex legacy, a blessing and a burden. Sara has regained access to the melody of Jewishness, but the price has been a need to confront the "shadow" of Jewish suffering. This final scene marks, then, not so much some return to a stable identity as the acceptance of a burden. Indeed, despite the tidy rebellion/return structure of *Bread Givers,* the novel is hardly definitive in any of its ostensible statements and conclusions. In place of any gradual sense of development, we find sudden shifts, radical changes of heart, an ambivalent sifting through of options. But within this mobility itself—this ability to make enormous changes at the last minute—we find what might be considered Yezierska's "solution" to the problem of Jewish identity.

Yezierska's "solution" to this problem comes more sharply into focus when we consider a phrase that crops up again and again in her work, borrowed from Matthew Arnold's poem "Stanzas from the Grande Chartreuse" (1855). Arnold's poem narrates a visit to the ruins of a monastery in Southern France, once home to the ascetic Christian sect, the Carthusians. As Arnold's speaker enters the abandoned halls and silent courts of the monastery, he dwells upon the singular piety of its former inhabitants. He then bemoans his inability to believe, his youth having been seized by "rigorous teachers" who "purged its faith, and trimm'd its fire."[17] In the most famous lines of the poem, the speaker posits himself as an impossible kind of pilgrim, moving through a godless world with no hope of deliverance: "Wandering between two worlds, one dead / The other powerless to be born." Yezierska deploys these lines at various moments in her work to characterize the essential position of the Jew. In *All I Could Never Be,* the protagonist says of herself and her fellow Jews, "[t]he old world is dead behind us, and the new world . . . is not yet born" (39); in the autobiographical *Red Ribbon on a White Horse,* just as she rejects Samuel Goldwyn's contract, she describes herself as "lost in chaos, wandering between worlds";[18] and in *Bread Givers,* she calls her transitional middle book "Between Two Worlds." This trope of in-betweenness reflects a different modality of Romanticism than the Pater-esque emphasis on flame-like burning. Here the emphasis falls on incompleteness, on exile, on liminality.[19] Even when Yezierska's heroine *does* come home, what she discovers are indelible traces of other places and other times. She feels "a shadow still there over me" (BG 297).

The difference, however, is that unlike Arnold, who represents his pilgrim as irredeemably estranged from *his* religious tradition, Yezierska represents in-betweenness as itself constitutive of Judaism. This, then, is the key to Yezierska's revision of Arnold: in place of Arnold's "forlorn" speaker who, like Dewey, becomes a spectator of tradition he cannot join, Yezierska's Jews are epitomized by their status as wanderers. Where Arnold's speaker emphasizes that the fire of his faith was extinguished by the teachers of his youth, Yezierska's Jews reclaim their "fire." What I am suggesting is that because Judaism stands for a collective history as well as a theology, it affords Yezierska the possibility of a different response to modernity than what we find in Arnold's poem. Where Arnold's post-Christian speaker testifies solely to the agony of loss, Yezierska's text concludes with a gesture of affirmation. It is not God or the religious tradition, narrowly defined, that is affirmed, however, so much as the possibility of remaining loyal to the memory of previous generations.

For another intertext for Yezierska's trope of betweenness, we may consider S. Ansky's *The Dybbuk,* subtitled *tsvishn tsvey veltn* (Between Two Worlds). It is possible that Yezierska knew of Ansky's play, since it was performed in New York City in 1924, a year before the publication of *Bread Givers.*[20] Ansky's sense of betweenness is close to Yezierska's: it signals not a position of stasis as in Arnold's poem but a position of tension and flux, where disparate realms (heaven and earth; past and present) seem on the verge of being conjoined. One might indeed gloss Yezierska's construction of Jewishness by considering the notion of a dybbuk, a spirit or ghost that occupies the body of the living and that speaks in its own voice. In Yezierska's texts, the Jewish past itself functions as a dybbuk inhabiting the body of America. It speaks through the "crying waste" of Hanneh Breineh's life and through the "fading chant" of Sara's father. Its language is a particular blend of the vernacular and the ornate, a Yiddish-inflected English that gives way to the pure biblical cadences of Isaiah. As in Ansky's play, this dybbuk is a force that disrupts convention and social decorum. When it speaks, the present is opened back onto the past, and the future suddenly appears as a horizon filled with promise.

To conclude, we might return to the lines from Waldo Frank that serve as the epigraph to this section: "Jewish thought has always been crisis thought." We might gloss this by saying that Lewisohn, Frank, and Yezierska each turn to Judaism to find a language of response to a crisis in the American democratic project, a palpable xenophobia in their midst. In their fictional and autobiographical writings, they represent the "return" to Jewishness as a gesture of defiance and a triumph over despair. But "Jewish thought" is "crisis thought" here in another sense as well. For Jewish tradition becomes a metaphor for a sublime force that *produces* a crisis. To invoke Jewish tradition is for these writers to signal dissent, to inspire a withdrawal from a corrupt world in the name of a future redemption.

Given its significance as a forerunner to today's multiculturalism, it is worthwhile considering the ways in which Lewisohn, Frank, and Yezierska all participate in the movement for "cultural pluralism." This movement, associated with Horace Kallen, emerged during this period as a critique of the nativist exclusion of nonwhites and "ethnics" from the category of Americanness. But while they affirm cultural pluralism, the Romantic dimension of these writers' sensibilities takes them in directions decidedly different from Kallen's thoroughly secular perspective. Recall that Kallen trained as a philosopher in the pragmatic school: he wrote his dissertation under William James and in an early book praised James to the skies while deriding Henri Bergson as an imprecise mystic.[21] Kallen emphasized the ties that bind the individual to his or her familial past, following James in theorizing identity in pragmatic terms, as something that was pieced together and formed through experience alone. In Kallen's writings on Zionism and Jewish culture, he labors to emphasize the empirical or naturalistic grounds of Jewish identity: the idea, in short, that Jewishness comprises an ethnicity like any other. "The fact of being a Jew," he writes, "is the fact of being a member of a natural social group."[22] What emerges in the writing of Lewisohn, Frank, and Yezierska, by contrast, is a view that goes well beyond Kallen's pragmatic cultural pluralism. More than "identity," they offer an ideal; more than ethnicity, ethos; more than a set of rituals or group behavior, a mandate and a mission. The emphasis in their writings, as we have seen, is not on some anthropological Jewish milieu so much as it is on the challenge of self-formation. More than annotations of experience, then, these are parables of *becoming*. In the next chapter we will see how a group of American Yiddish writers imagined their relationship to the same currents in American literary culture that inspired and shaped Lewisohn, Frank, and Yezierska. We will discover once again that Jewish writers in America entrust their own words with the task of bringing forth the prophetic vision first expressed in the Bible. This time the medium for this transmission will be Yiddish, the language of the Ashkenazi Diaspora.

Emma Lazarus. MSS 8827, Clifton Waller Barrett Library of
American Literature, Special Collections, University of Virginia
Library.

Mary Antin, circa 1916. Courtesy of Picture History.

Ludwig Lewisohn, circa 1922. Courtesy of The Jacob Rader Marcus
Center of the American Jewish Archives.

Waldo Frank, 1920s. Waldo Frank Papers, Rare Book
and Manuscript Library, University of Pennsylvania.

Anzia Yezierska, printed in *Literary Digest International Book Review,* December 1923.

איך װײס, איך בין אומשטערבליך. — װאַלט װהיטמאַן.
(צו זײן הונדערט יאָהריגען געבורטסטאָג.)

Walt Whitman, printed in *Shriftn,* 1919. Caption reads "I
know I am deathless—Walt Whitman. (On his hundredth
birthday)." The quotation is taken from "Song of Myself."

Israel Jacob Schwartz reading before the Provisional Committee of
the Histadrut, Havana, Cuba, March 3, 1947. Courtesy of YIVO
archives.

Irving Howe at Brandeis University, circa 1954. Courtesy of
Robert D. Farber University Archives and Special Collections
Department, Brandeis University.

Alfred Kazin in Brownsville, 1950. Courtesy of Berg Collection, New York Public Library.

PART 3

YIDDISH INTERLUDE

Bay di taykhn fun Niu York bin ikh gezesn
Un der nayer, frayer breyter luft mayn troym fartroyt.

By the rivers of New York I sat down
And confided my dream to the new, free, wide-open air.
—A. Leyeles. "A troym unter volknkratsers"
(A Dream under Skyscrapers), translated by
Benjamin Harshav

In the last chapter, we considered how Anzia Yezierska creates an "ethnic" literary discourse by evoking a shadow Yiddish syntax behind her English. Yezierska evokes Yiddish to symbolize an unassimilated, inner Jewish self, whose "fire" and passion cannot be contained by conventional English. The presence of Yiddish in subsequent English-language writings and cultural performances by American Jews is an extremely complex affair, but generally speaking when Yiddish surfaces—through syntax, terms of endearment, expletives, quotations, and so on—it symbolizes a break-through of an Old World Jewish self.[1] Consider the passages in the middle of Saul Bellow's *Herzog* where Herzog's recollections of his youth on Montreal's Napoleon Street bring long phrases of Yiddish into the text; or the scene in Mel Brooks' *Blazing Saddles* when a Sioux Indian chief, played by Brooks, suddenly holds forth in Yiddish. If Indians are the "native" Americans and if the quintessential "native" language is Yiddish, at least for Brooks, it would follow in his absurdist universe that Indians would speak Yiddish. Or consider Irene Klepfisz's bilingual poems, where English and Yiddish alternate and comment on one another, as if to dramatize the shifting grounds of modern Jewish identity itself.[2] Once again, the point is that the Yiddish signals an older stratum of Jewish existence. Its break-through into an English-language text signals a triumph over amnesia, which is to say assimilation.

But of course Yiddish is not merely a symbol that can be evoked or deployed in an English-language context to signify Jewishness. It is also a language in its own right, with its own complex internal history of de-velopment and transformation. In this "Yiddish interlude," I will explore some of the ways in which the themes we have been tracing—the dialogue between Jews and American literary culture, the reclamation of Jewish tradition, the quest for new forms—have played themselves out in Yiddish literature in America, particularly during the 1920s. Even though Yiddish writers belong in many ways to a separate literary tradition, with a dif-ferent set of challenges and a different range of options, it is nevertheless possible (and important) to consider the two traditions side by side. The key American literary figure here will once again be Walt Whitman, who was enthusiastically read and emulated by multiple generations of Yiddish poets. My goal is to explore points of convergence that might shed further light on the predicament of and possibilities for the Jewish writer in America.

6

The Yiddish Poets Come to America

Mir raysn zikh arayn in a velt a nayer,—
A mekhtike, an andershdike velt.
Frish un shtark iz undzer nay-farkhapte velt
A velt fun marsh un arbet.
     Pionern! O, pionern!

All the past we leave behind,
We debouch upon a newer mightier world, varied world,
Fresh and strong the world we seize, world of labor and the march,
     Pioneers! O pioneers!
   —Walt Whitman, "Pioneers! O Pioneers!" translated by Louis Miller

In 1940, the Yiddish Cooperative Book League of the Yiddish International
Worker's Order published the most substantial collection of Walt Whitman's poetry and prose to appear to date in Yiddish translation, complete
with a biographical sketch, photographs, and an appended monograph.

The collection was called *Lider: fun bukh: bleter groz* (Poems: From the Book: Leaves of Grass), and its translator was Louis Miller, a poet associated with the neo-Romantic school of American Yiddish poets, *Di yunge* (the Young Ones). As the name of the publishing-house alone would suggest, the image of Whitman presented in Miller's volume deviates somewhat from more familiar images of the "good grey poet" that circulated in English-language contexts at this time. What Miller's collection brings un-ambiguously to the fore is the revolutionary political dimension of Whit-man's work—a dimension that is only hinted at in F. O. Matthiessen's influential *American Renaissance: Art and Expression in the Age of Emerson and Whitman* (1941).[1] Here is the summary of Whitman's achievement that Miller offers his Yiddish readers: "Singing in a newer and freer form, the song of the average working man, he created a healthy and robust lyricism, which carries within it the promise of a truly socialistic poetry."[2] For Miller, and for several generations of like-minded Yiddish readers and writers, Whitman represented a long-awaited socialist prophet; to read his paeons to solidarity and freedom was to experience a renewal of their own deepest hopes. It was also to have their confidence restored that their own Yiddish-speaking immigrant community—marginal and insulated though it may have appeared to outsiders—was in fact at the vanguard of history and human progress.[3] Small wonder, then, that Whitman had already been translated numerous times into Yiddish, and that a long line of Yiddish poets, from Morris Rosenfeld to Israel Jacob Schwartz to H. Leivick to Reuben Ludwig, all considered themselves heirs to his vision and mantle.[4]

In this chapter, I discuss the uniquely productive encounter between Yiddish poets and the American bard. Having already explored how Waldo Frank positioned himself as Whitman's spokesman in the Young Americans' battle against the "genteel tradition" in the second and third decades of the century, we will discover surprisingly similar forms of self-positioning at this same moment among Yiddish poets. In both cases, these are *Jewish* writers in America who find common cause with Whit-man, and who see themselves as secret sharers of the deeper spiritual and political vision emanating from his work. One reason they feel this affinity is that they trace Whitman's vision back to prophetic traditions of the Bible, which they claimed as their own cultural heritage—even despite their thorough and often defiant secularization. Before exploring the en-counter between Yiddish poets and Whitman, I pause to reflect on another poet who figured prominently in the Yiddish literary imagination, Hein-rich Heine. I propose here that the trajectory of Yiddish poetry in America might indeed be charted by examining the symbolic roles played in the Yiddish literary imagination by these two iconic nineteenth-century poets.

Drawn to Heine for his elegant use of High Romantic forms, his political radicalism, and his biting satires of European culture, they saw their own destiny as lying along different lines, bound up with the promise of America. To imagine this destiny, they turned to Whitman for inspiration and for new models of self-expression.

The Problem of Tradition in Modern Yiddish Poetry

Since we are exploring instances of a complex problem in literary history, that of poetic influence moving across linguistic lines, let us momentarily consider the broader question of influence itself in modern Yiddish poetry. The larger question is how Yiddish poets have shaped an aesthetic between indigenous Jewish influences and "outside" sources. This is admittedly a topic for a separate book (or several books), but a few brief notes will have to suffice here. While previous generations of East European Jews had used Yiddish in a variety of literary genres, including biblical commentaries, homilies, ballads, fables, and prayers (the genre of *tkhines*—the prayers of early modern and subsequent Jewish women—being a case in point), these precedents only offered a partially serviceable tradition for modern Yiddish poets, who began to appear toward the end of the nineteenth century.[5] Writers of prose could and did draw on the motifs of the storytelling tradition that flourished in Yiddish and that was an integral aspect of Hasidism. The seminal neo-Hasidic stories of Isaac Leib Peretz and Isaac Bashevis Singer demonstrate how Yiddish writers could forge their own modern literary culture by secularizing the Hasidic *mayse*.[6] Prose writers also drew extensively on non-Jewish contemporaries such as Maxim Gorky, Anton Chekhov, Emile Zola, and William Thackeray. For Yiddish poets, particularly lyric poets, it may be argued that there were even fewer "indigenous" Yiddish sources for their art, and that therefore this kind of dependence was more pronounced. We might postulate that Yiddish lyric poets—whose aim is not to relate a tale but to crystallize their private vision of the world—have as a class been *more* dependent on "outside" literary models than writers from other European literary traditions and than Yiddish prose writers.[7]

In their lack of necessary or inevitable literary forebears, Yiddish poets pose something of a special case of Harold Bloom's "anxiety of influence" model of poetic creation. On the one hand, they often expressed an acute self-consciousness and feeling of dispossession, which they associated with being newcomers to the world of secular literary history. Here, the anxiety comes not from a surfeit of influences—as in the Bloomian model—but from a paucity of poetic forbears, the condition of the orphan, not the

Oedipal son. H. Leivick describes this fate in "Yiddish Poets" as that of "slink[ing] on God's earth like alien guests!"[8] The predicament of the Yiddish poet is read here through the trope of Diaspora: the Yiddish poet is as a guest among inhospitable hosts, an abject figure without a home. In "To the Gentile Poet," Mani Leib writes enviously of the "bard of the gentiles," who is the "[h]eir of Shakespeare, shepherds, and cavaliers." From Mani Leib's perspective, the gentile poet leads a charmed life, possessed of a long tradition in which to place himself. By contrast, the Jewish poet is stranded in limbo and anonymity: "But I, a poet of the Jews—who needs it!" His destiny is to sing "to a foreign world the tears of desert wanderers."[9] Interestingly, Mani Leib's failure to mention Hebrew-language precedents, such as the Psalmist or the poets of medieval Spain, suggests that for him at least, the tradition of Hebrew verse is part of an unusable past. To be a Jewish or a Yiddish poet (the terms are seemingly interchangeable for Mani Leib) brings a dreary sense of anonymity, rootlessness, and irrelevance to the greater traditions of world literature.

But as much as Leivick and Mani Leib picture themselves in a crippling predicament, there may have been some advantages to this situation. Indeed, Yiddish poets may have been immune to some of the debilitating anxieties that Bloom describes. Since they had no necessary literary forebears from whom they needed to "swerve," they may have been freer to engage in more promiscuous sorts of borrowings and reformulations than writers in other traditions might have dared. The sense of being ignored expressed by Jacob Glatstein in his well-known quip—that being a Yiddish poet means that he needs to read Auden but that Auden does not need to read him—might also reflect the freedom of the second-born, the one who escapes the Oedipal burdens of the first. Glatstein had to read Auden, but he might do with Auden anything he wished. If for Bloom the goal of strong poets is to locate themselves in a "discontinuous universe,"[10] it might be said that Yiddish poetry always already exists in a relation of discontinuity—i.e., freedom—with respect to its precursors. And this may help explain the playfulness and experimentalism that typifies the work of so many modern Yiddish poets, for whom punning, interlinguistic word play, intertextual reference, and radical shifts in register are all common practice. The distinctive position of Yiddish poets in literary history helps explain the frequent recourse Yiddish poets have to the technique of prosopopoeia—speaking in the voice of the Other. In Leivick's twelve-poem cycle "Spinoza," for example, the poet meets the revolutionary philosopher, who has traveled from his grave in Amsterdam to a hospital room in a sanatorium in Denver, where Leivick has gone to recuperate from tuberculosis. In his private encounter with the archetypal modern Jewish icon-oclast (and architect of the Enlightenment), the Yiddish poet begs for recognition: "Holy one, I touch your sleeve. / Rise up. Recognize me."[11] In the poem, Spinoza becomes an ally whose voice merges with that of the Yiddish poet. Below, we will consider two additional instances of prosopo-poeia, involving Heine and Whitman, who also return to life through the agency of the Yiddish poem.[12] If they lacked a well-established literary tradition in their own language, then, Yiddish poets looked elsewhere for inspiration, either to Jews writing in other languages or to broader cur-rents of world literature.

All of this is to suggest that by force of linguistic circumstance, Yid-dish poets became *bricoleurs* par excellence—adroit assemblers consulting the traditions of the past and reconfiguring them for their own purposes. Since nearly all modern Yiddish poets have been at least trilingual, they have generally been in a position to avail themselves of texts and traditions produced in multiple languages. They also turned to the work of transla-tion as a natural extension of their craft. In the course of a single essay, for instance, the "sweatshop" poet Joseph Bovshover offers his own transla-tions of Goethe, Heine, Milton, Petrarch, and Whitman. Other resourceful translators include the poet Yehoash, known for his translations of Long-fellow's "Hiawatha," Omar Khayyam's *Rubiyat,* and Lord Byron's "The Gazelle," not to mention the entire *Tanakh;* and I. J. Schwarz, who trans-lated Shakespeare, Walt Whitman, and Hayyim Bialik among others. Nor was the work of translation the business of poets alone. Isaac Bashevis Singer translated Thomas Mann's *Magic Mountain,* Knut Hamsun's *Hun-ger,* and Erich Maria Remarque's *All Quiet on the Western Front.* The work of translation was in many ways an effort to expand the literary possibili-ties of Yiddish and to rehearse strategies writers might themselves use (as well as to earn some money). Their dependence on translation was in this sense precisely the reverse of what we will see in chapter 9, when we will explore how postwar Jewish writers whose primary language is English turn to Yiddish for *their* serviceable tradition. Yiddish writers turn out-ward—the question is what they make of their discoveries, how the heroes from world literature sound when they speak Yiddish.

Heine as Jewish Tragic Hero

An anecdote in Abraham Brumberg's memoir *Journey Through Doomed Worlds* (2004) underscores the honorary role played by Heine among Yiddish poets. Brumberg recalls a visit as a boy to the aging Abraham

Reisen, one of the most famous and beloved Yiddish poets of all time, then living in a high-rise apartment in the Bronx. Brumberg came from a Bundist family that escaped Poland during World War II and was himself an active member in the "Club of Jewish Youth from Poland" in New York (later named *Hemshekh*). He knew many of Reisen's verses by heart, having sung them as a boy in his Yiddish elementary school in Vilna. Now he was being led by the legendary figure into a book-lined study in the Bronx, where Reisen proposed to read a selection from "the greatest poet who ever lived." What Brumberg discovered surprised him. "This [greatest poet] turned out to be Heinrich Heine," Brumberg writes, "whose verse [Reisen] read to me in German. I hardly understood a word but felt terribly excited that Reisen would treat me so respectfully, while also marveling that he would so adore a German poet."[13] Brumberg's surprise derives, no doubt, from the more common conception of Reisen as archetypal *Yiddish* poet, as the voice of a specifically East European Jewish cultural and religious milieu. Such a view has circulated widely, as in the introduction to *A Treasury of Yiddish Poetry*, where Irving Howe describes Reisen as "a poet crystallizing the feelings and values of *Yiddishkayt*," adding that "anyone who wishes to grasp the world outlook of the Eastern European Jew, both in the *shtetl* and in the immigrant world, must turn to Reisen."[14] As it turns out, the wisdom Reisen has to convey, or at least his ideal for poetry, comes from the world of European high culture: though Heine was himself a Jew, he was hardly the voice of the indigenous folk. Part of the "world outlook of the Eastern European Jew" is evidently a desire to enlarge the scope of this very identity through the imaginative resources of German Romanticism, or at least the version of it offered by Heine.

Reisen's admiration for Heine was shared by several generations of Yiddish poets in Europe and America. One would be hard-pressed to find another European poet who exerted as palpable an influence on the poetics of Yiddish verse.[15] The lyrics of Isaac Leib Peretz are replete with echoes of Heine, as in "Romanzero" and "An Edom," which take their titles from Heine. The compressed ballad form of "Monish" suggests a direct borrowing from Heine, as can its dark and satirical mood. Other notable Heine disciples include David Edelstadt and S. S. Frug, both of whom, like Peretz, gained popularity during the 1880s, and the slightly later Yehoash, whose love lyrics, ballads, versified legends, and essays show Heine's influence.[16] Heine's apotheosis as precursor poet can be found in a translation project of singular proportions undertaken by the leading poets of *Di yunge*. The project, a near-complete translation of Heine's work in eight volumes, was published in 1918, at a moment when Yiddish writers in

America were branching out in varied and ambitious directions, making a bid for their language as a medium for world-class art. The anthology included translations by the main poets of *Di yunge* (Mani Leib, Reuben Iceland, I. J. Schwartz, Joseph Rolnick, Zishe Landau, Moyshe-Leyb Halpern, and Mark Shayd) as well as figures associated with an earlier generation (David Frishman, David Pinski, and Abraham Reisen). The dean of modern Hebrew literature, Hayyim Nahman Bialik, also made a contribution, in the form of a translation of "Prinzessin Sabbat," suggesting that at least one point on which Yiddishists and Hebraists might concur was on the cultural significance of Heine.[17]

Heine's significance for Yiddish poetry is not difficult to fathom. The linguistic similarities between Yiddish and German made German verse forms a natural resource for Yiddish poets; Heine's political radicalism made him a hero among leftist writers and intellectuals in Europe and America in general; and, as we have seen, Heine was particularly serviceable as a modern Jewish culture hero—described by Heinrich Graetz as a subversive figure who struck at Christendom from within (see chapter 1). Heine's conversion, indeed, was often interpreted not so much as a sign of antipathy to Jewishness, but rather as a symptom of the Jew's inherently ambiguous position in Christian society. Heine was seen at once as an archetypal Jewish hero and an archetypal Jewish victim. Nowhere is this duality clearer than in Nachman Syrkin's introductory essay for the eight-volume collection of 1918. Syrkin (1868–1924), an architect of Socialist Zionism and a leader of the Poalei Zion party in America, calls Heine "a tragic Jewish poet, perhaps the most tragic poet who has ever ascended the mountain of the muses."[18] To Syrkin, Heine embodies the psychological confusion of the newly emancipated German Jew, whose "ghetto faith" had been undermined by enlightenment rationalism but who had yet to discover any new spiritual or national ideals. Syrkin points to a brief period in the 1820s when Heine allegedly reached his own version of Jewish nationalist pride, a Zionism avant la lettre ("How amazingly national, almost Zionistic, sound Heine's letters in 1823 to his friend Vulvel!").[19] Heine's works from this time, including the unfinished novel "The Rabbi of Bacharach," briefly established what Syrkin considers a link to the Golden Age of Spanish Hebrew letters. But the central motifs in Heine's life, for Syrkin, are finally inner conflict, self-betrayal, and ultimately the desperate return to roots when it was already too late.

So even as a generation of Yiddish poets evoked Heine through their rhetoric, prosody, and tone, many sought ways to escape the slide toward cynicism and capitulation they saw in Heine's life. The multiple varieties of secular Jewishness (Zionism, Bundism, etc.) had as a common denominator an impulse to affirm some system of values against the awareness that nihilism and despair were imminent possibilities for the modern Jew, cut off (or set free) from the continuities of tradition. Perhaps for this reason, the line from Heine's "Gedaechtnisfeier" that no Kaddish would be uttered over the poet's grave (*Keinen Kadosch wird man sagen*) became such a haunting and recurrent refrain in Yiddish writings about Heine, exemplified by Syrkin's essay, which concludes by imagining Heine's unvisited grave.

How did Yiddish poets writing from the standpoint of the *goldene medine,* the "Golden Land" of America, conceptualize their relationship to the tragic Heine? One place to look is the work of Joseph Bovshover (1873–1915), a figure associated with the "sweatshop" or proletarian school. A native of Lubavitch in White Russia, Bovshover moved on his own to Riga, where he acquired enough German to read the classics and to learn "all of Heine's verse by heart" (according to the *Lexicon of Yiddish Literature*). After immigrating to America in 1891, he became an ardent anarchist and a poet. Along with a series of works seeking to rouse his fellow sweatshop workers, he also produced a celebrated translation of *The Merchant of Venice,* which he entitled *Shaylok,* and which recast Shakespeare's comedy as a Jewish tragedy.[20] He also experimented with writing in English, including a strident hymn "To the Toilers," which was printed in the anarchist journal *Liberty* in 1896.

Bovshover's "Light and Shadow" (*Likht un shotn*) performs a complicated act of ventriloquism and revision, evoking Heine as both inspiration and fellow exile. The poem calls for a considerably more complex view of the poetics of "sweatshop" writing than critics have generally allowed.[21] The poem is composed of four-line stanzas with alternating lines of four and three beats, in imitation of one of Heine's most common verse forms. It imagines the poet Heine returning from the dead, visiting the Yiddish poet in his bedroom. Heralded by the strains of a heavenly lyre, Heine arrives just in time to relieve the Yiddish poet of his "melancholy dreams":

> Un plutsling hob ikh in'm tsimer bamerkt
> A shtilem, a vunderlikh veben—
> Un glaykh vi oyf fligel iz hayne aleyn
> Gekumen fun kever tsu shveben.[22]

> And suddenly I see in the midst of my room,
> A silent and marvelous form,
> As if flying with wings, 'tis Heine himself
> He's come to me straight from his tomb.

Harold Bloom has focused on moments in lyric poems when the poet's experience of loss and despondency is suddenly overcome by an influx of imaginative power. According to Bloom, the achievement of this "sublime turn" comes as a result of reconfiguring the rhetoric of the precursor, whose status as precursor must, however, be concealed.[23] The language of the precursor is liberating only when it can be usurped and stamped with the signature of the successor poet. In Bovshover's poem, by contrast, the ability to speak is enabled by the appearance of Heine *himself* in the poem, as if Bovshover were laying bare the conditions of his own rhetorical power. This is not so much the anxiety as the ecstasy of influence. Poetic agency is gained not by disguising the precursor, but literally by bringing him into the poem, establishing commerce with a broader literary history.

But what does Heine have to offer the anarchist Yiddish poet in New York besides company in his tenement room and a verse form he can use? As it turns out, it is Bovshover who has something to teach Heine, who in the poem expresses an ardent desire to see New York. During his lifetime, the historical Heine comically derided America in his poem *Jetzt Wohin* (Whither Now) as "a land where the men are 'baccy chawers, where they bowl without a king."[24] In Bovshover's poem, Heine is prepared to reconsider his cynicism. Rephrasing "Whither Now?" Bovshover has Heine say: "Here in the land where they chew their tobacco / I wonder will I like the smell?" The first site Heine wants to visit is the "Jewish ghetto," the prospect of a Jewish subculture in New York being particularly intriguing to him. As he implores the Yiddish poet to act as his tour guide, Heine gives over his blessing and sanction:

> Un vestu mir yede zakh vayzn genoy
> Di lumpen di groyse un kleyne,
> Als erlikher mensh vestu vern gekroynt
> Fun'm oremen haynrikh hayne. (71–72)

> And you shall reveal to me everything here,
> The blemishes, large and small,
> And you will be crowned as a good, honest man
> By me, the poor Heinrich Heine.

What the poem enacts, then, is the transfer of poetic agency from Europe to America and from German to Yiddish. Even as Bovshover affirms his indebtedness to Heine, he carves out a space for himself as an *American* Yiddish poet, with his gaze fixed firmly on the future. As a Jew in America, Bovshover sees himself as freer than Heine, who in the poem becomes the "poor" figure, dependent on the American Jew to glimpse the promise of freedom. Bovshover reiterates this idea elsewhere in the poem by evoking the fate of an actual statue of Heine. In 1893 a German American sculptor named Ernst Herter had completed a monument to Heine, which was rejected by Heine's hometown (Dusseldorf), purchased by a group of German Americans, and donated to the city of New York. Bovshover's Heine interprets the rejection of his statue exclusively on the grounds of his Jewishness: "They won't take [my statue] in Dusseldorf / I suppose it's because of my faith" (*Mir dakht zikh, dos kumt durkh mayn gloybn*). Just as his statue has been placed in New York, so too has his poetic legacy been transferred there. In bringing Heine across the ocean, the poem restages the Jewish migration from intolerant Europe to the New World, a place of possibility and at least potentially a new home for the Jews. Bovshover's poem and Syrkin's essay show how Heine's legacy could serve as both inspiration and warning to Yiddish poets in America. As these poets worked through questions surrounding emancipation, acculturation, secularization, and Jewish nationhood, they saw Heine as the embodiment of the failed attempt to find a home in European culture. The Zionist response to Heine's tragedy was to see in it further proof of the necessity for a Jewish homeland. But there were many who envisioned America as a place where a new kind of Jewish creativity could flourish. And for a brief interlude, a period lasting approximately from the turn of the century until the Second World War, Yiddish literary culture blossomed in America, moving in directions hitherto untested by Yiddish writers. And it was, among other things, the "gong of revolt," sounded by Whitman's poetry, that strengthened their faith in America as a possible home for Yiddish culture.

Walt Whitman among the American Yiddish Poets

The first translations of Whitman into Yiddish were produced, in 1897, by the very same Bovshover who played imaginative host to Heine in America.[25] In an essay on Whitman, where his translations appear, Bovshover celebrates Whitman as an artist of the highest order, on a par with Shakespeare. He underscores specifically the biblical sources and resonances of Whitman's rhetoric: "Whitman writes in the style and very often the tone of the Bible. He sings as the prophets once sang . . . he is a defender of true freedom . . . a Moses of free thought" (GS 330). In the words of a Yiddish poet/critic, this emphasis on Whitman's biblical resonances has the effect of bringing Whitman into a Judaic frame of reference. Bovshover names Moses according to the traditional appellation "Moyshe Rabeynu"

(Moses, our teacher), recalling the intimate terms Jews have traditionally assigned their biblical progenitors. Whitman is thus inserted into a familiar, Jewish context, as the recipient as well as the originator of a literary and spiritual tradition.

Another key moment in the Yiddish reception of Whitman was I. J. Schwartz's translation of Whitman's "Salut au Monde!" in 1912 in *Shriftn*, a journal described by Leonard Prager and A. A. Greenbaum as devoted to a "distinctly American, esthetically self-conscious school of Yiddish writing."[26] Schwartz (1885–1971) was a native of Petroshon, near Kovno in central Lithuania. He immigrated to America at the age of twenty-one and became active as a poet and translator among *Di yunge*. Drawing on extensive Jewish learning (his father was a respected rabbi), he became one of the main translators of Hebrew poetry into Yiddish, publishing book-length translations of Bialik, Saul Tchernichowsky, and Judah Halevi, as well as collections of *midrashim* on the meaning of Shabbat and on the figure of Moses.[27] In his translation of Whitman's "Salut au Monde!" with its catalogue of nations from around the world, Schwartz confronts the challenge of opening Yiddish poetic discourse to encompass previously unknown territory. The poem alludes to peoples, places, and rituals that could have scarcely had any precedent in Yiddish literature, terms such as Kamtschatkan, Berber, and Soudanese. Schwartz's translation is thus a demonstration that Yiddish literature is up to the task of encompassing the world at large—of saluting the *monde*.

Another point about Schwartz's translation is that the Yiddish itself tends to move closer to the vernacular language, in terms of both vocabulary and syntax. In this sense, the interest in Whitman can be linked to a broader impulse among the poets of *Di yunge* to eschew the heavily Germanized Yiddish (*daytshmerish*) used by previous poets and to use a more vernacular Yiddish. This is a point that deserves to be stressed: the revolutionary aspect of Whitman's poetics in English was to shift the register of poetic speech downward. In order to create a form of poetry to mirror what he considered the radical novelty of American democracy, Whitman sought to remove from his work any trace of the ornamental or the mannered, and to make poetry out of the American vernacular, such as the vocabulary he assiduously collected for his *American Primer*. He famously remarked in a letter to his friend and biographer Horace Traubel, "I sometimes think the *Leaves* is only a language experiment."[28] For Yiddish poets who sought to model themselves after Whitman, it was no small task to reproduce this experiment in Yiddish, since the division between registers in Yiddish is in many ways less clearly demarcated than in English. One way to replicate Whitman's "experiment" was to use a less formal syntax and to move from pretentious-sounding Germanic terms in the direction of spoken Yiddish, with its sizable vocabulary from *loshn-koydesh*, Hebrew, and Aramaic, evocative of the daily life of East European Jews. This means that the Yiddish poet who would follow Whitman's lead might end up including more terms derived from religious tradition: the Yiddish Whitmanian becomes, in this specifically linguistic sense, more bound up with things *Judaic*. Thus at a climactic moment of "Salut au Monde!"—to choose but one example—Whitman writes of a "divine rapport" that has equalized the poet with lovers in all lands. Schwartz renders Whitman's "divine rapport" as *hazhgokhe* (Providence), a term from Hebrew that evokes a specifically Judaic conception of providence. The word might very well have struck earlier poets as excessively parochial, and therefore nonpoetic. Schwartz's use of this and analogous terms suggests that Whitman provides a license for Yiddish poets to explore the full range of their language.

In addition to translating Whitman, Schwartz wrote an epic poem, *Kentucky* (1925), which represents the most sustained effort to celebrate Whitman's "open road" in Yiddish poetry. Schwartz lived for approximately eleven years in Lexington, Kentucky, where he ran a millinery store with his sister, and in this powerful work he proposed to tell his Yiddish readers about life in the South. A comment made by the poet A. Leyeles on the occasion of Schwarz's sixty-fifth birthday provides a context for reading this work. Leyeles is recalling a debate among American Yiddish writers concerning their proper relationship to their new home: to its culture, landscape, and body politic. He paraphrases a statement allegedly made to him fifty years earlier by the novelist Joseph Opatoshu:

> "I have recently met with several younger writers," Opatoshu told me. "Among them were Mani Leib, Zishe Landau, David Ignatoff and others. None of them finds it particularly necessary to know the language or the literature of this country. How can this be? Do they want to remain forever immigrants, forever foreigners? Or is this just some kind of affectation? Whatever it is, it's the wrong approach."[29]

Leyeles proposes that it was Schwartz who most dramatically overcame this pitfall, absorbing himself in the local scene, and rendering into Yiddish the contours of American life. At the same time, he praises Schwartz for being "deeply and authentically Jewish (in a national sense)" (*tif un ekht natsional-yidish*).[30] Schwartz was also praised by Leyeles's fellow Introspectionist, Jacob Glatstein, on account of Schwartz's biblical resonances. "Schwartz's portraits of nature possess a biblical grace because he is so absorbed with the language of the Bible that he thinks biblically, so to speak" (*er trakht tanakhish*).[31] Of course, the biblical and the American need hardly be imagined as antitheses. In the case of Schwartz, his biblical sensibility and his Americanism reinforce each other, and lead to an aesthetic that resonates powerfully with Whitmanian Romanticism and simultaneously establishes continuities with the Jewish past.

Schwartz's *Kentucky* was serialized in the New York socialist monthly *Di tsukunft* from 1918 to 1922, a time when New York City was unquestionably the hub of American Yiddish culture, even as other cities and regions beckoned as possible homes for Yiddish. One of the work's implicit goals is to prove that Yiddish literature is up to the task of representing a landscape and social milieu with no precedent in Jewish history. It begins with an introductory poem, whose title, "Blue Grass," is given in English. These will be the only words in Schwartz's work in Latin script; they serve as a reminder that the world that has given rise to the poem speaks English. In the context of the Yiddish poem, these lone English words stand out as strange and foreign, as if by including them Schwartz were reproducing the disorienting experience of coming to America. And of course the phrase "blue grass" is itself a surprising juxtaposition, as if we have suddenly entered an enchanted world, where nature's colors have been rearranged. "Blue Grass" begins with an evocation of the poet's new home but then immediately recalls his origins in the old country (where the rivers are blue, not the grass):

> Un ikh, an eynikl fun vander
> Vos hot got's velt dershpirt in lite
> Mit ire umetike velder
> Un bloye kheynevdike taykhn.[32]

> And I, a grandchild of wander,
> Who first touched God's world in Lithuania,
> With its solitary forests
> And blue rivers of grace.

This tender recollection of being at home in God's world is then offset by the jarring memory of his arrival in America, where he became lost in the "maelstrom of New York" (*malshtrom fun nyu-york*). Old and new worlds are identified by words expressive of different registers of Yiddish: a term from the Hebrew (*kheynevdik* or "filled with grace") codes the old country as the familiar; the international term (*malshtrom*) codes the new city as strange and alienating; indeed, it is a kind of Babel.

The poet's dislocation in America persisted, he tells us, until he learned to love it in its manifold contradictions:

> Geven a shprits fun zayne valn
> A blits tsvishn zayne blitsn.
> Biz tayer iz er mir gevorn
> Mit zayne ziger un bazigte
> Mit zayne umglikn un glikn,
> Mit zayne raykhtimer un dales
> Mit zayn farshtiktn krekhts un yubl. (K 5)

> I was a spray from its waves
> A flash among flashes,
> Until the city's restlessness became dear to me,
> With its victorious and its vanquished,
> With its tormented and its joyous,
> With its riches and its squalor,
> With its silenced moaning and its gaiety

This catalogue of opposites given in parallel syntactic units directly evokes Whitman's signature catalogue form. Specifically, Schwartz's evocation of the vanquished (*bazigte*) along with the victorious (*ziger*) echoes section 18 in "Song of Myself": "I play not a march for victors only . . . I play great marches for conquered and slain persons." This intertextual reference links the poet's personal triumph in America—his ability to recover agency—with his assumption of Whitman's rhetoric and angle of vision. The speaker of the poem can adore the New World when he recognizes what it stands for, and this recognition is expressed through Whitman's catalogue form, which provides a strategy for holding together opposing terms and concepts in a "democratic" balance. The experience of loss in the maelstrom of New York can be overcome when the poet understands the deeper meaning of America, its underlying spiritual principle.

This movement from loss to vision is recapitulated in the narrative of *Kentucky*, which traces the rise of a Jewish family in Lexington, Kentucky, through three generations, beginning with the arrival of the founding patriarch, Joshua. The early life of this Joshua is constructed as a pastiche of different biblical episodes. First, during his journey through the wilderness, he sleeps along the way and has a dream reminiscent of Jacob's dream of the angels and the ladder. In Joshua's dream, however, there are "black demons" (*shvartse sheydim'lakh;* K 14) ascending and descending the ladder, prefiguring the travails his family will endure in their new home. Later, some time after Joshua's arrival in what the text calls "the new land of

Canaan," he has to bury his first daughter, who figures as a symbolic sacrifice required by the New World. In words that mimic Abraham's request to the Hittites for a plot to bury Sarah he begs the local townsfolk for a place to bury her: "I am a stranger here among you. . . . Grant me a grave for my child." Schwartz's line, *Ikh bin a fremder do tsvishn aykh* (K 53), echoes the biblical *ger vetoshav anokhi imakhem* (I am an alien and resident among you; Gen. 23:4). These references evoke equivocal passages from the Book of Genesis precisely where narratives of the Jewish (and Puritan) experience in America more commonly evoke the triumphant Exodus narrative, as we saw in our discussion of Antin. Schwartz simultaneously maintains different versions of Canaan, both as promised land, a refuge reached after long suffering, and as the land of the Hittites, where Abraham buries Sarah and remains an alien. When the biblical Joshua comes to the Land of Canaan, he arrives as a conquering hero; in Schwartz's poem he is a stranger who must beg mercy of the local inhabitants. The kind of teleological narrative we saw in Antin's *The Promised Land* is undercut by the lingering sense of being a "stranger here among you."

Joshua manages to amass a tiny fortune in the scrap business, a form of labor that allegorically associates him with the debris and excess of capitalist production. The image of the Jew as a dealer in old wares also evokes the Christian view of Judaism as an outmoded form of belief. Schwartz calls these associations into play as a way of suggesting that the ills of Europe have followed the Jew to America. And there are new problems as well, for the price of merging into American economic life is cultural attenuation: pictures of grandparents together with old Talmudic volumes are laid to rest in the attic; Joshua learns that "in Columbus's country / It's not a sin to work on the Sabbath" (GD 86).[33] The process is exacerbated in the next generation: Joshua's son can hardly read Hebrew and, to the even greater dismay of his father, he has internalized the racial biases of Southern whites, condemning Lincoln for his folly in freeing the slaves. Joshua appeals to the Bible in hopes of instilling a moral view in his misguided son: "He tells him stories from the Bible, / About Noah with his sons . . . that Ham is not responsible for his black skin" (GD 53). But the son is lost to Southern mores, a sacrifice like his dead sister. The text expresses sympathy for the father, even as it emphasizes that he has lost the authority to sustain what Schwartz evidently sees as the core social values of Judaism. The son marries a gentile; and eventually Joshua, who has long left any form of Jewish practice, discovers his own "soul dried up with his body" (GD 141). Here, Schwartz's text sketches what might be called the narrative of melancholy acculturation, reminiscent of Asch's *Keyn Amer-*

ike (To America; 1911) or Abraham Cahan's *The Rise of David Levinsky* (1917).[34] Such narratives tell a generational story, linking Americanization with cultural loss and anomie.

But in *Kentucky,* the narrative ultimately resolves itself in a note of serenity analogous to what we heard in the opening poem, "Blue Grass." The first positive sign comes when a younger daughter of Joshua, Dorothy, returns from Chicago (where she has been sent to "mingle with Jews") as a newly devout Jew:

> fraytog-nakht's
> Fleg brenen ir likht antkegn mame's.
> Es hobn in'm hoyz fun altn dzshosh
> Araynkumen genumen naye bikher
> Fun idisher geshikhte, religyon,
> Di lider fun der tsarter ema lazarus. (K 132)

> Friday nights
> Her candles burned alongside her mother's.
> And into old Josh's house there arrived
> New books on Jewish history, religion,
> The poems of the gentle Emma Lazarus.

This is a specifically American scene of "return," to be sure. Dorothy's relationship to Judaism is mediated by "new" books. The reference to *fraytog-nakht* instead of *shabes* further suggests her distance from East European Judaism. Most striking is Schwartz's canny evocation of "the gentle Emma Lazarus" as a figure associated with the new American Judaism. Lazarus appears as symbol of New World piety, a refined poetess who embodies the Jewish American synthesis.

Dorothy's son is named David, which Schwartz spells according to its anglicized version (*deyvid*), foregrounding his Americanization. And yet the boy comes uncannily to reflect his biblical namesake: he bodies forth a triumphant new phase in Jewish history. As a young boy, David shows signs of intellectual sharpness, linking him to "the generations of elders whose life was steeped / In the house of Torah" (GD 147). His mother harbors the hope he will devote himself to traditional learning. But after a sojourn in an unnamed "distant city" and despite his mother's protestations, David returns home and resolves to be a farmer. The text stands back from this decision and marvels at it as a miraculous transformation:

> Fun vanen iz der gayst gekumen afn yung
> Dem zun fun doyres un fun doyres hendler
> Vos zaynen vayt un fremd geven fun erd

Un opgerisn fun ir zaft un kraft un reyekh?
Ken zayn, s'hot zikh genumen fun instinkt,
Nor unbavustzinig far im aleyn
Tsu opfrishn mit erd di shvakhe kreftn? (K 161–162)

From whence did this spirit come into the youth,
Of generations upon generations of tradesmen born
Who were strangers and aliens to the earth and soil
Uprooted from its source and powers and scent?
Perhaps it came instinctively
An unconscious impulse from within
To revive through the earth his weakened powers?

The vision of the earth as a regenerative force, and of working the land as the antidote to "weakened powers," recalls the central motifs of Zionist rhetoric from this period. But this David's Zion is in the fields of Kentucky, which now, two generations after his family's arrival, can be embraced as a genuine home. The new Jewish hero overcomes generations of alienation by discovering a spiritual power in the American landscape.

This spiritual revival via the soil sets up the final sequence of Schwartz's epic, in which the old patriarch Joshua suddenly has his own reawakening, inspired by his grandson. After resolving to assist his grandson with the purchase of the farm, Joshua, now far along into his dotage, comes alive to the true splendors of the New World:

Dos oyg vert loyter
Derzet azoyns vos er hot nisht gezen biz dan—

. . . .
Es iz geven, vi s'volt a dike hoyt
Zikh opgesheylt fun altn's oygn, un zayn blik
Iz klor un sharf un likhtig-hel gevorn;
Un zayne oyern vos zaynen shver geven,
Zey plutsim ongehoybn lebn. (K 169–170)

The eye is purified
He sees into what he had not seen—

. . . .
It was as if skin were peeled away from his aged eyes
And his view became clear and sharp and bright;
And his ears, which had grown weak of hearing
Suddenly returned to life.

Schwartz adds to the previous themes of rerootedness and psychic regeneration an image that recalls Emerson's famous "transparent eyeball" passage in "Nature." The old Jew becomes an Emersonian seer. This is not figured as the negation of Judaism, moreover, but as its return and unlikely fulfillment. A Jewish hero named David has established a new kingdom, characterized not by military might but by purified vision. In the final lines of the work, Joshua's mind is portrayed as a meeting-ground for multiple scenes and traditions, including "fragments of Psalms" (*shtiklakh tilim*) and "thoughts and feelings without beginning and without end" (*gedanken un gefiln on onheyb un on sof*). After his travails in the New World, after wandering through the wilderness, and after witnessing the disintegration of traditional Judaism, the Jewish patriarch experiences an unexpected triumph, a lifting into the space of mystical knowing. Schwartz even evokes in this final phrase (*un on sof*) the kabbalistic idea of the *eyn sof*, the infinite as if to hint at a synthesis between Transcendentalism and Jewish mysticism.

Thus Schwartz's American Yiddish epic *Kentucky* rehearses another version of the narrative of return that we have traced through texts by Lazarus, Lewisohn, Frank, and Yezierska. In each of these cases, America enables a new formulation of Judaism, which is also figured, at least potentially, as its purification. In each case, the discourse of Transcendentalism provides a bridge for the writer to bring Judaism back into the text. That is, precisely when the texts represent an experience of heightened inner vision, they also move toward a specifically Jewish frame of reference. The evocation of "fragments of Psalms" at the end of *Kentucky* performs a role analogous to the quotation from Isaiah 6 at the end of Lazarus's "By the Waters of Babylon"; the evocation of the Israelites' "tents" in the wilderness at the end of Lewisohn's *The Island Within;* and the image of the Jewish patriarch reading scripture at the end of Yezierska's *Bread Givers.* In each case, a journey through America has culminated in an image that stands metonymically for the survival and reassertion of Judaism. Also, these narratives all move toward some kind of mystical or "spiritualized" Judaism: what the protagonists recover above all is a form of "vision" defined as centrally Jewish. To recognize that these moves happen in the work of a Yiddish poet—and one who grew up steeped in the rationalism of Lithuanian Orthodoxy like Schwartz—suggests the powerful effect of American Romanticism on the representation of Jewishness.

Yiddish as Utopian Space

Countless other American Yiddish poets also claimed Whitman as a major influence and inspiration. Indeed, the interest in Whitman among Yiddish poets cuts across different literary schools, implying perhaps more common ground among these schools than is generally admitted. Speaking for

Yiddish poets as a group, A. Leyeles writes in "A Dream under Sky-scrapers" that Whitman unveiled for them the true power and promise of America: "Not in vain have we read the American poem / And inhaled, absorbed the Whitman tone" (*Nisht umzist geleyent s'lid amerikaner / un gezapt in zikh dem nusakh dem Vitmaner*).[35] In the Yiddish, Leyeles rhymes "Whitmanian" with "American," suggesting that for these poets the real America is the imagined place in Whitman's poems. In H. Leivick's "To America," the poet writes that he has carried within him the bounty of American freedom, which has been sanctified by the blood of Lincoln and the hymns of Whitman.[36] Again, the point I wish to make is not so much that responding to Whitman makes Yiddish poets American, but that Yiddish poets construct a new *Jewish* discourse, using Whitman as a model. Not only does Yiddish poetry itself inevitably imply a Jewish writer and a Jewish reader, but these poets also generally read Whitman as a modern version of the biblical prophet, a tradition they see as their own.

Yet another Yiddish Whitmanian we should consider is Reuben Ludwig (1895–1926), associated neither with Bovshover's "Sweatshop School" nor with Schwartz's *Di yunge*, but rather with the modernist-oriented *Inzikhistn* (Introspectionists). Ludwig emigrated from Kiev at the age of twelve and devoted himself to writing in Yiddish only after publishing his first poetical works in English in the socialist periodical *The New York Call*. Ludwig insisted on the possibility of writing in Yiddish about the American scene: such poems include "To a Negro" (*Tsu a neger*) and his cycle "Indian Motifs" (*Indianer motivn*), works that express solidarity with America's archetypal victims.[37] In "Symposium," Ludwig creates an imaginary community in which first Walt Whitman, and then John Brown and Abraham Lincoln all return from the grave to cast judgment upon America through the medium of a Yiddish poem. Like Bovshover's "Likht un shotn," he presents an instance of prosopopoeia that shows the Yiddish poet creating his own voice by imaginatively summoning figures from the past.

The first half of the poem is constructed as Whitman's responses to the question, "What do you see?" which itself comes from "Salut au Monde." This question is given in English, as though the poet had thought to summon Whitman in his own language only to discover that in the afterlife, Whitman has come to speak Yiddish. Whitman opens his discourse by describing the countryside using his characteristic long line: *Ikh ze breyte vegn fun nyu-orlins bizn hodson. / Ikh ze gele sof-zumerdike grez-lekh baflekn zeyere bregn* (I see open roads stretching from New Orleans to the Hudson. / I see golden, late-summer grass spotting the road's edge).[38] But, while Whitman may speak in his own familiar cadences, the present-day America he encounters horrifies him. The cities where he hoped to see a new society based on true fraternity have become rotten and crumbling (*tsefoylt un tsebreklt*); farmhands have become bound to their iron ploughs (*tsugebundn tsu aker-ayzn*). His dream of universal brotherhood has been "trampled upon by trembling feet," destroyed by the forces of capitalism, hauntingly embodied in the image of a "giddy-faced gold miner from California / With thinning yellowish skin and deeply sunken eyes." The Yiddish Whitman recognizes the vulnerability of his vision in a land taken possession of by the ethos of capitalism. Some redoubled, and possibly miraculous, effort will be necessary to steer the nation back on track.

In the second half of the poem, Whitman is joined by John Brown and Lincoln, who, just as in Waldo Frank's *Our America,* figure as Whitmanian prophets of democracy. Like Whitman, they too observe an America undone by selfishness and violence. Brown is portrayed as a persecuted "poor Jesus" (*oremen yezus*) who is being hunted down: "They want to hang me again in Virginia. . . . At the entrance of the nearest church" (*Zey viln mikh nokh a mol hengen in virdzshinye. . . . Bay der ershter kirkhn-shvel*). Lincoln can only remark that the land, without its leader, has spun into chaos.

The final lines of the poem resolve this crisis through a redemptive image of nature:

> Nor di lange stenge fun der misisipi
> Bindet zey in a shvern garb tsuzamen,
> Un eybik lebedik, eybik gants,
> Iz undzer kenigin misisipi,
> Eybik zingendik, tif un gants—
> Iz undzer kenigin misisipi.[39]

> Only the widely stretching ribbon of the Mississippi
> Binds all together in a single tight sheaf,
> Eternally living, eternally whole,
> Our Queen, the Mississippi,
> Eternally singing, deep and whole,
> Our Queen, the Mississippi.

Here, Ludwig evokes a symbol deeply interwoven with the language and metaphorics of American democracy. Evocative of Twain, the Mississippi stands not so much for personal escape but for the principle of interconnectedness. The Mississippi becomes a naturalized messianic force. By evoking the river as "Queen," Ludwig inverts the traditional Jewish representation of the redemptive, messianic figure as "King." This is a messiah already present within the forces of nature. Interestingly, it is unclear who is meant to speak these final lines, an ambiguity that reflects the idea of timelessness conveyed by the lines: we no longer hear a specific singer but an *eternal singing* in which all of the voices of the poem become indistinguishable. The voices of Whitman, Brown, and Lincoln gather together in the space of the Yiddish poem, which becomes a forum for holding a "symposium" on the future of America. Here the Yiddish poem itself becomes a utopian space of togetherness, where the "I" of the poem's first lines can be transformed into a "we." Within the "eternal singing" of these final lines, the divisions of time and place are overcome, and the dead are given new life.

The movement from Bovshover's "Light and Shadow" to Ludwig's "Symposium" reflects the movement from Heine to Whitman as guiding lights for Yiddish poetry. Both poems attest to the power of the Yiddish language to renew and reinvent itself in the New World. Both of these poets, it should be reiterated, were more than proficient in other languages, suggesting that to at least some extent, the decision to write in Yiddish was itself a declaration of cultural allegiance, an affirmation that a sustainable Jewish culture, structured around socialist values and expressed in Yiddish, was possible in America. We might say that it was their grounding in the Bible coupled with their progressive political ethos that enabled Yiddish American poets to see themselves as spokespeople for the American Idea. The Yiddish Whitmanians propose, in particular, that they possess a special ability to speak for Whitman's goal of blending voices and languages. Yiddish, we might say, becomes itself a symbol for a truly democratic communal space. The Yiddish Whitmanians, I am suggesting, saw themselves not only as part of the American bard's flock. They also appointed themselves as his necessary, ministering angels, with a special mission to renew his dream. And as they renewed Whitman's dream, they also imagined—and for a time, at least, seemed honestly to believe—that they were staking a claim for a politically progressive Yiddish literary culture in the America of the future.

PART 4

"ORATING IN NEW YORKESE":
THE LANGUAGES OF JEWISHNESS
IN POSTWAR AMERICA

Why did I always have to fall among theoreticians!
—Saul Bellow, *The Adventures of Augie March*

In 1963, the scion of New England Puritans and reigning poet-hero Robert Lowell attended a public symposium on Hannah Arendt's controversial new book about the Eichmann trial, published earlier that year. The symposium was sponsored by *Dissent* magazine and chaired by its polemical editor in chief, Irving Howe. Among those in attendance were a number of the writers and critics known today as the "New York intellectuals," including Daniel Bell, Lionel Abel, Mary McCarthy, Dwight Macdonald, and Alfred Kazin; also present was a veteran of the Warsaw ghetto uprising and a former leader of the revolutionary Jewish labor Bund.[1] Arendt's bold thesis that the Eichmann trial revealed nothing so much as the "banality of evil" was roundly attacked by many, supported by a few (Arendt herself did not make an appearance).[2] For many, the symposium was a watershed event, one of the first public airings of long-suppressed emotions about Nazi crimes against Europe's Jews.[3]

For Lowell, a Boston Brahmin with a taste for the exotic, the event was noteworthy for other reasons. In a letter to his friend and fellow poet Elizabeth Bishop, he noted his astonishment and delight: "One was suddenly in a pure Jewish or Arabic world, people hardly speaking English, declaiming, confessing, orating in New Yorkese, in Yiddish, booing and clapping."[4] This captivating scene inspired Lowell to reflect more broadly on the role of New York Jews in American culture. "There's nothing like the New York Jews," he wrote to Bishop. "Odd that this is so, and that other American groups are so speechless and dead." At a moment when a generalized weariness had settled upon the nation, Lowell was struck by the vitality of these debaters—all the more striking since the occasion that had prompted all this booing and clapping was a symposium on the single-most tragic episode in modern Jewish history.[5]

Lowell's comments reflect an attitude held by many on the postwar literary scene. This was a period that witnessed the rise of a new generation of Jewish writers, critics, and scholars to national prominence, among them Delmore Schwartz, Saul Bellow, Harold Rosenberg, Leslie Fiedler, Isaac Rosenfeld, Paul Goodman, Bernard Malamud, Grace Paley, Allen Ginsberg, Philip Roth, and Norman Mailer.[6] All were noisily interceding in a literary climate presided over by T. S. Eliot's icy persona, and in which John Cheever's terse *New Yorker* style had seemed the only imaginable way to write fiction. The Jewish writers introduced an innovative style marked by bursts of fury, flights of fancy, and jarring shifts between high and low registers. Howe later described this writing as a "yoking of street raciness and high-cultural mandarin."[7] This disorderly form was matched by an equally disorderly content. Emotions were expressed at a high pitch of intensity, epitomized by Tommy Wilhelm's spontaneous flood of tears at the end of Bellow's *Seize the Day* (1956); by a landlord's sudden transformation into a self-immolating penitent at the end of Malamud's "The Mourners" (1958); or by Aunt Rose's life-affirming declaration at the end of Grace Paley's "Goodbye and Good Luck" (1959) that she will finally have a husband ("which everyone should have sooner or later before the story's over").[8] What Lowell called "New Yorkese," then, was everything that "English," with its air of seriousness, its ancient, ancestral ties to the Mother Country, was not.[9] And in the context of the staid, buttoned-down 1950s—the period Howe famously dubbed "this age of conformity"—New Yorkese offered a glimpse of freedom, or at least a breath of fresh air.[10]

The postwar Jewish style was also marked by bold, explicit, and unapologetic assertions of Jewishness. Suddenly every reader of American fiction, Jewish or not, was expected to understand at least a smattering of Yiddish. Terms were left untranslated, lending the same authority to Yiddish that had been previously been reserved for French, German, or Spanish. Stories about New York Jews were offered up and read as parables for the national soul. The figure of the schlemiel became a hero, and the Jewish mother an object of nostalgic fantasy (or a castrating demon).[11] In one of his short stories, "Angel Levine" (1956), Malamud suggested that any act of genuine kindness turned one into a Jew, revealing just how broad the symbol of the Jew could become. "Believe me," the hero says to his wife after she has been saved by a black Jewish angel. "There are Jews everywhere."[12]

How might we explain this insurgent, uproarious sensibility in postwar Jewish American writing? Many commentators have looked to the specific predicament of second-generation American Jews—a generation positioned at an equal distance from the Jewish past and the American present. In *Prodigal Sons: The New York Intellectuals and Their World* (1986), historian Alexander Bloom argues that their own historical position created a heightened self-consciousness, which fostered a speculative frame of mind and a penchant for cultural analysis. "The feeling of loss of their connection to the immigrant community led . . . to the next logical conclusion, the assessment of their ties to their parents and the process by which they had broken away."[13] According to this analysis, the postwar writers stand for the quintessential *transitional* generation. They oversaw the transition, as it were, from the immigrant experience, with its Brooklyn or Newark streets, Yiddish-speaking homes, heders, and storefront shuls, to the post-ethnic, assimilated experience of other white Americans. In the terms of this generational account, an implicit equation is generally made between "immigrant life" and "Jewishness." As the immigrant community dissolves, there sets in a kind of period of restless adjustment, which fuels creativity, innovation, and an impulse to overturn the pieties both of home and of American society at large. New Yorkese, from this standpoint, is the expression of post-immigrant Jews who are deeply familiar with two worlds, but neither quite of one nor the other.

While compelling in many ways, this generational narrative has limitations. By treating the sociological context as the exclusive or final cause for cultural work, we obscure the active creative processes that go into the shaping and reshaping of a literary voice and vocabulary. And we lose sight of the strategic uses—political, psychological, artistic—to which constructions of Jewishness can be put. If we consider Jewish American writers not as figures fated by generational positioning to write in a certain way, but as figures engaged in dialogue with multiple traditions, we can move beyond the determinism that creeps into cultural analyses rooted in sociological paradigms. We can also see that Jewish writers living before *and* after World War II reimagine the significance of Jewishness in the midst of profound engagements with the meaning of America and with its classic literary tradition. By thus taking the long view of Jewish American literary culture, as we are doing here, we can recognize the limits of the familiar generational model. We can see how the Jewish encounter with America has been animated by recurring features, including the dialectical movement of identification and dis-identification with America and the turn toward heightened forms of Jewish identification to find a language of moral and political critique. To be sure, such highly specific postwar phenomena as the need to mourn the Holocaust, the entrance of unprecedented numbers of American Jews into the middle class, and the decline of socialism go a great distance toward shaping the sensibilities of postwar Jewish American writers; but there are also cultural dynamics affecting Jewish American writers in general that have a longer history.

Two writers associated with postwar Jewish American culture—who commented on and simultaneously embodied its new prominence—were Alfred Kazin and Irving Howe. Both were expert, prominent critics of American literature. Both were also responsible, at least as much as anybody else, for putting Jewish American literature on the cultural map and for establishing the terms within which the Jewishness of those writers was read. Both understood themselves as representative Jews of their generation, and they wrote voluminously about their experiences growing up in Brooklyn and the Bronx and about their subsequent experiences, once they had "made it," in Manhattan. Indeed, criticism and autobiography are frequently conjoined in their writing—sometimes explicitly, as in Kazin's *New York Jew* (1978), and sometimes implicitly, as in Howe's *World of Our Fathers* (1976).

In addition to the Holocaust, which implicitly or explicitly informs everything they wrote about Jews, another historical development that was pivotal in their self-understanding was the weakening of socialism in mid-century America. As Howe wrote in his autobiography, "Had American socialism not reached an impasse in the postwar years, I might have continued to think of myself as a cosmopolitan activist of Jewish origin, rather than a Jewish intellectual with cosmopolitan tastes."[14] I will propose that in different ways Kazin and Howe turned to the figure of the Jew to sustain many of the kinds of critique that socialism had offered.[15] They will describe Jewish culture as a force of resistance to the prevailing ethos of modern American life and as a model for collective life, grounded in history and memory.

7

"MY PRIVATE ORTHODOXY"

Alfred Kazin's Romantic Judaism

No matter how time and space were defined, I thought, it is impossible to
be simultaneously in Brooklyn and Manhattan.
—Isaac Bashevis Singer, "A Day in Coney Island"

When he died in 1998 at age eighty-three, Alfred Kazin left behind a
smattering of notes for a book he was preparing on the cultural history of
the Jews. Drawing on the work of his lifelong literary hero William Blake,
he called his work-in-progress "Jews: The Marriage of Heaven and Hell."
He had also already chosen an epigraph for the book, which came from
Philip Roth's *The Counterlife:* "The bastard has Jew on the brain."[1] Based
both on these quotations and on everything Kazin *did* write—which included numerous critical books, scores of critical essays and reviews, four
autobiographical works, and a voluminous private journal—it is tempting
to imagine his unwritten book on the Jews as seeking somehow to unify
Blake and Roth. It might very well have brought together the visionary

intensity of Blakean Romanticism with Roth's insistence on the shaping role of the American Jewish ethnic community. Kazin encompassed both of these poles in his writings on Jews, evoking what he called the "divine mystery of being Jewish" on the one hand while seeking on the other to understand how this mystery had been revealed to him in his everyday experiences in the Brownsville of his youth.[2] In this chapter, we will explore Kazin's journey from the first pinnacle of his career, when he made a name for himself as a brilliant young commentator on American literature, to his later efforts to work through the meanings that Jewishness might hold in modern America.

Going Native

When Kazin started out in the 1930s, he was consumed by the idea that literature might offer a moral compass in a world on the brink of chaos. Similar to Howe, Nathan Glazer, Daniel Bell, and other New York intellectuals, Kazin was a student at City College; but unlike these others, he was repelled by the sectarian fighting that defined student life. While others refined their moral and political outlooks in the alcoves of the City College cafeteria, where it was de rigueur to be a socialist and where the order of the day involved shouting down the Stalinists, Kazin saw socialism from the beginning as more of an overall ethical orientation than a specific position to be defended. "Although I was a 'socialist', like everyone else I knew," he later wrote, "I thought of socialism as orthodox Christians might think of the Second Coming—a wholly supernatural event which one might await with perfect faith, but which had no immediate relevance to my life."[3] Among second-generation New York Jews, Kazin might thus be considered part of the first wave of "deradicalization." Suspicious of doctrine from the start, he invested more faith in the spontaneous responses of the human imagination, and looked to art, not class struggle, as the agent of social and cultural renewal.

While working as a freelance book reviewer in his early twenties, Kazin was encouraged by Columbia professor Carl Van Doren to undertake a study of modern American literature. In response, Kazin wrote *On Native Grounds: A Study of American Prose Literature from 1890 to the Present* (1942). In this book, a rhapsodic, synoptic account of the rise of modern American writing, Kazin revealed to the surprise of not a few that a Jew from the bowels of Brooklyn, the son of a dressmaker and a housepainter, could gain mastery over a half-century's worth of literary, social, and political history. At a moment when Jews still had an uneasy status in American society, Kazin himself had seemingly laid claim to genuine "native" status by speaking on behalf of the indigenous culture, by tracing its itineraries from north to south and east to west, and by placing its triumphs and failures into a grand historical narrative.[4] In the wake of the publication of *On Native Grounds,* Kazin was suddenly looked to as a spokesman for American culture. The book launched him on a career that would include teaching posts at Harvard, Smith, Black Mountain College, and the City University of New York.

How can we reconcile Kazin's passion for American literature in *On Native Grounds* and his lifelong role as American literary ambassador with his later claim that "nothing has as much emotional and spiritual value for me as the Jewish experience"?[5] Or with the fact that he moved from his analysis of American literature to a sustained set of meditations on the world of Jewish Brownsville where he grew up? Or with the fact that he became a central advocate for Jewish writers from Isaac Bashevis Singer to Bernard Malamud and gave the final installment of his autobiographical trilogy the title *New York Jew?* Let us review the argument of his debut work as a context for these later developments.

On Native Grounds begins from the premise that literary criticism as it had emerged out of the 1930s had reached an impasse. The field was divided into two critical orthodoxies: the "textual–aesthetic" approach of the New Critics and the "sociological approach" of the doctrinaire Marxists.[6] As Kazin saw it, neither had proven fit to do more than chasten the reigning values of the day. "Allen Tate's South was remarkably like Michael Gold's Russia," he wrote, "a community to be used as a standard of order and fellowship against the Enemy" (ONG 330). Kazin dismisses the genteel Southern Agrarian and the scrappy Jewish Communist in the same breath for their ideological rigidity. Neither is willing, Kazin argues, to let literature speak on its own terms. As he wrote to Van Doren just as he was finishing the book, the age was "caught between the zealots and the grammarians, the politicos and the *precieux;* it is gasping for critical leadership, for tone, for a belief in literature that will begin with something so obvious as—a poet is a man speaking to other men."[7] Kazin hoped in *On Native Grounds* to reinstate precisely such a belief. To move beyond the politicized and polarized 1930s, he hoped to develop a form of criticism rooted in the idea that literature might provide a compass for living; his criterion for literary quality was the extent to which a work availed the reader of the "pang of individual experience" (ONG 327).

In his reading of American literature, Kazin proposes that the quintessential gesture of the American writer was and had remained one of revolt, not so much against any specific regime or ideology, but against the idea of limitation itself. Kazin's view recalls the insurgent spirit of the

"Young Americans" of the second decade of the 1900s, Waldo Frank's *Our America* being a key precedent for *On Native Grounds*. But whereas these earlier critics had generally celebrated the triumph over Victorian styles and mores, Kazin seeks to temper this view: "To speak of modern American writing as a revolt against the Genteel Tradition alone, against Victorianism alone, against even the dominance of the state by certain groups, does not explain why our liberations have often proved so empty; it does not tell us why the light-bringers brought us light and live themselves in darkness" (ONG ix). Looking back three decades after Frank had proclaimed that American writers had discovered their true calling, Kazin discovered that the "Young Americans" had spoken too soon, simplifying the formula for success.

In his alternate reading of American literary history, Kazin proposes a cyclical view in which breakthrough is followed repeatedly by failure, liberation by exhaustion. The bold American writer plunges forward, seeking to capture "a true north in our moral history" (ONG 228), but the final word is elusive. Some excess in rhetoric or failure of insight undermines the work. Kazin finds evidence for this pattern in the careers of writers as varied as Edith Wharton, H. L. Mencken, Sinclair Lewis, Ernest Hemingway, John Dos Passos, and Thomas Wolfe. Each one sets out propelled by massive energy and dreams of self-liberation. But at the height of success, when purity of vision seems to have been won and all bounds seem ready to burst, each writer somehow loses momentum, proving unable to provide a sustainable vision commensurate with the vicissitudes of actual living. Thus, Hemingway's heroic search for "the real thing" leads to an initial triumph: "He could rise above the dull submissive sense of outrage which most men felt in the face of events" (ONG 258). But Kazin finds Hemingway lapsing into "melodrama and sick violence" (ONG 259). The nihilistic hardness Hemingway developed in response to World War I seemed inadequate when applied to the Spanish Civil War and the threat of a fascist takeover of Europe. What had started out for Hemingway as a courageous encounter with "reality" had hardened into a pose that paradoxically created a barrier to reality in its actuality. Another version of this pattern is exhibited by James T. Farrell, whose style Kazin sees as perfectly calibrated to record the brutality of modern urban experience. But Farrell's harsh realism ultimately proves *too* harsh; his worldview is so "riddled with determinism" that he cannot offer any vision beyond brutality. Of the figures in Kazin's book, it is perhaps H. L. Mencken who most dramatically embodies these extremes of brilliance and failure. On the one hand, he is the "great cultural emancipator, the conqueror of Philistia" (ONG 161); on the other, he is "eccentric" and "willful" and frequently proved "cheap and cruel" (ONG 161). In each of Kazin's case studies, he shows how the American drive toward self-liberation and authenticity founders when it comes to developing a genuinely responsive moral vision. Gestures of defiance become emptied of significance; lofty pronouncement devolves into mere rhetoric and a drift toward nihilism.

But Kazin himself hardly sounds a note of despair as he sketches these portraits. For what endures through each failing episode is America "as an idea" (ONG 381), and in itself "America" retains value as a spur toward cultural and personal renewal. "Our modern writers," Kazin asserts, "have had to discover and rediscover and chart the country in every generation, rewriting Emerson's *The American Scholar* in every generation . . . but must still cry America! America! As if we had never known America. As perhaps we have not" (ONG x). Kazin endorses Emerson's "America" as essentially a spur to new creation and a promise of imminent deliverance. But this deliverance must be sought ever anew; Emerson must be rewritten in every generation. Responding to the beginning stages of World War II, Kazin argues that the pressure of the times can only be resisted by redoubling those "explorations of the human imagination" that literature alone can provide and alone can lead beyond the stifling formulations of the past.

A crucial backdrop for *On Native Grounds* is the outbreak of the war and the spread of fascism. And this is perhaps where Kazin chiefly differs from Frank and company as well as from the Marxists and the Southern-agrarian New Critics: the danger he seeks to remedy is neither Victorian repression, nor capitalist domination, nor industrialism run amuck, but the threat to what he calls "our whole modern democratic culture" posed by "the Axis Ministers of Culture—the half-men, the death's-heads grinning over their spoil of our time" (ONG 405). Even if the "light bringers" had failed in the past, the essential premise underlying their efforts—that the self *can* be unencumbered—this, more than anything else, has to be preserved as a vital principle in the face of fascism. *On Native Grounds* is thus a celebration coupled with a warning—a celebration of the idea of America as a spur for new creation, and a warning that the final deliverance, sought for so passionately and earnestly by generations of American writers, may not be quite as imminent as had been supposed.

Kazin's attraction to American literature, along with that of fellow Jewish critics of his generation, including Philip Rahv, Leslie Fiedler, and Howe, has sometimes been theorized under the sign of assimilation, as a reflection of the immigrant's desire to merge with the native culture, to insinuate himself on "native grounds." Russell Jacoby has written that the New York intellectuals exemplify certain attitudes typical of immigrant groups in general: "The 'foreigner'—the Jewish intellectual—embraced his new cultural home . . . [as a response to] anxiety of illegitimacy or persecution."[8] According to this view, an engagement with American literature becomes one of various tactics of integration, the strategy in this case being to gain legitimacy through eloquence. A problem with this argument is that it tends to conflate *American literature* with *American society*, as if "America" itself were a univocal totality, oriented to a single purpose. To associate an engagement with American literature with the drive for social integration is to forget that, for Kazin, the writers discussed in *On Native Grounds* remain figures of revolt. The "native" in Kazin's title may be read not in the sense of "nativist" but in the sense of "wild," a reminder that Whitman's "barbaric yawp" is sounded not by Whitman alone. Hence, Kazin may be seen not so much as trying to insinuate himself into a new social world (though he clearly managed to do this), but as celebrating the radical and experimental currents he has discovered within American culture. Indeed, the project of American writers (and here we might count Kazin himself) is to *rewrite* Emerson, not merely to pay homage to his greatness. Kazin's own critical style—with its forceful declamations and dazzling range of reference—bears witness to his own drive for innovation, his efforts to embody in his writing the dynamism and vitality of American literary culture.

Reflections on the Shoah

When Kazin wrote *On Native Grounds*, he had already worked for a number of years as a book reviewer for the *New York Times* and *The New Republic*, specializing among other areas in books on Jewish themes. This is not to say that he was any sort of unequivocal advocate for modern Jewish culture. In his review of Mordecai Kaplan's *Judaism as a Civilization* (1936) for the *Times*, we hear the ambivalent note that characterizes many of his reflections on Jewish culture from this period. While praising the passion behind Kaplan's efforts to "reconstruct" Judaism, he concludes somewhat sardonically that "Dr. Kaplan's clarion call [to American Jewry] to return to itself may provoke only a limp, if sympathetic response."[9] In *On Native Grounds*, Kazin's response to Jewish American writing is far more limp than sympathetic. In Ludwig Lewisohn's attempt to revive the "Hebraic genius," Kazin sees misguided sentimentality; writers like Daniel Fuchs and Clifford Odets are mentioned but are barely discussed. Henry Roth goes unnoticed altogether. The world of Yiddish creativity remains invisible, as if his father had never brought home a single edition of the *Jewish Daily Forward*. These omissions are striking in light of Kazin's subsequent career, a fact he himself underscored when he later wrote that during the late 1930s he and his wife were both "in a terrible rush to get away from everything we had grown up with."[10]

At times, this ambivalence toward American Jewish culture veered toward open hostility. In 1944, Kazin was asked to contribute to a symposium in *Contemporary Jewish Record* entitled "Under Forty." The symposium focused on what the editors considered an important new development: "With the coming of age of the children of the Jewish immigrants, we find that quite a few of them are taking their place in the front ranks of American literature. . . . [American Jews] are spectators no longer but full participants in the cultural life of the country."[11] The respondents—who included Muriel Rukeyser, Lionel Trilling, Delmore Schwartz, and Kazin— were asked to comment on their own attitudes toward their "Jewish heritage." Of the respondents, many of whom express tepid and vague sorts of affirmations, Kazin sounds the loudest note of discord, doubting whether he had been shaped in any significant way by his Jewish past. Kazin goes on to attack American Jewry in general for its "dreary middle-class chauvinism," and for its association with the cheap products of popular culture: "I have never seen much of what I admire in American Jewish culture, or among Jewish writers in America generally. . . . I see the Broadway boys making the over-eager jokes in our self-defense; and the music of Tin Pan Alley and Hollywood; and the sickening plays of the George S. Kaufmans" (10). As for his own identity, he announces that he learned long ago "to accept the fact that I was Jewish without being a part of any meaningful Jewish life or culture" (11). He associates himself instead with the tradition of protest he describes in *On Native Grounds*, explaining that his own life has followed an arc of his own making. Having rejected a faith merely imposed, he has pieced together his own personal culture, which he associates with Blake, Emerson, and Melville.[12]

But even as Kazin was declaring his independence from the Jews he grew up around, he was becoming increasingly attuned to the fate of the Jews of Europe. And here Kazin's response was anything but limp. "Every day and every week, for exactly eleven years more," he later recalled, "Hitler was to be at the back of my mind like a bad dream" (SOT 11). Elsewhere he wrote that in his "private history of the world," he noted down "every morsel of fact and rumor relating to the murder of my people" (NYJ 30). His enthusiasm for American literature, with its progressive spirit and emphasis on self-fashioning, could hardly insulate Kazin from these pained recognitions. This obsessive concern for the Jews of Europe set Kazin apart to some extent from others in the *Partisan Review* group, many of whom were focusing less on the mass murder of Jews than on the dangers of global militarism. The New York intellectuals in general seemed to have had a delayed reaction to the Holocaust.[13] Howe points out that even in 1946, when it was impossible not to know, he and other "sensitive people" he knew "often fell into a shared numbness, a blockage of response, as if to put aside the anguish that was lying in wait" (MH 249). Howe also admits that in his efforts to interpret the war through the lens of class struggle and capitalist domination—categories that he had embraced during the ideological 1930s—he had been unable to recognize the unprecedented nature of the extermination camps. Kazin was atypical in this regard, openly discussing the reality of the death camps during the war years. His rejection of orthodox Marxism made him less inclined, perhaps, to fit every new historical development into its overarching terms, and so he was better able to recognize and register the horror of the Holocaust as it was occurring. But, after distancing himself so decisively from the Jewish community, how would Kazin find a way to respond to the Holocaust while sustaining his critique of middle-class American Jewish life? And, to put the same question differently, how would the Holocaust complicate and transform his sense of himself as a Jew?

Kazin's first public response to the Holocaust was an essay he wrote early in 1944, while serving as literary editor for *The New Republic*. Kazin had come across a brief article in *The New York Times* that contained a description of the suicide of Shmuel Ziegelboim, the representative of the Jewish Worker's Bund in the Polish government in exile, along with Ziegelboim's suicide note. Ziegelboim's wife and child had been killed by the Nazis, and he had been trying from London to summon an active response from the world to the Nazi assault on Jews. In desperation over the liquidation of the Warsaw ghetto and the failure of Allied statesmen to respond to his calls for intervention, Ziegelboim committed suicide, leaving a letter addressed to the Prime Minister of Poland, General Sikorski. The letter culminated with a plea for world action: "Perhaps by my death," he wrote, "I shall contribute to the indifference of those who may now—at the last minute—rescue the few Polish Jews still alive from certain annihilation."[14] Kazin was moved to reprint Ziegelboim's suicide note in *The New Republic*, on January 10, 1944, and he appended an essay in which he tried to draw out the larger implications of Ziegelboim's act.

Throughout 1943, *The New Republic* had printed a series of articles describing the fate of Jews in the war and reviewing possible courses of action that might save the remaining European Jews.[15] Kazin used Ziegelboim's letter as an opportunity to speculate more broadly on the persecution and murder of Jews, and to offer a plea not merely to the Allied governments but to all responsible bystanders. In this striking essay, Kazin anticipates a view that would gradually surface in later philosophical and theological speculation on the Holocaust: that the Nazi crimes represent a rupture in human history, that they call for a fundamental rethinking of inherited moral and political categories:[16]

> Historically, no massacre was ever so unexpected, no act of cruelty ever so great that it violated the professions of a civilization. . . . But surely there was never so much self-deception about our essential goodness or our dream of "social security," so little philosophic (or moral) searching of the lies our hopes build on our lack of community, as there is today. . . . Something has already been done, by us the bystanders and not just the Nazi killers—which can never be undone, except as we seek to understand it and to grow human again (or expectant or merely wise) through it. (45)

The senseless murder of Jews proves that enlightenment ideals have failed. No "social contract" has managed to protect Jews. The liberal faith in "essential goodness" must also be rethought. Kazin's emphasis on a broader complicity moves his discourse out of the sphere of politics, toward the problems of ethics, empathy, and individual conscience—the problem, in short, of what he calls "growing human again."

Having framed the crisis as a loss of basic humanity, it makes sense that Kazin would respond by redoubling his efforts to inspire "belief" in literature, which he looked to as the sole means of recovering the "pang of experience." Throughout the war years, Kazin was immersed in the work of William Blake, preparing the manuscript of *The Portable William Blake*, which came out in 1946. As a coda to his article about Ziegelboim, Kazin appends the final stanza of Blake's powerful song of experience, "London" (London being, also, the site of Ziegelboim's death). The lines Kazin quotes read: "In every infant's cry of fear / In every cry of every man, / In every voice, in every ban, / The mind-forg'd manacles I hear." By presenting this pastiche of texts—Ziegelboim's suicide note alongside Blake's "London"—Kazin links the self-martyred Polish Jew and the Romantic visionary poet. Both are fundamentally alike, he implies, in their impulse to liberate humanity from their blindness. This use of Blake allows Kazin to universalize the message of Ziegelboim's suicide note and the war as a whole: the center has not held, and we are all implicated in the disaster. Nevertheless, while presenting Ziegelboim as a Blakean prophet, Kazin also describes him as the embodiment of the particular spiritual achievement of East European Judaism. In Ziegelboim's self-sacrifice, Kazin sees a courageous and selfless gesture: "Shmuel Ziegelboim came from a ghetto-driven, self-driven, but spiritually generous culture; and I honestly believe that he was thinking not only of his own people at the end, but of the

hollowness of a world in which such a massacre could have so little meaning." Ziegelboim's Bundist affiliations or the political culture of Poland are
of less account to Kazin than the broader Jewish cultural matrix—the
"spiritually generous culture" of the ghetto—from which Ziegelboim
emerged.[17] Ziegelboim embodies at once victimhood, outsiderness, courage, and "spiritual generosity." Here, then, is another voice of protest, like
the writers Kazin discusses in *On Native Grounds*, with the difference that
protest is now grounded in East European Jewish life. The challenge of
becoming human again might be met, it seems, by recalling the world that
created Ziegelboim. In his article on the self-martyred Bundist Shmuel
Ziegelboim, we discover the beginnings of a new emphasis in Kazin's
writing: protest, if it is to mean anything besides sheer negativity, must
arise from a feeling for human community and an awareness of the past.

Back to Brooklyn

Almost immediately upon the conclusion of World War II, Kazin began
writing a series of autobiographical vignettes that eventually became *A
Walker in the City* (1951), a lyrical evocation of the immigrant Jewish
world of Brownsville and a major contribution to postwar Jewish American literature.[18] We have already seen this kind of shift from criticism to
autobiography—and from a meditation on Americanness to a meditation
on Jewishness—in the case of Lewisohn. In Kazin's case, he made the shift
at a moment at which a number of New York Jews began gravitating
toward questions relating to Jews, Judaism, and Jewishness. Irving Howe
describes the postwar moment as the beginning of his personal "recon-
quest of Jewishness."[19] Some began exploring the possibilities for Jewish
faith and practice in postwar America; others set out to discover the
specifically "Jewish" quality of cultural icons like Franz Kafka and Marc
Chagall; still others reevaluated the Western literary canon with an eye
toward antisemitic currents. Even when the Holocaust was not explicitly
mentioned in these postwar meditations, it was always an implicit backdrop, a kind of centripetal force drawing Jewish intellectuals to reflect on
an identity whose meaning had been dramatically reorganized in the span
of less than a decade. The newly formed *Commentary* magazine was one
important forum for these reflections. In his inaugural statement, editor
in chief Elliot Cohen announced that in the postwar era the center of
Jewish cultural production had now shifted from Europe to America:
"*Commentary* is an act of faith in our possibilities in America. With Europe devastated, there falls upon us here in the United States a far greater
share of the responsibility for carrying forward, in a creative way, our

common Jewish cultural and spiritual heritage."[20] Kazin's writings about growing up in Jewish Brownsville reflect this new sense of responsibility for Jewish culture that Cohen describes. Indeed, the first installment of *A Walker in the City*, "The Lady Downstairs," was printed in *Commentary* 1947—after being rejected by *The New Yorker*.[21]

Kazin's book contains only one reference to the Holocaust, but it is a striking passage, in which he discloses the connection between the destruction of European Jewry and his own impulse to tell the story of his upbringing as a Jew in Brownsville. It comes from the opening of chapter 2, "The Kitchen":

> The last time I saw our kitchen this clearly was one afternoon in London at the end of the war, when I waited out the rain at the entrance to a music store. A radio was playing in the street, and standing there I heard a broadcast of the first Sabbath service from Belsen concentration camp. When the liberated prisoners recited the *Hear O Israel, the Lord Our God, the Lord is One,* I felt myself carried back to the Friday evenings at home, when with the Sabbath at sundown a healing quietness would come over Brownsville.[22]

This passage directly precedes a long recollection of Kazin's mother and the Brownsville kitchen where she labored away at a sewing machine. It is, significantly, the only moment in the entire text that takes place outside of New York City, and it takes us back to London, the scene of Ziegelboim's suicide and Blake's poem. The prayer spoken by the liberated prisoners, the *Shema*, gathers special meaning in postliberation Belsen. Moving beyond the context of liturgy narrowly defined, it becomes a sign of Jewish survival and of an insistence on the part of the survivors to remain Jewish in spite of everything. It testifies not only to the relation between Jew and God, but also between Jews and their own cultural past. So moved was Kazin by this expression of Jewish perseverance that he repeats his description of this scene on at least two additional occasions in his subsequent writings. As Kazin relates the scene in *A Walker in the City*, the prayer uttered by the former prisoners comes to function as a mnemonic for his childhood. The *Shema* serves as a point of identification with the survivors, the saving remnant of European Jewry; and his own past experiences take on new value as part of a broader collective Jewish memory that has been rescued from annihilation. Recovering the memories of his youth becomes Kazin's way of participating in the refusal to surrender life, identity, and peoplehood to the Nazis. Writing the story of his life becomes for Kazin the symbolic equivalent of the prayer uttered by the survivors.

This theme of Jewish perseverance is conjured in a subtle way by the structure of Kazin's book, which eschews the narrative conventions of autobiography. Unlike in more standard autobiographies, the present tense in Kazin's text does not represent a position of stable, mature, and "enlightened" self-reflection. Instead, the present is a place of agitation, in which the adult Kazin is compelled by an unnamed force to "go over the whole route" of his past. There appears to be something unavoidable about Brownsville, as we learn in the opening words: "Every time I go back to Brownsville it is as if I had never been away . . . I am back where I began" (W 5–6). The landscape of Brownsville functions for the adult Kazin as a battleground of unresolved impulses: "An instant rage comes over me, mixed with dread and some unexpected tenderness" (W 5). Brownsville evokes an ambivalent response, and Kazin represents his journey there as a journey into his own unconscious. "I feel in Brownsville," he writes, "that I am walking in my sleep. I keep bumping awake at harsh intervals, then fall back into my trance again" (W 7). This trope of the urban landscape as personal unconscious has an analogue in Freud's metaphorical use of Rome as "a psychical entity with a similarly long and copious past."[23] Kazin's Brownsville is likewise represented as a container for the submerged origins of his adult self. Kazin is not so much the autobiographer as confident storyteller, but as analysand, divulging his memories and desires in their unworked-through complexity.[24] The point is that his past has remained, and it calls out to him as if in a dream.

Indeed, like the elusive latent content of a dream, Kazin's Brownsville cannot be known or encountered except in its specific details. It is evoked as an endlessly proliferating series of smells, colors, tiny objects, pieces of garbage, voices, and so on. Time itself is unhinged: sometimes the "I" is the adult writer, sometimes a boy of eight, sometimes an adolescent. We never quite know where we are in this text. The central metaphor is that of walking, which links Kazin to classic American protagonists on the move, from Whitman traveling down the open road to Huck Finn sailing on his raft. But unlike these figures, whose main impulse is to move outward, Kazin is impelled by an equally powerful centripetal force: "Brownsville is that road which every other road in my life has had to cross" (W 8). The old, Jewish neighborhood pulls Kazin back as if by its own force.

The first chapter of *A Walker in the City*, "From the Subway to the Synagogue," proceeds as a study in contrasts. The road to his childhood home is punctuated by two buildings: "On my right hand the 'Stadium' movie house—the sanctuary every Saturday afternoon of my childhood, the great dark place of all my dream life. On my left the little wooden synagogue where I learned my duties as a Jew" (W 39–40). These two buildings stand metonymically for opposite pulls on the young Kazin. The cinema represents a forbidden and exotic realm—"the very lounge looked and smelled like an Oriental temple" (W 40). The movies also introduce into his home the notion of romantic love, a dangerous and alien notion that keeps his cousin unmarried, perpetually longing for some ideal suitor: "there they were in our own dining room, our cousin and her two friends—women, grown-up women—talking openly about the look on Garbo's face when John Gilbert took her in his arms, serenely disposing of each new *khayimyankel,* poor wretch, my mother had picked out for them" (W 57). Hollywood's icons perform a destructive function, rousing an overwhelming feminine desire for romance that the hapless suitors cannot hope to satisfy. In a tragic coda to this passage, in Kazin's second autobiographical work, *Starting Out in the Thirties,* this same cousin is conned into a scheme by an attractive older man who inexplicably asks her to pose as his wife and then abandons her in the Midwest, precipitating her hospitalization for severe depression. Hanging over Kazin's memories, then, is a sense that danger awaits those who allow themselves to be lured away from Brownsville.

But the young Kazin manages somehow to avoid the dangers of fantasy. For all of its allure, the cinema remains a place he visits only temporarily. At some point during his Saturday afternoons at the movies, his conscience finally overtakes him with "the sudden alarm of a boy, who reminding himself at six o'clock that it was really time to get home" (W 40). As for the world of the synagogue, for all of its aesthetic failings, it continues to have a hold on the young Kazin:

> It was dark enough, but without any illusion or indulgence for a boy. . . .
> Whenever I crossed the splintered and creaking porch into that stale air
> of snuff, of old men and old books, and saw the dusty gilt brocade on the
> prayer shawls, I felt I was being pulled into some mysterious and ancient
> clan that claimed me as its own simply because I was born a block away.
> (W 42)

Linked to the community of Kazin's mother's hometown of Dugschitz, the synagogue is associated with the depths of history. If the cinema stands for the *exotic,* the synagogue stands for the *ancient:* "Old as the synagogue was, old as it looked and smelled in its every worn and wooden corner, it seemed to me even older through its ties to that ancestral world I had never seen" (W 42). Unlike the figures on the movie screen, this ancestral world hovers beyond representation, a locus of authority that commands as if from a primordial realm. Throughout Kazin's text, indeed, distinct worlds are signified by different senses: *seeing* connects Kazin to the American present, while *hearing* relates to the Jewish past.[25] In one typical scene, the young Kazin stands enthralled before an advertisement ("the Gold Stripe silk stocking ad teasing my eye from step to step"), only to have the spell broken by "the cries of old Jewish women selling salted pretzels" (W 98). These cries—and there are many such cries in Kazin's Brownsville—recall the errant boy to his filial responsibility as a Jewish son.

A key scene for understanding Kazin's relationship to Judaism occurs when he describes the morning of his Bar Mitzvah. After the service he "wearily unwound the stiff black thongs of the phylacteries from my left arm . . . . [and] removed from my forehead, for that is over the brain, the little black box in which is inscribed the *Hear O Israel, the Lord Our God the Lord is One*" (W 99). This is the same *Shema* prayer the adult Kazin hears over the radio in London, spoken by the liberated former prisoners of Belsen. In that scene, the prayer is associated with "healing quietness," but here it is associated with empty ritual and arbitrary authority. His Bar Mitzvah has left the young Kazin unmoved, confronting him with another demand for submission. But when he returns home, he walks onto his fire escape, and here he reads, for the first time, the English translations of the prayers, something he had previously imagined to be "not entirely proper" (W 100). What he discovers through this transgressive crossing from Hebrew to English sends him into rapture. "In an agony of surprise, as if I could distinctly hear great seas breaking around me, [I] read aloud to myself" (W 100). Now it is a sublime natural force, not merely the claims of conscience, that Kazin hears. From this day onward, Kazin writes, he devoted himself to decoding the wisdom of Judaism inscribed in the prayer book; it is this engagement with Judaism through solitary reading that Kazin calls "my private orthodoxy" (W 100). Here Kazin proposes a symbol for Jewish piety in the image of his young self sitting alone outdoors, on his fire escape, discovering hidden depths within his prayer book.

Interestingly, when Kazin excerpts the passages he supposedly read on the fire escape, he presents a rearranged version of the traditional liturgy. The first paragraph that he quotes comes from Psalm 95, which is the first prayer in the Kabbalat Shabbat service (the prayer for the welcoming of the Sabbath):

> Harden not your hearts, as in the day of strife and temptation in the wilderness, when your fathers provoked me, and proved me, though they saw my wondrous work. Forty years was I grieved with this generation, and said, it is a people of erring heart, for they have not considered my ways. Then I swore in my wrath that they should not come to the place of my rest. (W 100–101)

Citing the words of God, the psalmist recalls God's wrath and dismay over the Israelites' waywardness in the wilderness. The point is to renew faith amidst an awareness of the sinfulness of previous generations. In the traditional Sabbath service, this Psalm is followed by Psalm 96, but the second paragraph Kazin quotes, *as if* it directly followed Psalm 95, is the paragraph that follows the recitation of the *Shema:*

> True and certain, established, sure, just, faithful, beloved, esteemed, desirable and pleasant, awful, mighty, regular, acceptable, good and beautiful, is this word unto us for evermore. (W 101)

According to the traditional order of the prayers, the "word" that is "true and certain" is precisely what has just been affirmed in the three paragraphs of the *Shema* prayer, namely the affirmations of God's sovereignty and justice, from Deuteronomy 6 and 11 and from Numbers 15. These paragraphs explain what will happen if Israel follows God's commands (e.g., "if you will diligently obey My commandments . . . I will give you rain for your land at the proper time" etc.). But whereas the emphasis of the original *Shema* falls on continuity and the importance of maintaining piety into the future generations (as in the dictum "You shall teach [these words] thoroughly to your children"), Kazin quotes Psalm 95, which characterizes the relationship between Jew and God as ongoing conflict: the generation of the desert "provokes" and "proves" God.[26]

By rearranging the liturgy in this way, Kazin has created a new version of the *Shema* that testifies above all to a broken covenant.[27] What is "true and certain" is that the fathers "hardened their hearts," and that they have been punished and kept from the Promised Land (i.e., "My place of rest"). Kazin's *Shema* is based on the very real possibility that a yawning gap might open up between God and His people. His people may be abandoned to a gruesome fate, either because of something they themselves have done or because of some obscure fact about His role in the universe. This is, we might say, a version of Judaism retrospectively crafted in response to the trauma of the Holocaust.[28] It offers, moreover, a way of interpreting the *Shema* uttered by the survivors of Bergen-Belsen, who also seem to testify to the ongoing relevance of Judaism in spite of God's apparent absence during the Holocaust. By rearranging the traditional liturgy in *A Walker in the City,* then, Kazin imagines a Judaism predicated on conflict and metaphysical strife more than any set of positive teachings. This idea that Judaism countenances disharmony between humans and God provides a way for Kazin to imagine himself back into a broader tradition. "I had never realized that this, this deepness, lay under the gloomy obscurities of Shabbes in our little wooden synagogue on Chester Street. . . . *When your fathers provoked me!* How many fathers I had!" (W 101). Kazin offers a similarly agonistic view of Judaism a few years later in his review of Elie Wiesel's *Night,* which Kazin reads as an "accusation of God": "It is exactly because of the child's demand for justice, because of his demand on God, because of his insistence that *the consummation has not been reached* and that history remains imperfect, that the book is so effective" (italics added).[29] Jewish faith is epitomized by the recognition of history as an ongoing site of conflict, among human beings and between the individual Jew and God. The impulse to question God, to accuse Him, even to doubt His very existence, become for Kazin characteristic expressions of Judaism itself, and it is this version of Judaism that Kazin embraces as his tradition.

In this heterodox mood, it is not surprising that Kazin offers the figure of Jesus as an emblematic Jew. In a scene near the end of the text, the young Kazin picks up a "little blue volume," a New Testament, which he covertly reads in the library. Once again, a transgressive act of reading yields a sublime meaning: "Each [word] seemed to burn separately in the sun as I nervously flipped the pages. . . . The initial shock of that language left no room in my head for anything else" (W 159). The passage Kazin quotes from is the famous section in Paul's First Epistle to the Corinthians that equates salvation with unmediated vision (13:9–12): "When that which is perfect is come, then that which is in part shall be done away. . . . For now we see through a glass darkly; but then face to face." Though uttered by Paul, Kazin links these words with the figure of Jesus, whom he renames "Yeshua" in a bid to reclaim him as a Jew: "I had been waiting for him all my life—our own Yeshua, misunderstood by his own, like me, but the very embodiment of everything I had waited so long to hear from a Jew" (W 161–162). By laying claim to Jesus as a renegade Jew, Kazin presents once again his view that a synthesis might be achieved between piety and iconoclasm.

Read in relation to his literary criticism, we might say that Kazin invents a version of Jewishness here that is aligned with the rebellious impulse he celebrates in *On Native Grounds.* He associates Judaism above all with a particular relation to experience. "The voice that spoke in the prayer book," he writes, "confirmed everything I had felt in my bones about being a Jew: fierce awareness of life to the depths, every day and in every hour: the commitment: the hunger" (W 103). Nevertheless for all of Kazin's emphasis on Jewish "hunger" and iconoclasm, he also describes Jewish tradition as a principle of historical continuity and communal togetherness. Alongside memoirs of walking through New York on his own, Kazin fondly recalls Friday dinners in Brownsville as a stay against loneliness and a foretaste of utopia: "Socialism would be one long Friday evening around the samovar and the cut-glass bowl laden with fruit and nuts, all of us singing *Tsuzamen, alle tsuzmen!*" (W 61). At one point Kazin recalls berating his father for not having accepted a homestead he was offered in Omaha, Nebraska. But his father's response trumps the naïve Kazin's fantasy America: "It would have been too lonely. . . . Alfred, what do you want from us Jews" (W 60). This phrase echoes elsewhere in the text, becoming the voice of Jewish tradition itself. It functions in the text as a gesture of self-mockery, showing that unlike the young Kazin, the mature autobiographer has come to value Jewish endurance and solidarity. He is, as we have seen, drawn by a centripetal force: his mode of walking in the city is determined and shaped as if by some imaginary compass pointing back to Brownsville and the Jewish past.

This point contrasts directly with Kazin's description of the American writers in *On Native Grounds,* who all embody different versions of the great American journey into an uncharted world. Jewishness, by contrast, is anchored in the past, and the forms taken by this culture are finally circumscribed in ways unimaginable to the American Adam. Solidarity—linked for Kazin to the "healing quietness" of Sabbath in Brownsville—is, after all, one thing that the Hemingways and the Menckens, for all their questing, never seemed to countenance. And if Blake's walker in London is an isolated prophet, the Jewish boy walking in Brownsville is finally linked to a community: "So it was: we had always to be together: believers and non-believers, we were a people; I was of that people. Unthinkable to go one's own way, to doubt or to escape the fact that I was a Jew" (W 60). Finally, Kazin represents Judaism in *A Walker in the City* as a tradition with two distinct aspects. On the one hand, it represents a tradition of iconoclastic spiritual seekers, hungrily immersing themselves in experience and raising their fists to God. On the other, it stands for historical memory, communal solidarity, and "healing quietness." This latter point must be read as a revision of Kazin's celebration in *On Native Grounds* of the American tradition of radical experimentalism. After the Holocaust and the manifold dislocations of postwar life, the project of rewriting Emerson no longer suffices, and Judaism offers him a symbol and a principle of historical continuity. The lesson of *A Walker in the City,* then, is that all roads lead to Brownsville just as, according to Freud, all dreams lead to the unconscious. For all the changes wrought by recent history, Kazin's Jewish past remains "live" material; Kazin will always be "back where [he] began." At the bleakest moment in modern Jewish history and in defiance of Hitler, Kazin has remained Jewish to the core, or at least *at* the core.

Beyond Modernism

Kazin's *A Walker in the City* enters into dialogue with another text about Jewish American boyhood, Henry Roth's modernist masterpiece *Call It Sleep* (1934). In *On Native Grounds*, Roth's novel goes unmentioned, though it seems that Kazin had read it by 1937, when he mentions it in passing in a review. But if Kazin had not seen fit to notice Roth's novel in 1942, he later became one of its champions. Invited in 1956 by *The American Scholar* to contribute titles for a feature called "The Most Neglected Books of the Past 25 Years," he enthusiastically praised *Call It Sleep*, as "something won, very far within, against the conventional cruelties of modern city life."[30] In *A Walker in the City* there are so many parallels with *Call It Sleep* that it seems likely that Kazin had the novel in the back of his mind when he began writing his own work. Both works describe the spiritual quest of a Jewish boy in Brownsville, and both texts portray an "illicit" discovery of a biblical text in English translation: David Shearl's fascination with Isaiah 6 parallels the young Kazin's ecstatic reading of Psalm 95. In each case, the Jewish boy salvages a fragment from the textual traditions of Judaism, and evinces a "private orthodoxy." Moreover, numerous specific scenes are repeated or evoked: Kazin includes a memory of the cellar where his family has a coal bin, reiterating the central motif of the first book of *Call It Sleep*: "I was afraid of the cellar," Kazin writes, "[It] was made up in even parts of silence and blackness" (W 111–112). Kazin's cellar, like Roth's, is invested with sexual significance, as it is there that "some wilder, rancid smell . . . told me someone was hiding away with a girl" (W 112). Other parallels are a scene in which Kazin's father refers to him as his "Kaddish" (W 37), a memory of playing follow the leader (W 87), scenes of walking alone out of Brownsville past chicken coops, and a scene in which an unsuspecting woman in the neighborhood bathes naked at her kitchen sink while Kazin watches from outside (138–139). These parallels suggest that Kazin turned to *Call It Sleep*—consciously or unconsciously—as a template for imagining his own life.

Among the differences between these works, however, the most conspicuous is that the terrifying sexuality of *Call It Sleep* has been somehow sanitized. The dark fear that pervades Roth's text overall has given way, in Kazin's text, to expressions of joy and contentment. Compare the following scenes where the sons watch their mothers cleaning the linoleum floors of their Brownsville apartments. In *Call It Sleep* we read the following:

> Then she got down on all fours and began to mop the floor. With knees drawn up, David watched her wipe the linoleum beneath his chair. The shadow between her breasts, how deep! How far it—No! No! Luter! When

he looked! That night! Mustn't! Mustn't! Look away! Quick! Look at—
look at the linoleum there, how it glistened under a thin film of water.[31]

Roth's young protagonist, David Shearl, recoils in panic when he realizes
he is gazing upon his mother in the same way as Luter, whose sexual
advances upon his mother caused disgust and terror in the boy. His turn
toward the linoleum suggests how sublimated desire expresses itself in
"aesthetic" contemplation. In contrast to this scene of emergent Oedipal
desire, we find the following in Kazin's text:

> I waited for the streets to go dark on Friday evening as other children
> waited for the Christmas lights. . . . When I returned home after three,
> the warm odor of a coffee cake baking in the oven and the sight of my
> mother on her hands and knees scrubbing the linoleum on the dining
> room floor filled me with such tenderness that I could feel my senses
> reaching out to embrace every single object in our household. (W 52)

The identical scene of the mother on hands and knees, scrubbing a linoleum floor, comes through in Kazin as a purely nostalgic memory.[32] Once
again the boy looks upon the objects of his household, but this time there is
no onrush of desire and self-disgust, no panic. Throughout *A Walker in the
City* sexuality is generally figured as a rite of passage ("sooner or later you
would have to prove yourself doing things to women" [W 29]), rather than
as unbridgeable crisis. The deeply troubled childhood sexuality in *Call It
Sleep* has been largely resolved, and, as a result, the representation of the
Jewish family in general is much less ambivalent: in Kazin's work there is no
castrating Jewish father, nor a sensually seductive Jewish mother.

One effect of this revision is that unlike Roth's Brownsville, Kazin's
Brownsville can function as a "healing" space, an alternative to the postwar
world he inhabited. That is, the "uses" to which Kazin puts his Brownsville
memories in the late 1940s were entirely different from Roth's in the early
1930s. Roth wrote his novel as his entry ticket into the avant-garde cultural
circles he had glimpsed through his patroness-lover Eda Lou Walton.[33] The
text ultimately proves that the early experiences of an immigrant Jew provide sufficient material to write a Joycean novel about urban life. For Kazin,
the point was not so much to move into some brave new world of his own
imagining but to discover a bridge back to the past. In the wake of the Holocaust, Kazin's Jewish memories have suddenly become poignantly relevant
as a token for a broader Jewish world that had been destroyed. For all of his
own experimentalism, Kazin implicitly distances himself from the kind of
modernism epitomized by *Call It Sleep*. When his Jewish past rises into his
memory, it provides a refuge from the violence and dislocations of history.

After writing *A Walker in the City,* Kazin returned repeatedly to the question of the Jewish writer's unique contribution to American literature. Having sifted through various possible meanings of his own Jewishness, he was in a special position to comment on the Jewish American writers who rose to prominence later in the decade. Kazin became a key advocate for writers such as Bellow, Malamud, Mailer, Philip Roth, and I. B. Singer—whom he linked together in his essay "The Earthly City of the Jews." A central idea in this essay that emerges in his reading of Singer is that Jewish tradition equips the modern Jewish writer above all with the power of *acceptance:* human nature, the world's wickedness, God's mysteriousness, all of this can be accepted and confronted head-on given the ultimate premise, which has survived even the secularizing force of modernity, that all is somehow God's will.[34] In another important essay, "The Jew as Modern Writer" (1966), Kazin adds that the complexities and anxieties of postwar society had made the period particularly ripe for the intervention of Jewish writers. "Never was interpretation, explanation, commentary, a vital new midrash, so much needed as in the period starting with the war.... In a time when the old bourgeois certainties have crumbled, the Jew is practiced in what James called 'the imagination of disaster'."[35] Jews have witnessed—and lived through—crises that had seemed insurmountable; and their accrued wisdom and tragic sense are now more necessary than ever.

Kazin's later autobiographical work, *New York Jew* (1978), asks whether the Jew in modern America can continue to be a bearer of wisdom. Here Judaism is increasingly represented as a lost tradition, as in the scene at Kazin's father's funeral, when he is called upon to read the Kaddish: "I mangle the ancient, awesome text, ashamed before the few of us left . . . that I read the words so badly" (NYJ 439). Kazin stands as the recipient of an "awesome" tradition that has almost completely dissolved. The final sequence of *New York Jew* moves toward an apocalyptic vision. Kazin describes in rapid succession the appearance of a book by a "Northwestern University professor" denying the Holocaust, the death of Kazin's father in the Coney Island Hospital, and a series of fires in Brownsville that have left the neighborhood in shambles. These events bring Kazin to the brink of despair. Having returned to Brownsville with the intention of writing about "a native's return," he loses heart when he recognizes signs of its decline: rusted blood covers a window, mounds of garbage stand in the streets, and "charred, blackened, firestreaked" apartment houses crowd out any remnant of *his* Brownsville. His "native grounds" have been disfigured beyond recognition. In *A Walker in the City,* it had been possible to return to Brownsville as a way of responding to the Holocaust; now Brownsville seems to have self-destructed.

But in the closing passage of *New York Jew,* Kazin creates a scene that evokes the moment from *A Walker in the City* where he discovers God on his fire escape. This time we encounter the adult Kazin, by now a distinguished professor and respected authority on American literature, standing on a balcony, "high over Lincoln Center," and again he is seized with a yearning for God. Turning his back on the frivolous conversations ("the people arguing about movie reviews"), Kazin notices that a fire has broken out on the Weehawken piers in New Jersey, and he alerts his fellow party-goers to the disaster:

> As they finally turn around to see it, a new party excitement takes over in the face of that blazing insistency over Jersey. The sky is all red, crazy-red. People reach out, feel each other hungrily. The sky over our heads has been loosened at last. I want to love again. I want my God back. I will never give up until it is too late to expect you. (NYJ 451)

This concluding exclamation—"I want my God back"—may be read in two separate ways: as the bootless cry of the alienated American Jew, filled with yearning but dispossessed of any guiding tradition; or as itself an avowal of faith. For Kazin, these positions turn out strangely to be complementary. The hallmark of Jewish faith, as he describes it, is not after all to possess any coherent set of teachings or any stable "knowledge" of God; the covenant has long been broken, and Jews belong to the "earthly city." They are, however, driven again and again to make sense of the God who "appears as fire" (NYJ 448). In this apocalyptic scene, with fires blazing over Jersey, Kazin becomes a prophetic figure. He insists on bearing witness to destruction, and he affirms that, as a Jew, he still remembers God, though He remains inscrutable (and may not even exist).[36]

Kazin died, as I have said, having begun work on a new book about the Jews. It is tempting to imagine this work as offering some definitive statement about his "Romantic Judaism." We might also imagine this book as offering a response in particular to the question left hanging at the end of his last published book, *God and the American Writer* (1997). There, after exploring the religious convictions of a line of classic (and exclusively non-Jewish) writers from Hawthorne to Dickinson to Faulkner, Kazin concludes that the impulse of so many American writers to claim primacy for the self had precluded any genuine relation with God. And he finds in this a serious deficiency: "There is no radiance in our modern writers, just stalwart independence, defiance of the established, and a good deal of mockery."[37] He asks whether our sensitivity to "radiance" has atrophied or whether it might somehow be retrieved. Given his lifelong obsession with the question of God and his interest in Jewish writers from Bernard Malamud to Elie Wiesel to I. B. Singer, it stands to reason that he would have turned to Jewish writers and thinkers in his final book to reconstruct a language for articulating a more vibrant religiosity—not some traditional version of Judaism, to be sure, but some way of orienting the self toward that placeholder for the divine that Kazin still called God. Of course, the unwritten book itself stands as a poignant symbol for us, a reminder that, for Kazin, the last word on the Jews had not been said or at least that Judaism still somehow called him forth and begged for his response.

Coda: Jewish Romanticisms

Among postwar Jewish American writers, Kazin was far from alone in constructing a "Romantic Judaism"—a Judaism based above all on concepts such as inwardness, spiritual agon, emotional intensity, and striving. Various critics, novelists, and poets similarly read Judaism into Romanticism and vice versa. Foregrounding a more meditative side of Romanticism, Lionel Trilling proposes in "Wordsworth and the Rabbis" (1950) that the great English romantic poet William Wordsworth may be elucidated through comparison with the "Judaic ethos," as embodied in the Mishnaic work *Pirke Avot*. "In Jewish tradition," Trilling writes, "the great Hillel has a peculiarly Wordsworthian personality, being the type of gentleness and peace, and having about him a kind of joy which has always been found wonderfully attractive."[38] In *Shelley's Mythmaking* (1959), Harold Bloom reads Romanticism alongside Martin Buber's dialogical philosophy in *I and Thou*, anticipating his later efforts to find in the Kabbalah a language for modern literary criticism. And in *Herzog* (1964), Saul Bellow's hero Moses Herzog is an intellectual historian and Jewish schlemiel who specializes in Romanticism and feels called upon to address and rectify the spiritual malaise of modernity. "Romanticism guarded the 'inspired condition,'" Moses writes in one of his countless letters, "preserved the poetic, philosophical, and religious teachings, the teachings of transcendence and the most generous ideas of mankind."[39] In his own spiritual yearnings and devotion to "Jewish suffering," Moses embodies an effort to preserve the same sort of teachings under the sign of modern Jewish identity. In the most general terms, these writers all conceive of Romanticism with Judaism both as embattled traditions of spiritual depth and moral seriousness—alternatives to the anarchic extremism and denials of historical continuity that characterize the modernist outlook.

Yet another Jewish romantic is Allen Ginsberg, like Kazin a self-styled heir to the romantic-prophetic poetics of Blake and Whitman. It may be surprising to link Ginsberg with Kazin, since generally speaking no love was lost between the New York intellectuals and the Beat underground. Nevertheless, the combination of Judaism and Romanticism in Ginsberg's work—particularly *Kaddish,* about his mother's madness, hospitalization, and death—reflects precisely the same kind of impulse we have seen in Kazin's critical and autobiographical writings. Like *A Walker in the City* (as well as Yezierska's *Bread Givers*), *Kaddish* dramatizes an act of returning to an "old neighborhood" linked with the Jewish past: "I walk toward the Lower East Side—where you walked 50 years ago, little girl—from Russia, eating the first poisonous tomatoes of America."[40] Ginsberg follows his mother's trajectory from being a passionate Communist—member of the Young Person's Socialist League, reader of the *Daily Worker,* singer of the "Song of the National Front" on her mandolin—to being a schizophrenic patient in a New Jersey State mental hospital, beset with paranoid visions of Hitler and spies at every door. Ultimately, Ginsberg's impulse to mourn his mother leads to his recovery of her radical impulse under Jewish auspices: "I've seen your grave! O Strange Naomi! My own cracked grave! Shema Y'Israel—I am Svul Avrum . . . Svul Avrum—Israel Abraham— myself—to sing in the wilderness toward God."[41] When Ginsberg identifies with his mother, he reclaims a Jewish name, as if to say that identification with the Jewish prophetic tradition enables him to sustain his mother's radicalism.

Read in relation to Ginsberg's Beat Generation anthem *Howl, Kaddish* suggests in its very title the transformation of a generic, almost subhuman sound (a "howl") into the language of Jewish liturgy (a "kaddish").[42] This transformation is mirrored by the change in self-identification: in *Howl,* Ginsberg locates himself horizontally as part of a "generation destroyed by madness"; in *Kaddish* he roots his identity vertically, back into the past, in relation to his mother and *her* madness. And the effect of this development is to shift the emphasis away from the violent and abstract apocalypticism of *Howl.* Now "madness" is no longer an abstract force threatening to overcome everything (". . . the best minds of my generation destroyed by madness"): it is instead part of an embodied history; it can be described and, if not necessarily understood, harnessed and rechanneled as creative energy.

This movement from an apocalyptic view of history to a view of historical and cultural continuity provides, I think, a way to elucidate the Jewish–Romantic connection we are exploring here. As different as all of these writers are, Kazin, Trilling, Bloom, Bellow, and Ginsberg all express wariness of a tendency toward apocalyptic thinking in postwar American culture, what Herzog refers to as the "wasteland outlook." Indeed, they all point to T. S. Eliot, author of the work that serves as an emblem for this outlook, as the embodiment of a particularly pernicious strain in the culture, an obsession with crisis and a fear of finality. If Eliot's *The Waste Land* emphasizes cultural breakdown and crisis, they will call attention to continuities. Romanticism, with its secularized language of transcendence, offers a way for them to reaffirm the relevance of Jewish tradition, even for contemporary Jews for whom conventional forms of belief and practice have become untenable. And with this reaffirmation, they gain a purchase on some kind of permanence, a stay against apocalypse.

8

THE JEWISH WRITER
FLIES AT TWILIGHT

Irving Howe and the Recovery of Yiddishkayt

Mayn beygzas laykhter guf
Maydt oys dem toyt fun faln,
Barirndik koys, koys dem sharf fun di kinzshaln.

Gracefully
I sidestep death
Barely touching the blades.
　　　　　—Celia Dropkin, "Di tsirkus dame"
　　　　　(The Circus Lady; translation by Faith Jones)

In 1952, the Yiddish linguist Nahum Stutshkov met with literary critic Shmuel Niger in New York City to discuss the idea of compiling a multi-volume dictionary that would encompass the totality of the Yiddish language. It was the first time a project on such a scale had been proposed, a Yiddish answer to the *Oxford English Dictionary,* showing the full depth and range of the language. Stutshkov and Niger hoped to provide a definitive reference work covering what they later called "the language of all classes of the Jewish people, from the language of the scholar to the language of the village Jew; from the cultured language of the intellectual to the slang of the uneducated."[1] Conceived in the wake of the Holocaust, the project inevitably took on the broader, symbolic function of paying homage to the destroyed world of East European Jewry and to a language that had lost over half its speakers in less than a decade. Nine years after the project was conceived, there arrived in print the first of ten proposed volumes of the *Groyser verterbukh fun der yidisher shprakh* (Great Dictionary of the Yiddish Language). In their enthusiastic introduction, editors in chief Yudel Mark and Chaim Gold wrote, "Our joy is enormous, because it has been our particular destiny to begin the honorable and historic task of erecting a roof over the building of our language, and thereby to ensure that a large portion of Yiddish will never fall into eternal oblivion."[2] Due to various editorial problems and lack of funding, the project was abandoned twenty years later, after redactors had completed only the four volumes dedicated to the first letter of the alphabet, *alef.*

In the same year (1952) and in the same city that the ill-fated *Groyser verterbukh* was conceived, Yiddish poet Eliezer Greenberg invited American-born literary critic Irving Howe to collaborate on a project of translating Yiddish short stories into English. Their meeting led to the publication of a lengthy anthology, *A Treasury of Yiddish Stories* (1954), which included stories from twenty-three different authors, drawings by the distinguished artist Ben Shahn, a glossary, and a ninety-three-page essay by Howe creating a detailed portrait of East European Jewry. Howe and Greenberg anticipated a readership that knew no Yiddish besides a few expressions and that had little familiarity, if any, with Yiddish literature. With its dedication "to the six million," the anthology might be seen as another way of memorializing the Holocaust dead. By presenting a collection of writings that expressed the ethos of East European Jewry, it offered American Jewish readers insight into a world that was no more. By contrast to Stutshkov and Niger's dictionary, Howe and Greenberg's anthology project was enormously successful. Praised in *The New York Times* by leading Yiddishist Uriel Weinreich as "the way Yiddish literature should be presented in English," the *Treasury of Yiddish Stories* has since become a classic in its own right, providing many American readers with their first, and often only, contact with Yiddish literature.[3] Howe and Greenberg followed their first anthology with five additional volumes: *A Treasury of Yiddish Poetry* (1969); *Voices from the Yiddish: Essays, Memoirs, Diaries* (1972); *Selected Stories: I. L. Peretz* (1974); *Yiddish Stories Old and New* (1974); and *Ashes out of Hope: Fiction by Soviet-Yiddish Writers* (1977).

This tale of two publishing projects, both begun in 1952, encapsulates a portrait of the culture of Yiddish in America at mid-century. On the one hand, the unfinished dictionary stands as an all-too-poignant symbol for the disappearance of East European Jewish life and the sharp decline in spoken Yiddish throughout the Jewish world. But if the "roof over the language" was never completed, a broad sampling of modern Yiddish literature in translation—fiction, poetry, and essays by writers from Mendele Mocher Sforim to Chaim Grade—was suddenly widely available in paperback editions. Yiddish literature gained a new lease on life among second- and third-generation American Jews for whom the language had suddenly become a poignant symbol for a distant but more "authentic" way of being Jewish. The American Jewish community, haunted by the Holocaust and dispossessed of the language of its forbears, was transforming into a self-conscious subculture defined through a connection to an "imagined" Jewish community—imagined both in Benedict Anderson's sense of a community defined more by the *idea* of commonality than by direct experience, and in the literary sense of a community whose self-understanding derives from the stories it tells about itself.[4] Howe and Greenberg's anthologies thus participate in the formation of what Jeffrey Shandler calls a "postvernacular" Yiddish, namely a language that has largely moved beyond its function as a medium of daily communication but that remains in circulation as a token and symbol.[5]

These anthologies reflect a similar impulse that led Alfred Kazin to write about his youth as a Jewish boy in Brownsville. Howe turned to the genre of the anthology to accomplish much of the same cultural work that Kazin tried to accomplish through autobiography: both summoned images of prewar Jewish life to establish imaginative connections with the past and to heal, in some way, the traumas of recent history. What did this turn to translation portend for Jewish culture in the America of the future? What sort of cultural past was being bequeathed to Jewish readers and writers and how would it be absorbed, modified, and reused? To approach these questions, let us explore Howe's own journey from being a firebrand socialist in the 1930s and 1940s to being a Yiddish anthologist in the context of Cold War America.

From Trotsky to Sholem Aleichem

The young Irving Howe (neé Horenstein) would have hardly seemed a likely candidate for his later role as Jewish cultural mediator. Coming of age in the East Bronx in the early 1930s, he became involved in socialist organizing in his early adolescence. It was at street-corner meetings that

Howe developed his taste for polemics and his talent for theorizing. He later referred to his adolescence as a period of total immersion in the struggle against capitalism: "Never before, and surely never since, have I lived at so high, so intense a pitch, or been absorbed in ideas so beyond the smallness of self . . . [The movement] gave my life a 'complete meaning,' a 'whole purpose'" (MH 42). Howe spent the years 1936–1940 at City College, but unlike Alfred Kazin, who preceded him by five years, he dove headlong into its partisan political battles, distinguishing himself as one of the vocal members of the anti-Stalinist left. Trotsky was his intellectual model, and he sharpened his rhetorical skills attacking Soviet apologists among the student body.

By the time he turned twenty-one in 1941, Howe was managing editor of *Labor Action,* a Trotskyite paper stridently opposed to America's entry into the war. Howe's view that World War II was "a war between two great imperialist camps to decide which shall dominate the world" was initially shared by radicals of various stripes in America.[6] *Partisan Review,* for example, had come out opposed to the war up to the bombing of Pearl Harbor. But Howe maintained his stridency even then, criticizing that journal's editors for "stumbl[ing] and equivocat[ing]" when they began rethinking their opposition to the war in 1942.[7] As for the significance of Jewishness, Howe dismissed it, in an article on the "Jewish Question," as at best a sentimental fantasy: "There is no such thing as 'the Jew,'" he wrote. "There are rich and poor Jews, Jewish workers and Jewish bosses."[8] Class trumped any other mode of affiliation; working-class consciousness must not be diluted by imaginary connections elsewhere.

During the war years, however, Howe gradually lost some of his ideological rigidity. He spent the latter part of the war as a soldier in Alaska, where a mixture of enforced isolation and steady reading brought about a shift in his thinking. As his interest in literature deepened, he developed what he described as "that taste for complication which is necessarily a threat to the political mind" (MH 95). Once established, this tension between measured reflection and ideological warfare would remain a recurrent preoccupation for him. It became, indeed, the central theme of one of his major works of criticism, *Politics and the Novel* (1957), which explores how political ideas are complicated, modulated, and sometimes neutralized when placed in the context of a narrative.

And if his own predilections were leading him toward "complication," the American cultural and political scene he reentered after the war pushed him even farther away from his previous ideological stance. The emergence of a triumphant and economically thriving America dramatically reconfigured the terms of engagement for nearly everyone in Howe's generation. As the Cold War took shape and the global political spectrum became polarized between Soviet communism and Western liberalism, the finely tuned position of the anti-Stalinist left was losing whatever foothold it may have had. Many New York intellectuals who had formerly considered themselves cultural and political dissidents now found themselves affirming the central thrust of American society, sometimes tentatively, sometimes with great enthusiasm.[9] In a symposium published in *Partisan Review* entitled "Our Country and Our Culture," the editors remarked that "for better or for worse, most writers no longer accept alienation as the artist's fate; on the contrary, they want very much to be a part of American life. . . . They now believe that their values, if they are to be realized at all, must be realized in America and in relation to the actuality of American life."[10] Many of the people Howe had gone to school with were accepting positions in universities, publishing houses, and think tanks. Some began drifting to the right. Howe's ongoing, fierce antipathy to capitalism set him apart from other members of the New York intellectual community. He retained enough of his former Marxist orientation that he could still write in 1952 that capitalism as a world system was "exhausted economically and spiritually."[11] But, despite this acute sense of crisis, he was equally convinced that revolutionary socialism needed to be reformulated. This reformulation would constitute the central challenge of Howe's intellectual life over the next four decades.

Another impasse that defined this period and that Howe reflected upon considerably has been described as the "end of the American avant-garde."[12] Modernist and avant-garde cultural styles that had flourished a generation or two earlier and that had spoken for creative freedom and resistance to the bourgeois order had been gradually absorbed into mainstream American institutions, from academia to major art museums to advertising. What had seemingly come to an end, at least according to Howe and many other New York intellectuals, was the period in which artistic experimentation could be regarded as a sufficient expression of cultural critique.[13] Once modernist heroes such as James Joyce and D. H. Lawrence had become required reading in English literature classes, their force as cultural rebels was necessarily curtailed. And once an exhibition of Abstract Expressionist paintings had been underwritten by the CIA (intent on emphasizing the "freedom" of the Free World), one had to think twice about any simple equation linking radical aesthetics with radical politics. Howe later described this dilemma as the "decline of the new," the recognition of which made Howe one of the first theorists of "post-modernism." The kind of unqualified celebration of the avant-garde we saw in Waldo Frank's *Our America* (1919) had come to seem anachronistic, and with it the idea that dissent and aesthetic innovation were necessarily aligned.

This reassessment of modernism was quickened for Howe and others by the debates that followed the nomination of Ezra Pound's *Pisan Cantos* for the Bollingen award in 1949.[14] Pound's antisemitic tirades over Italian radio during the war meant that the antisemitism evinced by his poetry could no longer be dismissed as benign eccentricity, and Howe, Clement Greenberg, and others insisted that Pound's nomination be reconsidered. In the shadow of the Holocaust, the moral and the aesthetic dimensions of a work of art could simply no longer be kept apart. Pound received his award, but the debate made clear that for Howe, at least, many of the central articles of modernist faith—that idiosyncrasy was aligned with freedom, that art belonged to an autonomous sphere immune from moral judgments—had come to seem untenable. It would not be quite right to say that Howe had come to reject modernism *tout court.* The point is that with the need to rethink the idea of an avant-garde and with the prospects of socialism increasingly uncertain, Howe's overriding feeling after the war was that a vacuum had been opened up in the intellectual culture of the American left and in his own life.

Howe expressed his loss of direction during the postwar years in a revealing letter to Lionel Trilling, who had suggested to Howe that he become a graduate student at Columbia University and earn his living by teaching:

> I feel isolated in the sense that the entire intellectual milieu of the present day is alien to me. At the risk of misunderstanding, I would say that I would have flourished better in the thirties. . . . I don't feel at home in any place: not among my radical friends who view me with suspicion, nor among literary people who hold the same view for diametrically opposite reasons, nor among the *Time* people who think of me as an "intellectual," nor even among the PR [*Partisan Review*] people . . . This bears on the teaching job problem. On the one hand, it attracts me because: I think I would love to teach, the security and time it might eventually mean are tempting, and perhaps (though I'm realistic enough to be skeptical about it) some sense of intellectual community might result from it. On the other hand: I fear, perhaps unreasonably, that it would continue a process of defanging that has already begun.[15]

Howe's hesitations did not prove powerful enough to keep him out of academia (he later found teaching jobs at Brandeis, Stanford, and the City University of New York), but the dangers of complicity remained a pressing concern for years to come. What is most illuminating about his letter, perhaps, is that Howe is expressing his fear of "defanging" to *Lionel Trilling*. Having been active in the very political culture that Howe recalled with nostalgia and having nearly lost his teaching position in 1936 for being "a Marxist, a Freudian, and a Jew," Trilling managed to become the first tenured Jewish professor in Columbia's English department.[16] At the time he received Howe's letter, he cut a figure of increasing gentility, his expressions of cultural critique being increasingly ambivalent, devoted to dialectical complexity more than political exigency. His critique of the "liberal imagination" suggested at times that a slippery slope connected liberalism itself with communism, leaving Trilling himself (so it seemed to Howe) to the right of center. Trilling thus represented one road that American Jewish intellectuals were taking, and Howe had grave misgivings about all it portended. For if Trilling had retreated into complexity, Howe continued to see himself as devoted to what he called a world more attractive. But now that the "complete purpose" he felt in "the movement" had fallen away, and nothing had come to take its place (besides the fear of defanging), what other fate could he imagine for a Jewish intellectual in America besides Trilling's quietism?

Alan Wald, Gerald Sorin, and others have explored Howe's formulation of a "democratic socialism" during the postwar years, a rigorously anti-Stalinist position that distinguished itself from liberalism through its ongoing insistence on class as the key to social analysis.[17] Part of this rethinking involved a turn inward, which also led him, interestingly, to reflect on the predicament of the Jew in postwar America. Having dismissed Jewishness as false consciousness, he began seeing it as an identity with its own history and inner dynamic. As with other Jewish writers (or *kultur tuers*) we have considered thus far, Howe's "return" to Jewish culture was informed by his reading of American literature. The terms in which he came to define modern Jewish identity did not come from the Romanticism of Emerson and Whitman, however, but rather from the idea of American regionalism as exemplified by the works of Sherwood Anderson and William Faulkner. In individual book-length studies of these writers—*William Faulkner: A Critical Study* (1952) and *Sherwood Anderson* (1951)—Howe reiterated his charge that American society had eroded the basis for genuine community. "Fraternity" had been lost in a country devoted to "a highly competitive ethic [and] a systematic suspicion of the past."[18] And in different ways, these writers' fictional portraits had poignantly borne witness to this loss. They described in tones at once angry, shocked, and elegiac the passing away of a previous form of life—an agrarian Middle West in the case of Anderson, and the gallant Old South in the case of Faulkner—and the development of industrial society. They cast an unflinching eye at the new "grotesque" forms that individual lives assumed in the wake of this upheaval. Nor did Howe see these writers as wistful romantics. In both cases, he sought to distill what he called the "implicit politics" contained in their work, the challenge they put forth to their readers to recall the significance of organic community amid a modern industrial society wholly given over to individualism.

Howe's reading of Faulkner is indebted in many ways to the poet-critic Allen Tate, a surprising point of reference for Howe given Tate's often brazenly reactionary politics (Tate was a member of the Southern Agrarians, one of twelve writers who contributed to the notorious cri de coeur of the fading Southern establishment, *I'll Take My Stand* [1937]). In a passage Howe quotes approvingly in his book on Faulkner (and that will later appear, slightly altered, in his reading of Yiddish fiction), Tate notes that "the distinctive Southern consciousness is quite temporary. It has made possible the curious burst of intelligence that we get at the crossing of the ways, not unlike, on an infinitesimal scale, the outburst of poetic genius at the end of the sixteenth century when commercial England had already begun to crush feudal England."[19] What Howe absorbs from Tate is what might be termed a master trope for literary production: the literary imagination is sparked by a "crossing of the ways," the erosion of one way of life and the emergence of some new, wholly other way of living. It gains urgency from the flux of history, and though it reports upon a world that has been lost, its testimony can provide an indispensable compass for others. Through Tate and Faulkner, Howe also glimpsed a theme he would later make much of: the nobility of failure and the value of attending to "twilight" cultures.

Howe's career as a Yiddishist officially began in 1952, when he reviewed a new translation of *Wandering Star,* a novel by Sholem Aleichem. Howe's review of Sholem Aleichem suggests that the model of "regional literature" he developed from reading Anderson and Faulkner might be applied to Yiddish writers as well. In this review, Howe ventures a broad definition of Yiddish literature, which he conceives of as a more-or-less unified tradition. He constructs Yiddish literature by opposing it to the "intense, recalcitrant, and extreme" literature that mid-century American readers have come to value, by opposing it, in short, to the ethos of modernism.[20] Yiddish writers, Howe proposes, have nothing to do with the extremities of vision one finds in D. H. Lawrence, nor with the images of catastrophe one finds in Eliot's *The Waste Land* (once again the ubiquitous *bête noir* of mid-century Jewish American intellectuals). Yiddish literature does not "confront the harsh finalities of experience, or strip each act to its bare motive, or flood us with anguish over the irrevocability of death" (270). Instead, in the work of Mendele, I. L. Peretz, and Sholem Aleichem, every individual act is represented as a meaningful gesture in an integrated culture. The Yiddish writers speak, Howe proposes, from a firm sense of identification with a community. They express fraternity with the poor, not out of "populist sentimentality" as in John Steinbeck, whom Howe distrusted, but because the conditions of East European life had generated the possibility—and the need—for genuine solidarity. "Who, in the ghetto world," Howe asks, "was not finally a *luftmensch*, a Menachem Mendel trading nothing for nothing and living off the profits?" (271). In Howe's formulation, the "ghetto Jews" are somehow insulated from the capitalist game of getting and spending.

Howe's review caught the eye of Yiddish poet Eliezer Greenberg, who was just at that moment looking for an ally in the English-speaking world in his private campaign for Yiddish. A native of the Besserabian shtetl of Lipkan, Greenberg arrived in America in 1913 and associated largely with the neo-Romantic school *Di yunge*. He played an important role in the formation of a Yiddish literary culture in America, writing monographs about the key Yiddish poets Moyshe-Leyb Halpern, H. Leivick, and Jacob Glatstein. He tended to be more aware of the American literary scene than other poets of his generation. "Among other Yiddish poets, he was sometimes called '*der Amerikaner*,'" Howe later recalled, "one who kept in touch with unseemly English-language things."[21] In the years following the war, Greenberg became concerned with the fate of Yiddish literature, but whereas others turned inward in despair, he considered ways to forge connections with the broader community of American Jews. Greenberg sent Howe a note inviting him to join forces on a project of translating Yiddish literature. As Howe describes their collaboration process as it developed, Greenberg would select stories out of "a briefcase of crumbling old books" and read them aloud to Howe (MH 260). Together they would decide which texts might work in translation and who might perform the translation work. Within two years, *A Treasury of Yiddish Stories* was published.

Constructing Yiddishkayt

One of Howe and Greenberg's primary aims as anthologists is to demonstrate the *seriousness* of Yiddish literature. The fact that Viking Press brought out the collection went some distance toward making this point. Viking Press was known at this time as the publisher of highbrow works, including a series of "Portable" editions of classic writers such as William Blake and Joseph Conrad, not to mention several books by Lionel Trilling. To bring out a selection of Yiddish stories in this context was to assert that these works had something to offer the serious, "intellectual" reader, an agenda clearly revealed in Howe's correspondence with his translators. Writing to the poet and translator Aaron Kramer during the preparation of *A Treasury of Yiddish Poetry* two decades later, Howe reveals the ongoing force of his crusading spirit: "I utterly hate, with a violence I don't quite grasp myself, the Rosten tone, which transforms everything in Yiddish into a *yok*."[22] If Leo Rosten's book, *The Joys of Yiddish* (1967), had emphasized the light side of Yiddish, Howe's anthologies will show the full scope of its expressive powers. Later in this letter to Kramer he adds: "My inclination is to try for purity of diction—given the cultural notions in the air about Yiddish. I think the most important objective is to make clear that it's not something quaint—*mein bubbes meinses*—but a poetry in many ways like all others." At the basis of Howe's thinking here is an opposition between the *quaint* ("mein bubbes meinses" translates roughly into "old wives tales"), and the "pure," linked to serious art.[23]

At the same time, however, more than any previous anthologizers of Yiddish literature in English, Howe and Greenberg insisted on the cultural distinctiveness of Yiddish literature, what Howe calls in the introduction to *A Treasury of Yiddish Stories* its "qualitatively unique . . . cultural aura" (TYS 29). The reader of Yiddish literature, he explains, must be willing to "enter an unfamiliar world and to adjust himself to literary modes and expectations that differ from his own culture" (TYS 2). He cites Maurice Samuel, who suggests that because of its unique fusion of Germanic, Slavic, and Hebrew and Aramaic elements, the Yiddish language itself has about it "a suggestion of an oriental bazaar" (TYS 47).[24] This is the balancing act at the center of Howe's construction of Yiddishkayt: to vouch for the quality and seriousness of Yiddish writing while also claiming for it a purpose and character alien to the norms of Western aesthetics.

Howe's lengthy introduction to *A Treasury of Yiddish Stories* marks the transformation of the City College radical into the postwar Yiddishist. In a pedagogical rather than strictly polemical tone, it leads the American reader through a crash course in modern Jewish history, beginning with the rise of Hasidism and focusing on the shtetl as a microcosm for Jewish life. The social world of the shtetl, Howe explains, was "unified, singular, contiguous" (TYS 3); it had "not yet split into sharply defined classes" (TYS 6). The inhabitants of the shtetl valued learning over acquiring, collective life over individual accomplishment, beautiful deeds over beautiful things. As for the religious dimension of Jewish life, Howe imagines a Judaism where the transcendent God has entered the empirical world: "God was a living force, a Presence, something more than a name or desire. . . . Toward Him the Jews could feel a peculiar sense of intimacy"

(TYS 8). In this elegiac portrayal of the Old Country, Howe's introduction resonates with other postwar works such as Marc Zborowski's ethnographic study, *Life Is with People* (1952) and Abraham Joshua Heschel's *The Earth Is the Lord's* (1949). All of these works forge a picture of the shtetl as the essential geography of prewar Jewish life, the site of what Heschel called "the golden period in Jewish history, in the history of the Jewish soul."[25] They spoke to a pervasive feeling among postwar American Jews of living *in the aftermath,* of having missed the defining phase of Jewish history that was abruptly destroyed in the Holocaust.[26] But unlike Zborowski and Heschel, Howe is less concerned with drawing a portrait of the shtetl as a timeless ideal than in exploring what happens when, under the combined pressures of urbanization, antisemitism, and the spread of secular ideologies, the shtetl begins to break apart. Howe argues that this period of breakdown is a uniquely productive and dynamic period in Jewish history, in which a secular literary culture began to take shape. The distinctive mark of this literature was its "precarious balance" (TYS 28) between the folk world and the modern world, its familiarity with shtetl life and its ability to reflect critically on that life. "Formal Yiddish literature," he writes, emerged during a "wonderful interregnum" when East European Jews were no longer within the grip of the traditional religious order, but had yet to lose their distinctiveness through acculturation to non-Jewish norms. It is this "twilight" culture that he calls "the culture of Yiddishkayt."[27]

Central to Howe's view is the notion that creative energy and insight coincide with historical crisis. "Yiddish reaches its climax of expressive power," he asserts, "as the world it portrays begins to fall apart" (TYS 28). This is the same point he previously made about Faulkner, also a figure whose creativity was sparked, according to Howe, by the decline of a once-stable world. As with Faulkner, the Yiddish writers Howe discusses discover a voice just when the world they know, the world of the shtetl, began to unravel. This is a moment that presents both an unavoidable theme—the breakdown of a culture rooted in tradition and belief—and an indispensable perspective, borrowed from the "alien" cultures that are themselves partly responsible for the breakdown of the shtetl world. As in Hegel's dictum that "the Owl of Minerva begins its flight at twilight," here, too, a heightened form of insight becomes available precisely when the traditional structures of society are breaking down.[28]

A useful analogy might be drawn here between the way Howe views Yiddish literature and the way Walter Benjamin theorized the art of storytelling in his famous essay "The Storyteller." Both Howe and Benjamin were essentially post-Marxist thinkers consumed with the problem of sustaining a critical perspective onto society in the face of dwindling faith in Marxist teleological versions of history. Both saw in the destruction of traditional folk cultures a parable for modernity, and both looked to storytellers as possible guides to the future precisely in their dissonant relationship to modernity. For Benjamin, the storyteller is a figure closely related to other kinds of teachers and sages. Like them, the storyteller is capable of *giving counsel,* which he accomplishes above all by "transmitting" experience. This relates to Howe's image of the Yiddish writer as part of an integrated community, bound together by memory and a spirit of fraternity. And like Howe, Benjamin is most interested in what happens when the community begins to come apart, when the disruptive forces of modernity create a shift in the very quality of experience, and the basis of the storyteller's art is suddenly endangered. In Benjamin's words, "[t]he art of storytelling is reaching its end because the epic side of truth, wisdom, is dying out."[29] At the same time, Benjamin proposes that it is now possible to "see a new beauty in what is vanishing," by which he seems to mean both that the forces of modernity make the storyteller a chronicler of decline, and that contemporary readers glimpse in the work of traditional storytellers a kind of twilight beauty. Benjamin's storyteller and Howe's Yiddish writers—though conceived on opposite sides of the Holocaust—are thus figures who preserve a kind of wisdom that is no longer fostered by the world but that remains vital to the possibility of reimagining the future.[30]

The arrangement of the stories in the *Treasury* is structured according to this narrative of historical decline.[31] A majority of the stories are grouped under a section called "Portrait of a World." In stories here by Sholem Aleichem, Isaac Leib Peretz, Abraham Reisen, and Isaac Bashevis Singer, the folk world of the shtetl is evoked through the voice of the traditional storyteller. This section is followed by another section entitled "Breakup," which contains narratives in a strictly realist mode. The key figure here is David Bergelson, whose somber works reflect Howe's argument about Yiddish literature as a response to cultural dissolution. For example, "In a Backwoods Town" follows a series of disaffected individuals cut loose from the moorings of community. The central figure, a "rabbiner," a rabbi officially appointed by the government, tries to overcome his lassitude through a liaison with a married woman. Throughout, the tone connotes desperation and exhaustion: "He dozed off with a hazy awareness that the autumn which prevailed in his rabbinical soul was now coming into being outdoors, and that somewhere beyond the godforsaken little border town there surely must be great bustling cities where men were active and alive" (TYS 473). Here is an encapsulation of Howe's argument about Yiddish literature: it focuses on a "border town"; its protagonist is stationed between worlds; it meditates on a better life elsewhere without a clear sense of where it might be or how to build it.

The final section, "New Worlds," draws into focus the destruction of Jewish Eastern Europe. Three of the stories here revolve around World War II—Singer's "The Little Shoemakers," Isaiah Spiegel's "A Ghetto Dog," and Chaim Grade's "My Quarrel with Hersh Rasseyner." The stories that take place in America—"The Little Shoemakers," Sholem Asch's "A Quiet Garden Spot," and Joseph Opatoshu's "The Eternal Wedding Gown"—are all studies in senescence and death. Pervading these works is the theme of a total incommensurability between the Yiddish-speaking world and the New World. In Singer's story, a shoemaker who personifies shtetl life does appear, after barely escaping the Nazis, to gain a new lease on life in the outskirts of New Jersey. But Singer's inescapable, if subtle, point seems to be that any sense of a "new life" in America can only be built on delusion. The story's final image of the family reunited around the awl, singing traditional melodies, appears deliberately calculated to draw the reader into a redemptive fantasy that the story itself insistently undercuts. America can only mimic paradise. The shoemaker's sons have really betrayed Old World Judaism, and became capitalists who market their wares as having the "touch of the old world." None of the children speaks Yiddish; the local temple inspires no piety.

The impulse to return enacted by Singer's Old World protagonist in "The Little Shoemakers"—an impulse that is desperate and impossible as much as it is irrepressible—suggests one of Howe's conclusions about modern Yiddish writers. As much as the outside world beckons, and as much as they are drawn to revolutionary movements and ideologies, these writers are close enough to the traditional structures of Jewish life that they seldom truly leave its province, just as Kazin does not break completely free from the orbit of Brownsville. And this helps explain, according to Howe, why the radical experimentation of literary modernism could never fully capture the allegiance of Yiddish writers. "Each of these writers, as he later went his separate way, retained something of what he learned from his youthful brush with modernism, yet almost all of them returned to traditional Jewish themes. Yiddish culture, by the very terms of its existence, allows only a limited receptivity to modernism" (TYS 69). At a moment when the avant-garde was losing its momentum and when socialism had seemingly reached an impasse, Yiddish literature provided Howe with a model for a life suspended between stabilities, a "precarious balance" that heroically clung to its deepest premises.

Howe and Greenberg's translation project may also be seen in the context of an emerging impulse in the postwar literary world at large to affirm and celebrate what according to our current nomenclature we would call "minor" literatures. Indicative of this new trend was the 25th International Congress of the P.E.N. Association of Writers, convened in Dublin in 1953, which was devoted to "the literature of people whose language restricts wide recognition."[32] Among the speakers at this conference were the Provençal writer André Chamsun, the Gaelic writer Michael MacLiammoir, and the very same Eliezer Greenberg who at that same moment was busily working with Howe to prepare the *Treasury of Yiddish Stories.* Greenberg's talk at the P.E.N. congress, entitled "The Literature of Small Peoples: A Special Problem," is a fascinating document that reveals how Yiddish literature could be imagined as part of a broader movement of cultural resistance at the height of the Cold War. It helps us recognize the political stakes involved in the project of recovery he had undertaken with Howe.

In his talk, Greenberg asserts that a common denominator shared by democracy and totalitarianism alike is a colonizing impulse to win over as allies the small nations of the world. To honor Yiddish literature is thus to take a stand against cultural imperialism and the overall leveling force of Cold War political culture. He continues by offering a characterization of Yiddish literature that harmonizes with the view Howe will place at the center of his introduction to the *Treasury* and all of his subsequent work on Jewish culture. Here is what Greenberg told his audience in Dublin:

> What characterizes Yiddish literature best is its profound humanism, its moral and ethical values, its deep compassion, and its tender aura of martyrdom and sanctification. For in Yiddish literature man is the measure of all things and man is universal and eternal. I. L. Peretz, one of the great founders of Yiddish literature, refused to acknowledge that "those who create cannot live." He insisted that "men of high aims do not outlive their aims; they are bound to eternity." And finally, he urged, "neither individuals nor nations can live by themselves."[33]

Greenberg helps us situate Yiddish literature alongside other expressions of local resistance at this Cold War moment. The values Greenberg affirms via Yiddish literature—humanism, fraternity, communality—were precisely ones that Howe was trying at this very moment to salvage from socialism.

Permanent Revolution or Perpetual Decline?

The importance of discovering in Yiddish literature a symbol, a figurative "address," for cultural resistance can hardly be underestimated. In Howe's literary and cultural essays over the next decades, we find that not only Yiddish literature, but also the "culture of Yiddishkayt" more broadly defined, functions rhetorically as a term of opposition, enabling Howe to demur from a cultural or political world given over (in his mind) to an insidious nihilism. Three examples we might cite are the essays "The Literature of Suicide" and "Auschwitz and High Mandarian," collected in *The Critical Point;* and his excellent short book, *The American Newness: Culture and Politics in the Age of Emerson* (1986). While treating very different subjects, they all lodge a similar complaint against worldviews taken to be extreme, irresponsible, and ultimately hostile to life. A. Alvarez is taken to task for uncritically accepting the nihilistic side of the modernist sensibility; George Steiner for disingenuously announcing the failure of Western culture; and Emerson, while treated much more respectfully than these others, for endorsing a wholesale renovation of life that will "banish every mode of social and moral oppression" in one quixotic fell swoop.[34] Emerson the utopian and Alvarez the nihilist come to sound alike in Howe's work for both rejecting the claims of history and the bonds of community. And what makes Howe's criticisms more than merely the cry of the skeptic is his rhetorical use, at some key moment in each argument, of a Jewish text to serve as an antithesis. Against Alvarez, Howe offers passages from Isaac Babel and Osip Mandelstam; and against Steiner, he invokes Jacob Glatstein and Aaron Zeitlin, Yiddish writers who bear out Howe's argument that among the survivors themselves, a dominant motif is not that of discarding traditions but rather of "reasserting them in defiance of Gentile history."[35] In all of these instances, Howe invokes a Jewish writer who expresses a sober, humanistic view, a contrast to the extremism and apocalypticism of Alvarez and Steiner.

Most surprising is a moment in *The American Newness* when Howe dissents from Emersonian individualism by way of an anecdote from Rashi's commentaries on the Bible (hardly a standard reference in the pages of *Labor Action*). The passage Howe quotes shows Abraham on the third day after his circumcision, waiting at the tent door for a passerby. God has brought out a burning sun to keep away company and give Abraham some peace and quiet, but when God sees that Abraham is grieved at the absence of visitors, He sends him angels in the guise of men. Howe explains that this touching story affirms the values of "sociability and solidarity" (CP 45), both of which have low priority in Emerson's hierarchy of values. This unlikely turn to Rashi reveals how broad the category of "Jewish literature" had become in Howe's lexicon. The rhetorical function played by Rashi and Isaac Babel are quite similar: both stand for fraternity and an affirmation of life, in its most basic sense, in the face of extremism of one sort or another.

But what about Jewish culture in America, produced in English? Is there any contemporary analogue of the antithetical force of Yiddish poetry, Isaac Babel, and Rashi? Throughout the 1950s and 1960s, a period in which Howe formed and edited the journal *Dissent,* he continued to inveigh against middle-class Jewish culture, most conspicuously in the damning review he wrote about the 1964 Broadway production of *Fiddler on the Roof.* What the musical disclosed was nothing less than "the spiritual anemia of Broadway and of the middle-class Jewish world which by now seems firmly linked to Broadway."[36] At the same time, he found much to celebrate in the rise of a new generation of Jewish writers in America, figures such as Saul Bellow, Bernard Malamud, and Tillie Olsen. By describing these writers as exemplars of a single worldview, a Jewish version of the regional literature of the South, Howe created a paradigm for Jewish American literature that has remained prevalent and useful. His was also one of the loudest voices in the rediscovery of Henry Roth's *Call It Sleep,* which came out in paperback form in 1964, just as Howe was bemoaning Broadway's debasement of Jewish memory. Before long he began work on his massive social history of American Jews, *World of Our Fathers* (1976), which explored once again the "culture of Yiddishkayt," this time as it had manifested itself during a brief transitional period on the Lower East Side. All of this suggests that Jewish creativity did manage to cross the ocean— and temporarily to express itself in English.

Still, a dominant motif in Howe's writings on Jewish American literature is the same narrative of decline that structures his reading of Yiddish literature. This time the tradition moves from the immigrant writings of Abraham Cahan and Henry Roth through second-generation figures such as Bellow and Malamud, before finally becoming exhausted in the work of Philip Roth. "His importance in the development of American Jewish writing," Howe writes about Philip Roth, "was that, finally, he seemed to be cut off from any Jewish tradition."[37] As for the future, Howe saw only a depletion of resources, a loss of any overpowering subject—in short, the end of a Jewish American literary tradition and indeed of a vital Jewish culture in general. In an address before a *Tikkun* conference in 1988, he announced, "The American Jews constitute a drained community, drained of its animating passions and energies, of its faith that it possesses a self-subsistent ground for its being. . . . They have lost their bearings."[38]

This view is expressed notoriously in the introduction to *Jewish-American Stories,* where, in a passage that has gained a certain amount of notoriety for its pessimism (and apparent lack of foresight), he sounds the death knell of Jewish American literature:

> Insofar as this body of writing draws heavily from the immigrant experience, it must suffer a depletion of resources, a thinning-out of materials and memories. . . . The sense of an overpowering subject, the sense that this subject imposes itself upon [writers'] imaginations—this grows weaker, necessarily, with the passing of the years.[39]

It has almost become a ritual of recent Jewish American criticism to argue that Howe has been proven wrong. Many have pointed out that though he saw no future for Jewish American writing, the slew of recent literary productivity provides ample testimony to the contrary.[40] Some have noted that while the great immigration of 1881–1924 may no longer furnish an "overpowering subject," more recent developments in American Jewish life have provided new sorts of subjects. Among these developments, one might include the recent Russian immigration, which has recreated the conditions for an "immigrant" sensibility; the rise of modern Orthodoxy, which has led to heightened reflection on the sacred–secular divide; and the increased prominence of the Holocaust in American public culture, which has led to postmodern reflections on mediation, memory, and simulation.[41]

My proposal here is not so much to take on Howe's claims as a rival critic and to use the recent efflorescence of Jewish American writing as evidence to prove him wrong. Rather, I propose to view him as someone who paradoxically sustained the very tradition he saw as ending. Rather than read Howe exclusively as a commentator, we can see him as the *creator* of a discourse. This discourse is structured according to an opposition between Yiddishkayt, which stands for collective memory and ethics, and some version of nihilism on the other. What makes Howe's version of this opposition so forceful is that he always writes from the standpoint of desperation, when the continuities of history are quickly dissolving and we are left with an almost impossible challenge to remain sane. What I am suggesting, then, is that Howe's prognosis of decline can be read as itself a literary trope. Howe's own writings—with their brooding seriousness, their restless searching among old texts, their pained admissions of defeat—constitute in themselves a compelling image of a Jewishness striving to find its bearings. For Howe, literature at its most poignant and meaningful is an expression of crisis; it tells us what has been lost, what we are losing, and, perhaps, what we might hope for again. The dialectical force of Howe's own writing is such that his own texts seem to confirm his view of Jewish literature as a tradition that speaks most poignantly as a chronicle of decline.

One of the striking features of the idea of decline is that it can provide the animating center around which to construct a literary text and, arguably, a culture itself. As Simon Rawidowicz notes in "Israel: The Ever-Dying People," the trope of lastness has played a key role in diasporic constructions of Jewish identity. "The world makes many images of Israel," he writes, "but Israel makes only one image of itself: that of a being constantly on the verge of disappearing."[42] This trope goes all the way back to the Talmud itself where, at the end of tractate *Sotah,* we encounter a chronicle of all that has been lost: "When Rabbi Meir died, there were no more makers of parables. When Rabbi Azzai died there were no more diligent students. When Rabbi Zoma died there were no more expounders. . . ."[43] The time of plenitude, when wisdom could flourish freely, is behind us: we are always already losing the essence, gathering fragments. This paradoxically is a foundational statement and sentiment of rabbinic Judaism, which establishes the basis for a way of life *after* a time of plenitude, specifically when the Temple still stood. Another way of saying this, perhaps, is that the elegiac mode also offers a way of participating, at least imaginatively, in a culture whose end has been declared.

Found in Translation

Indeed, although he reads modern Jewish culture as slated for disappearance, Howe has himself become a foundational figure for further, and unlikely, forms of Jewish creativity. In addition to providing a link back to the world of Yiddish creativity, Howe's translation project provided, in concrete terms, a forum for Jewish writers and readers to interact with this past. By briefly surveying some of the responses to Howe and to his translation project more broadly, we might gain a sense of what this ongoing, though inherently embattled, Jewish creativity looks like. The census of Jewish American writers whose own imaginations were sparked by their direct involvement with Howe and Greenberg's translation project is long and illustrious. What it underscores is the productive role of translation in the unfolding of Jewish literary culture in America after the war.

Saul Bellow was corralled by Howe into doing the translation of Singer's "Gimpel the Fool" for *A Treasury of Yiddish Stories* ("Gimpel" was published in *Partisan Review* a year before the *Treasury* came out). The result was not only an immediate embrace among "sophisticated" English-language readers of Singer, but a new direction in Bellow's own writing style. In 1953, Bellow had just finished *The Adventures of Augie March,* a rambling, ecstatic account in which the Jewish hero plays the role of a modern-day picaro, exploring the social world in its manifold forms. After the Gimpel translation, Bellow wrote *Seize the Day,* a much more compressed work that focused on the schlemiel hero Tommy Wilhelm who, in Gimpel-like fashion, is taken in by those around him—particularly by the charlatan Dr. Tamkin, whose financial advice proves disastrous for Tommy. But like Gimpel, Tommy surfaces as the only deeply human character in the novel, whose ability to feel for others reflects an ultimate triumph.[44] Bellow's translation of Singer thus coincided with and may very well have caused Bellow's shift to a new model for the Jewish hero, based on faith in others and often expressed through suffering. This kind of schlemiel figure would develop further in *Herzog* (1961), whose hero Moses Herzog becomes a moral center in a world spinning out of control.[45]

Bernard Malamud was by his own account moved to write his story "The Magic Barrel" directly after reading through a series of Yiddish folk tales at the instigation of Howe. "The idea for the story itself, the donné, came about through Irving Howe's invitation to me to translate a story from Yiddish."[46] Howe was hoping to lure Malamud into the work of translation; instead he provided the materials out of which Malamud fashioned a story in English. In Malamud's story, a hapless marriage broker expresses skepticism over the idea of a "love match" in terms that directly recall one of these tales. (The punch line in the tale Malamud cites is: "A love-match? I can get you that kind too!") Malamud's development in this and subsequent works of a symbolic mode—akin to what we might call "magical realism"—also comes out of his engagement with Yiddish texts. Thus, in a note in Malamud's journal, dated March 8, 1954, just after his perusal of Yiddish writings at Howe's behest, we find Malamud rethinking his own aesthetic: "Go back to the poetic, evocative, singing—often symbolic short story. Use all you've got. Go for more than story—but make story good."[47] Here Malamud is entrusting his own writing with the task of sustaining, in English, an ethos and sensibility that he connects to East European Jewish culture. In Howe's own estimation, the experiment seems to have worked. In *World of Our Fathers,* as if forgetting his own role in Malamud's development, Howe describes "The Magic Barrel" as nothing less than a "miraculous salvage . . . [a work which] can only be called the Yiddish story in English."[48]

Howe and Greenberg's collection also provided Philip Roth with the epigraph for his first published work, *Goodbye, Columbus* (1959). The epigraph reads "The heart is half a prophet," which Roth attributes to "a

Yiddish proverb" (the *Treasury,* published six years earlier, offers the same line with the same attribution). Its effect in Roth's volume is to suggest that underlying these biting satires of modern Jewish life, the stories finally affirm ideals and values associated with the culture of immigrant Jews. The reader is encouraged, in effect, to draw a connection between Howe's *Treasury,* which culminates with the Yiddish proverbs, and Roth's collection, which begins with one of them. In Roth's later novel *The Anatomy Lesson* (1983), Howe is himself woven into the narrative, in the character Milton Appel. In an early passage of the novel, Zuckerman is so inspired by Appel's translations from Yiddish that he undertakes to learn Yiddish himself. What most inspires Zuckerman (and Roth as well, we assume) was the exhilarating stand Appel/Howe's Yiddish translations took against the "snobbish condescension of those famous departments of English literature from whose impeccable Christian ranks the literary Jew . . . had until just yesterday been pointedly excluded."[49] Howe becomes a trailblazer for the postwar American Jew as subversive literary intellectual, a forerunner for Roth's own self-fashioning.

Finally, we should consider that Cynthia Ozick's substantial work for Howe on *A Treasury of Yiddish Poetry* (1969) coincided with the period in her career when she was beginning to identify more and more as a *Jewish* writer. Her translations of Glatstein, in particular, lead directly to many of her recurrent themes, such as the conflict between Judaism and paganism and the problem of faith after the Holocaust. Many of her fictions and essays from the 1970s onward are directly informed by Howe's translation project, both literally and symbolically. In works such as "Envy, or Yiddish in America" (1969) and *The Messiah of Stockholm* (1987), the problem of translation has itself become a key motif around which to structure her meditations on modern Jewish culture. Both narratives center around the haunting image of Jewish texts written in "obscure" languages (Yiddish and Polish) and languishing without a readership—in the first case because there aren't enough translators of Yiddish, in the second case because even if an adequate translator for the Polish were found, the text in question, Bruno Schultz's manuscript "The Messiah," has disappeared. In these narratives, the motif of the obscure or somehow unreadable text sets off frantic quests—for translators and for texts. And in Ozick's world, these quests are always finally fruitless: the "Jewish" text remains somehow in obscurity. Read in relation to Howe and Greenberg's project—and postwar American Jewish readers they catered to, Ozick seems to be confirming his view of translation as the key to the Jewish past while deepening—if this were possible—his skepticism that the generations can really speak to one another. Finally she will propose that some deeper spiritual challenge must be faced if Jewishness is to have any continuing relevance.

Ozick ultimately critiques Howe's secularism, and Roth will ultimately parody his Howe stand-in for assuming a stance of false gentility. But there are important similarities linking all of the writers who were somehow shaped by Howe's translation project. All were Jews who were born and bred in America and who found themselves, in the middle of the road of the American century, bereft of language for expressing their ultimate concerns and commitments. In different ways, all have turned toward some version of "Jewishness" to uncover the resources with which to construct such a language. In Howe's elegiac renderings of Yiddishkayt, in Bellow's schlemiels, and in Ozick's turn to religious discourses, we find a common revisionary stance toward "tradition"—a common insistence that "Jewish" somehow equals resistance to the inhumanity of contemporary life, whether to capitalism and anomie, to the repressions of the WASP order, or to aesthetic paganism. And here we return to Robert Lowell's point while observing the debates surrounding Arendt's book on Eichmann. At precisely the moment one might have expected silence or surrender, there is speech. Jewish culture has continuously renewed itself, we might say, by virtue of a faith in human language, a faith that loss might be compensated for by commentary, debate, and invention. The confidence placed by postwar Jewish American writers in literature itself— in what we generally construe as secular literature—reveals how new genres, and new languages, can be entrusted with various old tasks. We learn from their active responses to Howe and Greenberg that at least some part of East European Jewish culture has continued to speak through translation, which functions here in its most literal sense of "carrying over," though what is retained is always suspected of somehow not being quite enough. By reading Kazin's Romantic Judaism alongside Howe's Yiddishkayt, we can recognize two impulses that have combined in the formation of Jewish American literary culture. The first bespeaks an ongoing preoccupation with transcendence, a willingness to rise to the challenge of imagining divinity and our relationship to it. The second bespeaks more secular concerns, an awareness of the shaping role of community, history, and of the unique angle of vision offered by Yiddish. Both impulses have sustained a fascination with Jewishness, an effort to hear in its echoes a lesson in survival.

CONCLUSION

The place where all tracks end
is the place where history was meant to stop
but does not stop   where thinking
was meant to stop but does not stop
where the pattern was meant to give way at last
                                        but only
becomes a different pattern
                            terrible, threadbare
strained   familiar   on-going
                —from Adrienne Rich, *Sources*

This passage from Adrienne Rich's autobiographical poetic cycle, *Sources,*
may be read as an allegory of the story of Jewish cultural continuity offered
by this book. In Rich's poem, history was "meant to stop," either because
America enforces cultural amnesia on all who enter, or because the "tracks"
evoked by the poem are those that led to the Nazi extermination camps, or

because modern historical consciousness itself leaves Jews feeling stranded in time, cut off from the wellsprings of a tradition that appears once to have been sufficient and authoritative. For all these reasons, contemporary Jews—and American Jews in particular—have been frequently harassed by an acute perception of *living in the aftermath*. Nevertheless, Rich's poem also asserts that "the pattern"—whatever it was—has not simply given way; something is "on-going." The passage itself, a succession of clauses, unimpeded by punctuation, attests to an irrepressible vitality, a force of transformation and renewal. Rich's own career bears witness to this process: having started out in the 1950s as a brilliant young poet praised by W. H. Auden for her control and modernist irony, she reclaimed her place in the continuity of Jewish life, in the midst of intense engagement with questions surrounding feminist politics and the meaning of ethnic, sexual, and racial identity in American culture.[1] At the same time, Rich knows too much to be overly sanguine about the sturdiness of this new/old pattern: while it may be "familiar," it is also "threadbare" and "strained," hardly a simple renegotiation with the past. In another section of "Sources," Rich proposes a paradoxical image to describe her feeling of solidarity with Jews across time: "The Jews I've felt rooted among / are those who were turned to smoke."[2]

The impulse to root oneself among Jews at the moment history was meant to stop reflects a subtheme that has appeared again and again in the foregoing chapters. This theme is that the turn toward Jewish identification offers a response to the radical dismissal of history and a concomitant tendency toward extremism and nihilism that have characterized American culture. In various ways, the writers we have considered all distance themselves from those currents in American culture that speak for the severing of all ties to the past and for antinomian assertions of the imperial self. Their engagements with Judaism and Jewish culture and history then offer what I have called a "stay against apocalypse" because they provide a vantage point from which to see the present as a point along a long trajectory, reaching back into the past and pointing toward the future.

The case studies I offer in this book reveal some of the ways in which Jewish American writers have participated in the process Rich describes, the process by which the "pattern" of Jewish life transforms and persists just at the moment it seems to be dissolving. In each instance, the writer in question attests somehow to a gulf dividing the present from the past, with "authentic" Jewish identity associated generally with the past and almost always with Eastern Europe. But each writer also goes on to elaborate some set of images, tropes, or metaphors through which the past manages to speak once again—and in the American present. Lazarus writes a poetic cycle in which the East European immigrant appears as a vessel in which the "jewel of the Law" has been preserved. Antin recreates the world of the shtetl in her fiction, celebrating the idealism and uniquely forceful faith of East European Jews. Lewisohn describes the deep soul of even the most assimilated Jew as a repository for an abiding Jewishness. Frank affirms the "Jewish Word" as a perpetually available spiritual teaching. Yezierska envisions the Jewish past as a chorus of generations of ghosts, all clamoring for expression. I. J. Schwartz and Reuben Ludwig develop a Whitmanian poetics in Yiddish, nominating Yiddish as a privileged medium for transmitting Whitman's "prophetic" vision. Howe represents Yiddish and, ultimately, all Jewish literature as a meditation on crisis and decline, in effect turning crisis into a master trope for Jewishness itself. Even the mournful declaration that the tradition has ended, or the cry of longing, as at the end of Kazin's *New York Jew,* have the positive effect of creating a language of Jewishness. In all of these cases, "tradition" is neither repossessed once and for all nor rejected. More to the point, it is synthesized into an image and thereby given renewed currency, even in the guise of an elusive, threadbare, or ever-diminishing resource. In many cases, the idea of an elusive and vulnerable Jewishness has lent a sense of urgency to the work of cultural production, fueling an impulse to rediscover old traditions and to create new forms in which to express them.

I have described these varied expressions and affirmations of Jewishness as responses to specific historical developments—from pogroms in nineteenth-century Russia to the rise of xenophobia in post–World War I America to the Holocaust in Europe to the decline of the anti-Stalinist Left in America during the Cold War. But I have also emphasized how Jewish American writers have been profoundly influenced by their dialogue with American culture—both with the abstract "Idea" of America and with the classic American literary tradition that has given shape to this Idea. If Jewish American writers have inquired into the meaning of Jewishness, they have done so from the perspective of Main Street and by looking through lenses crafted by local optometrists. In this sense, their work exemplifies the process by which Jewish cultures have been formed throughout history.

This process might be described as the ongoing redefinition of Judaism and Jewish identity through terms offered by the "outside" culture. Maimonides' effort to unite rabbinic theology with Aristotelian philosophy is perhaps the best known instance of this process, but openness to the outside world and creative interaction seem to be the rule, not the exception, throughout Jewish history. David Biale argues in the introduction to his *Cultures of the Jews* that "rather than the *Mekhilta*'s explanation for why Jews survived in exile—as well as in their own land [resistance to assimilation and avoidance of 'idle gossip']—perhaps our supposition ought to be just the reverse: that it was precisely in their profound engagement with the cultures of their environment that the Jews constructed their unique identities."[3] All of the writers in this book have engaged profoundly with American literary culture, posing in many instances as its most forceful advocates, but they have also adapted the language(s) of American culture to describe their own predicament as Jews.

I have suggested that the American literary tradition has been particularly productive for certain kinds of Jewish self-imagining because it has nurtured an *oppositional* idiom, linked in direct and indirect ways to the tradition of biblical prophecy. If the quintessential American writer is a prophetic outsider crying in the wilderness, Jewish writers have often seen fit to inhabit this position as well, since, after all, the prophetic tradition is indigenous to Judaism itself. In some cases, then, Jewish writers identify with the post-Puritan American literary prophetic only to discover the possibility of speaking for and from this tradition *as a Jew*. We see this most clearly perhaps in the cases of Emma Lazarus, Ludwig Lewisohn, and Waldo Frank, all of whom imagine their work as a conduit for the biblical tradition, that of the prophets above all. It is also important to note that when Anzia Yezierska has her Jewish patriarch quote from Jewish texts, what we hear is neither in *Bread Givers* Hillel nor the Baal Shem Tov, but the prophet Isaiah. And with the Yiddish poets we considered, the same principle applies: the more "American" they are, the more biblical and "prophetic" they seem to become. Recall Jacob Glatstein's point that what distinguishes I. J. Schwartz is both that he has opened himself to American literary culture and that he "thinks biblically" (*er trakht tanakhish*). This biblical cast to the Jewish American imagination is fostered and reinforced by American literary culture even as it introduces a critique of this culture's skepticism about the claims of historical memory.

Indeed, the texts of the prophets have a very different sound and status when summoned by Jews and from the standpoint of Jewish historical experience, that is, from the standpoint of exile. If the Christian reading of Isaiah finds in him the anticipation of Jesus, the traditional Jewish reading sees an expression of yearnings that have yet to be realized. The famous image of the "man of sorrows" or "suffering servant" from Isaiah 53:5 has been read by Christian exegetes as a figure for Jesus, but Jewish commentators have tended to read it either as an anticipation of a messiah who has not come or, indeed, as a portrait for Israel itself.[4] And thus, having imbibed the prophetic tradition through American and essentially Christian or post-Christian sources, the Jewish writer can reclaim this tradition as a language of unfulfilled Jewish aspiration and longing.[5]

Even when these writers are not familiar with the specific exegetical traditions of Judaism, they do know that whatever else it stands for, Judaism understands that the cycle of exile and redemption has yet to complete itself.

Before exploring some final implications of this Jewish American "prophetic mode," it is worthwhile briefly to consider two additional examples. Like Allen Ginsberg's *Kaddish*, E. L. Doctorow's *The Book of Daniel* (1971) is also ostensibly a work of mourning, its fictitious premise being that it is an autobiographical text composed by the son of two Communists executed for "conspiracy to commit espionage." Based directly on the historical Rosenbergs—here renamed the Isaacsons—the text restages history through the template of the biblical Book of Daniel. The central allusion and framing device links the author/son to Daniel himself, whose visions and defiance of the Babylonian establishment make him a serviceable hero for the Jewish activist in modern America. As with *Kaddish*, the text sketches out a conversion narrative, with the protagonist discovering a mission by resituating himself as heir to the tradition of the Jewish prophetic. In one of the novel's most chilling scenes, just as Daniel's mother is to be killed in the electric chair, she heralds her son's mission: "Let my son be bar mitzvahed today. Let our death be his bar mitzvah."[6] Within the framework of the novel, this gruesome image associates Daniel's mission and initiation into Jewish manhood with the act of bearing witness to his parents' murder in the name of divine justice.

Written in the context of the apocalyptic tenor in America during the late 1960s—when the idealism and sense of purpose of the early New Left was coming apart under the strains of cooptation, exhaustion, and repression—Doctorow's novel underscores how Jewish prophecy can provide a language for sustaining a sense of purpose amid the dissolution of ideological certainty. At the novel's conclusion, Doctorow quotes a long passage from the Book of Daniel that looks beyond the chaos of the present toward a future redemption, an end when "the people shall be delivered."[7] When the biblical frame of reference is reintroduced, the novel's despairing view suddenly appears as but a moment of negation along a much broader redemptive trajectory.

A final example, which once again returns to the history of Jewish radicalism in America (and the Rosenbergs in particular), is Tony Kushner's celebrated play *Angels in America: A Gay Fantasia on National Themes*. Written in response to the repressions of Reaganite conservativism and its failure to address the AIDS epidemic, Kushner also stages the birth of a "prophet," drawing upon language(s) derived from the traditions of Judaism—in this case the language of mysticism. Here, the figure elected as prophet is in fact the Mayflower WASP, Prior, a victim of AIDS who appears to transform into a Jew precisely when his prophetic vocation unfolds.[8] (Prior is explicitly and repeatedly hailed as "prophet.") His ancestors visit from the heavens and proceed to chant kabbalistic formulas (88); his nurse inexplicably begins reciting the *El Male Rachamim* prayer in Hebrew (98); and he discovers a giant book with a burning *Aleph*, a sign in Kabbalah for the divine power of creation (99). Prior's "Jewish" status is confirmed at the moment he refuses to relinquish his mortal body, despite his summons by the angels. By insisting on returning to earth for "more life," he rejects Christ-like status, opting instead to struggle with the almighty, which epitomizes "the Jewish way" (135), according to the rabbi in the play, Isidor Chemelwitz. The final sequence in the play shows Prior ascending and descending a ladder to the heavens: he has chosen to enact the destiny of Jacob, confirming the existence of the angels even while wrestling with them.

In both of these examples, a set of images and metaphors borrowed from Jewish history, liturgy, and biblical literature arrives to supplement a political discourse that has somehow lost traction. In particular, these texts enact a movement from Communist politics to prophetic vision. Both draw attention to the history of the Rosenbergs, who function in these works as archetypal victims of America's periodic witch-hunting mania as well as symbols of a Jewish tradition of protest. We might say that the prophetic rises on the ashes of the political, rescuing a glimpse of hope despite the failure of ideology.[9] Thus for Doctorow and Kushner and in different ways many of the writers we have considered here, the return to Jewishness provides a perspective from which to reclaim and renew the American democratic project under different auspices.

One way to conceptualize the Jewish difference within American literature is to contrast the stance of Adam with that of Abraham. As R. W. B. Lewis observes in his classic study *The American Adam* (1955), nineteenth-century American writers characteristically appropriated for themselves the authority of Adam in the garden, naming the flora and fauna as if for the first time and according to their own predilections.[10] To be sure, this motif identified an ideal more than any actual existential or linguistic condition, but the point is that these writers' greatest hopes were linked to the idea that history might start over in the New World, and in their own minds. For Jewish writers—at least those who came to align themselves with the particularistic traditions of Judaism—the ideal has veered closer to Abraham, who heard the commanding voice of God and responded by leaving his home. (Abraham is, incidentally, the first figure in the Bible named according to the Hebrew word for prophet, *navi*.) To the extent that they bring Abraham to the fore over Adam, Jewish American writers diverge from the radical individualism and rejection of history that characterizes the American ethos and that receives its classic formulation in Emersonian Transcendentalism. These Jewish writers affirm the notion— or at least the validity of the notion—of a commanding word, located outside of the individual, at a significant remove from the capriciousness of sheer whim (to evoke a central Emersonian concept). And even when these writers seem unsure about that status of their own belief, they affirm the tradition that has transmitted this commanding word; in a word, what they affirm is historical memory, a triumph over amnesia.

The effect of this affirmation is not to promulgate a set of laws that must be obeyed, but more broadly to instill a sense of hope. What Abraham receives, after all, is not a decalogue but a commandment to depart the condition he currently inhabits ("Get thee out of thy country . . ."), along with a promise that blessings will follow ("I will make of thee a great nation, and I will bless thee . . ."). So too the writers I have discussed establish themselves not as advocates for any narrow definition of Judaism, but as the recipients of a tradition centered on the basic premise that a moral force exists and that human life might be rearranged in line with its dictates.

Let us consider a final implication of the Abrahamic mode I have described. In the epilogue to *The American Jeremiad,* Sacvan Bercovitch offers an incisive critique of the "symbol of America." Bercovitch proposes that the "ritual of the Jeremiad" has been at once liberating and confining for American writers—liberating because it has released "titanic creative energies"; confining because this freedom has always been expressed as a reaffirmation of the American myth. He then argues that the power of the American myth has made it impossible for American writers truly to divest their allegiance to America, even as they have tried to envision a genuine alternative to the status quo. As he writes, "the terms of renewal remained locked in the same symbolic structure" (194); or, as Greil Marcus writes in a passage Bercovitch cites, "American is a trap: its promises and dreams . . . are too much to live up to and too much to escape" (204). The offering of the Jewish writer, as I have outlined it here, might provide a way out of this impasse. From the perspective of the "Jewish Jeremiad," America may be an attempt to manifest the ideal, but it neither guarantees success nor furnishes the sole basis of hope. The "American Idea," indeed, can be bracketed as but a version, a single instantiation, of a much broader tradition, one that starts all the way back at Sinai—or at least in Polotsk. And if history does not begin anew with America, we can also begin to imagine that it will not end there either. The

Jewish prophetic situates America along a long trajectory whose beginning is the word spoken first to Abraham and whose end is still glimmering somewhere over the horizon. By affirming the continuities of history, the Jewish prophetic offers a way out of the American impasse. What I offer in this book, then, is not merely a reminder that the present generation of Jews has inherited and carried forward the legacy of ambivalence and dialectics, positioning and self-fashioning, alienation and return, bewilderment and revelation, and belatedness and renewal that past generations have endured and wrestled with. It is also a proposal that the radical impulse known as the "American Idea" need not drain away into the symbol of America. Instead it can be—it has been—reclaimed and redirected.

NOTES

INTRODUCTION

1. The question of the influence of Puritan ideas on Jews remains a background theme in this study more than a central focus. For a more sustained discussion, see Michael P. Kramer, "New England Typology and the Jewish Question," *Studies in Puritan American Spirituality* 3 (1992): 97–124. See also Sam B. Girgus, *The New Covenant: Jewish Writers and the American Idea* (Chapel Hill: University of North Carolina Press, 1984), esp. 10–18.

2. See, for example, Hasia Diner, *Lower East Side Memories: A Jewish Place in America* (Princeton, N.J.: Princeton University Press, 2002); Arnold M. Eisen, *Rethinking Modern Judaism: Ritual, Commandment, Community* (Chicago: University of Chicago Press, 1998); Norman Finkelstein, *A Ritual of New Creation: Jewish Tradition and Contemporary Literature* (Albany: State University of New York Press, 1992); Sylvia Barack Fishman, *Jewish Life and American Culture* (Albany: State University of New York Press, 2000); Andrew Heinze, *Jews and the American Soul: Human Nature in the Twentieth Century* (Princeton, N.J.: Princeton University Press, 2004); Eli Lederhendler, *Jewish Responses to Modernity* (New York: New York University Press, 1994); Jonathan Sarna, *American Judaism: A History* (New Haven, Conn.: Yale University Press, 2004); Jeffrey Shandler, *Adventures in Yiddishland: Postvernacular Language and Culture* (Berkeley: University of California Press, 2005); Donald Weber, *Haunted in the Promised Land: Jewish American Culture from Cahan to the Goldbergs* (Bloomington: Indiana University Press, 2005); Hana Wirth-Nesher, *Call It English: The Languages of Jewish American Literature* (Princeton, N.J.: Princeton University Press, 2005); Stephen J. Whitfield, *In Search of American Jewish Culture* (Hanover, N.H.: Brandeis University Press, 1999).

3. See Alan M. Dershowitz, *The Vanishing American Jew: In Search of Jewish Identity for the Next Century* (Boston: Little, Brown, and Co., 1997). Consider also the disparaging view of American Jewish culture expressed by Israeli novelist A. B. Yehoshua in the talk he gave at the American Jewish Committee's Centennial Symposium, May 1–2, 2006. These remarks and responses to them were published in a pamphlet entitled *The A. B. Yehoshua Controversy: An Israeli–Diaspora Dialogue on Jewishness, Israeliness, and Identity* (American Jewish Committee, August 2006).

4. By tracing a central motif through successive generations of Jewish American writers, in this case the encounter with American literary culture, my study complements a number of recent studies that have constructed other narratives, focusing on different motifs. On the theme of Zionism and Diaspora, see Andrew Furman, *Israel through the Jewish American Imagination: A Survey of Jewish-American Literature on Israel* (Albany: State University of New York Press, 1997) and Ranen Omer-Sherman, *Diaspora and Zionism in Jewish American Literature* (Lebanon, N.H.: Brandeis University Press, 2002). On the theme of gender identity and masculinity in particular, see Warren Rosenberg, *Legacy of Rage: Jewish Masculinity, Violence, and Culture* (Amherst: University of Massachusetts Press, 2001). On the theme of language, see Hana Wirth-Nesher, *Call It English: The Languages of Jewish American Literature* (Princeton, N.J.: Princeton University Press, 2005).

5. See Stephen Greenblatt, *Renaissance Self-fashioning: From Moore to Shakespeare* (Chicago: University of Chicago Press, 1983), especially 1–9.

6. See Harold Bloom, *The Anxiety of Influence: A Theory of Poetry* (London: Oxford University Press, 1975).

7. Interestingly, Bloom's career itself points to the cultural dynamics I will be tracing: he immerses himself in the Emersonian visionary tradition and subsequently embraces the language of Kabbalah, remapped as an allegory for poetic creation. Eventually he fashions a hybrid identity for himself as a "Jewish gnostic," and identifies himself at once as a spokesman for the Western canon and as exponent for a heterodox, but insistently *Jewish* cultural tradition. See, for example, the introduction to Harold Bloom, *Agon: A Theory of Revisionism* (New Haven, Conn.: Yale University Press, 1982); and *Kabbalah and Criticism* (New York: A Continuum Book, 1975). For an illuminating discussion of Bloom's relationship to Judaism, see Norman Finkelstein, *A Ritual of New Creation: Jewish Tradition and Contemporary Literature* (Albany: State University of New York Press, 1992), 27–48.

8. A complete history of the relationship between Jewish literary critics and American literature has yet to be written. For useful studies highlighting some of the key episodes and figures in this history, see Jonathan Freedman, *The Temple of Culture: Assimilation and Anti-Semitism in Literary Anglo-America* (Oxford: Oxford University Press, 2000), 155–209; and Rael Meyerowitz, *Transferring to America: Jewish Interpretations of American Dreams* (Stony Brook: State University of New York Press, 1995).

9. Sacvan Bercovitch, *The American Jeremiad* (Madison: University of Wisconsin Press, 1978), 180.

10. Clifford Geertz, *The Interpretation of Cultures* (New York: Basic Books, 1973), 5.

11. Leslie Fiedler, *Fiedler on the Roof: Essays on Literature and Jewish Identity* (Boston: D.R. Godine, 1990), 60.

12. Ruth Wisse, *The Modern Jewish Canon: A Journey through Language and Culture* (New York: Free Press, 2000), 322.

13. See Sander Gilman, *Jewish Self-Hatred: Anti-Semitism and the Hidden Language of the Jews* (Baltimore, Md.: Johns Hopkins University Press, 1986) and *The Visibility of the Jew in the Diaspora: Body Imagery and Its Cultural Context,* the B. G. Rudolph Lecture for 1992 (Program in Jewish Studies: Syracuse University, 1992).

14. Michael Rogin, *Blackface, White Noise: Jewish Immigrants in the Hollywood Melting Pot* (Berkeley: University of California Press, 1998), 102.

15. Walter Benn Michaels, *Our America: Nativism, Modernism, Pluralism* (Chicago: University of Chicago Press, 1997).

16. See Werner Sollors, *Beyond Ethnicity: Consent and Descent in American Culture* (Oxford: Oxford University Press, 1987), 195–207. See also Werner Sollors, Introduction, *The Promised Land* by Mary Antin (New York: Penguin, 1997), xi–1.

17. Amos Funkenstein, *Perceptions of Jewish History* (Berkeley: University of California Press, 1993), 98–120.

18. Ernest Rubinstein, *An Episode of Jewish Romanticism: Frank Rosenzweig's The Star of Redemption* (Stony Brook: State University of New York Press, 1999).

19. David Roskies, "S. Ansky and the Paradigm of Return," in *The Uses of Tradition: Jewish Continuity in the Modern Era,* edited by Jack Wertheimer (New York: Jewish Theological Seminary of America, 1992), 260.

PART 1 (INTRODUCTION)

1. Abraham Cahan, *The Rise of David Levinsky* (New York: Penguin Classics, 1993), 530.

2. Sholem Asch, *Uncle Moses,* in *Three Novels,* translated by Elsa Krauch (New York: Putnam's, 1938), 175.

3. Donald Weber explores multiple versions of this melancholic, nostalgic mode in Jewish American culture in his book *Haunted in the Promised Land: Jewish American Culture from Cahan to the Goldbergs* (Bloomington: Indiana University Press, 2005). His reading of Cahan and Asch dovetails with my own (see Weber, 69–71).

4. Mary Antin, *The Promised Land,* edited by Werner Sollors (New York: Penguin Books, 1997), 35. Hereafter cited in text as PL.

5. *The American Transcendentalists: Their Prose and Poetry,* edited by Perry Miller (New York: Anchor Books, 1957), ix.

1. SONGS OF A SEMITE

1. Emma Lazarus, *Selected Poems and Other Writings,* edited by Gregory Eiselein (Peterborough, Ont.: Broadview, 2002), 233. Hereafter cited in text as SP. Eiselein's collection is an outstanding source for anybody interested in exploring Lazarus's works.

2. For a close reading of the "Jewish" aspects of Lazarus's most famous poem, see Daniel Marom, "Who Is the 'Mother of Exiles'? Jewish Aspects of Emma Lazarus's 'The New Colossus.' " *Prooftexts* 20, no. 3 (2000): 231–261.

3. See Sandra M. Gilbert and Susan Gubar, *The Madwoman in the Attic: The Woman Writer and the Nineteenth-Century Literary Imagination* (New Haven, Conn.: Yale University Press, 1979). See also Tricia Lootens, "Hemans and Her American Heirs: Nineteenth-Century Women's Poetry and National Identity," in *Women's Poetry, Late Romantic to Late Victorian: Gender & Genre, 1830–1900,* edited by Isobel Armstrong and Virginia Blain (New York: St. Martin's, 1999), 243–260.

4. Bette Roth Young, *Emma Lazarus in Her World: Life and Letters* (Philadelphia: Jewish Publication Society, 1995), 194. Hereafter cited in text as Young.

5. Any claim about the "beginning" of Jewish American literature is, of course, open to debate and bound to be inexact. It will also be hard to escape circular reasoning, since it will depend to some extent on one's operative definition of "Jewish American literature" in the first place. Nevertheless, it is useful to reiterate that the writers I am considering here may be seen as "Jewish" not only because their parents or the parents of their characters happen to be Jewish, but because in their writing they explicitly allocate to Jewishness or Judaism some specific and often positive set of associations. I am wary of using this premise as some sort of litmus test for the "Jewishness" of a text, however, because of the large field of important and challenging works it would leave out. For an illuminating discussion, which proceeds from a broader definition of Jewish American literature than the one I use here, see Michael P. Kramer, "Beginnings and Ends: The Origins of Jewish American Literary History," in *The Cambridge Companion to Jewish American Literature,* edited by Hana Wirth-Nesher and Michael P. Kramer (Cambridge: Cambridge University Press, 2003), 12–30. See also the generously inclusive canon assembled by the editors of the indispensable *Jewish American Literature: A Norton Anthology,* edited by Jules Chametzky et al. (New York: Norton, 2001).

6. For biographical information on Lazarus I have relied primarily on the following sources: Bette Roth Young, *Emma Lazarus in Her World: Life and Letters* (Philadelphia: Jewish Publication Society, 1995); Diane Lichtenstein, *Writing Their Nations: The Traditions of Nineteenth-Century American Jewish Women Writers* (Bloomington: Indiana University Press, 1992); Dan Vogel, *Emma Lazarus* (Boston: Twain, 1980); and Eve Merriam, *Emma Lazarus Rediscovered* (New York: Citadel, 1956). Esther Schor's recent biography of Lazarus appeared too late to be included in this study: *Emma Lazarus* (New York: Schocken Books, 2006). Subsequent references to Young's biography will be cited in the text as Young.

7. Hasia Diner, *A Time for Gathering: The Second Migration, 1820–1880* (Baltimore, Md.: Johns Hopkins University Press, 1995).

8. This encounter has been often noted and marveled at. Alfred Kazin supposes that Lazarus was the first Jew Emerson ever met. While this speculation is evocative, it remains unsubstantiated. Alfred Kazin, "The Jew as Modern Writer," *Commentary* 44, no. 4 (April 1966): 37.

9. Anne Boyd, *Writing for Immortality: Women and the Emergence of High Literary Culture in America* (Baltimore, Md.: Johns Hopkins University Press, 2004), 18–24.

10. Ralph L. Rusk, ed., *Letters to Emma Lazarus* (New York: Columbia University Press, 1939), 4. Hereafter cited in text as Rusk.

11. Ralph Waldo Emerson, *Selections from Ralph Waldo Emerson,* edited by Stephen Whicher (Boston: Houghton Mifflin, 1957), 21. Further citations refer to this edition.

12. Matthew Arnold, *Culture and Anarchy,* edited by Samuel Lipman (New Haven, Conn.: Yale University Press, 1994), 86–96.

13. Lazarus's continued enthusiasm for Emerson also suggests that this self-image was not fundamentally tarnished by an episode that occurred in 1874, when she found herself left out of the poetry anthology *The Parnassus,* which Emerson edited. This episode has attracted attention because of the surprisingly direct letter she wrote to Emerson expressing her supreme disappointment, her feeling of being treated with "absolute contempt" by the very person from whom she had received praise. Some have seen in this rejection the origin of Lazarus's subsequent embrace of her Jewish identity. Nevertheless, the fact remains that Lazarus never fully abandoned her sense of herself as an American writer nor did she withdraw her initial admiration for the Emersonian vision. Having written herself into the Transcendentalist tradition, she never really wrote herself out of it. For a different view, see Max I. Baym, "Emma Lazarus and E.," *Publications of the American Jewish Historical Society* 38 (1949): 261–287.

14. For a useful discussion of Lazarus's relationship to Zionism, see Ranen Omer-Sherman, *Diaspora and Zionism in Jewish American Literature: Lazarus, Reznikoff, Syrkin, Roth* (Hanover, N.H.: University Press of New England, 2002).

15. The first analyses of Lazarus's Jewish turn can be found in a series of essays printed in a special memorial edition of the *American Hebrew,* 1887. See also Josephine Lazarus's preface to the posthumously published two-volume collection *The Poems of Emma Lazarus,* edited by Josephine and Anne Lazarus (Boston: Houghton Mifflin, 1888).

16. Walt Whitman, "Doings at the Synagogue," in *Walt Whitman of the New York Aurora: Editor at Twenty-Two,* edited by Joseph Jay Rubin and Charles H. Brown (Corralltown, Pa.: Bald Eagle, 1950), 34.

17. William Dean Howells, "An East-Side Ramble," in *Impressions and Experiences* (New York: Harper & Bros.), 147. For a sustained analysis of Howells' attitudes toward Jews, see Sarah Alisa Braun, "Becoming Authorities: Jews, Writing, and the Dynamics of Literary Affiliation, 1840–1940" (Ph.D. diss., University of Michigan, 2007).

18. Henry Wadsworth Longfellow, "The Jewish Cemetery at Newport," in *The Complete Poetical Works of Henry Wadsworth Longfellow* (Cutchogue, N.Y.: Buccaneer Books, 1993), 191–192.

19. Jonathan Freedman offers a reading of Oliver Wendell Holmes's poem "At the Pantomime," bringing up a number of analogous themes. See *Klezmer America: Jewishness, Ethnicity, Modernity* (New York: Columbia University Press, forthcoming).

20. For a discussion of nineteenth-century discourses of Orientalism in relation to Jews, see Ivan Davidson Kalmar and Derek Jonathan Penslar, eds., *Orientalism and the Jews* (Waltham, Mass.: Brandeis University Press, 2005).

21. Nathan Glazer, *American Judaism* (Chicago: University of Chicago Press, 1989), 23.

22. See Matthew Frye Jacobson, *Whiteness of a Different Color* (Cambridge: Harvard University Press, 1998), esp. 171–200; Noel Ignatiev, *How the Irish Became White* (New York: Routledge, 1995); Karen Brodkin, *How Jews Became White Folks and What That Says About Race in America* (New Brunswick, N.J.: Rutgers University Press, 1998); and Eric Goldstein, *The Price of Whiteness: Jews, Race, and American Identity* (Princeton, N.J.: Princeton University Press, 2006).

23. It would be a mistake, of course, to presume that the notion of a Jewish race was exclusively a product of the nineteenth century. During the period of the Inquisition the notion had emerged of *limpieza de sangre* (purity of blood), with Jews regarded as inherently inferior to their Spanish Christian neighbors. See Benzion Netanyahu, *The Origins of the Inquisition in Fifteenth Century Spain* (New York: New York Review of Books, 2001).

24. Bette Roth Young discusses this episode in some detail in *Emma Lazarus in Her World,* 46–47.

25. "Judge Hilton's Position," *The New York Times,* June 10, 1877: 1.

26. See Gilman, *Jewish Self-Hatred.*

27. For a more general discussion of the ways Jewish American writers draw upon and recast the theoretical innovations of German Jewish culture, see my article, "Brooklyn Am Rheim? Jewish American Writers and German Jewish Culture," in *Jewish Texts and Contexts,* edited by Anita Norich and Yaron Eliav (Hanover, N.H.: University Press of New England for Brown University, forthcoming).

28. Yosef Hayim Yerushalmi, *Zakhor* (Seattle: Washington University Press, 1982), 86.

29. Emma Lazarus, *An Epistle to the Hebrews,* edited and introduced by Morris U. Schappes (New York: Jewish Historical Society of New York, 1987), 8. For a discussion of the role of Graetz and the turn to history in nineteenth-century Jewish culture, see Ismar Schorsch, *From Text to Context: The Turn to History in Modern Judaism* (Hanover, N.H.: Brandeis University Press, 1994), 266–302.

30. Heinrich Graetz, "Constructions of Jewish History," in *Ideas of Jewish History,* edited and introduced by Michael Meyer (Detroit, Mich.: Wayne State University Press, 1988), 221–222.

31. Ibid., 222.

32. Graetz himself played a key role in the struggles of German Jews against the new waves of antisemitism that appeared in late nineteenth-century Germany. During the very years that Lazarus was reading Graetz's history, he was engaged in heated disputes with the historian Heinrich von Treitschke over the alleged anti-Christian sentiments in his work. See Schorsch, *From Text to Context,* 292–293.

33. For a discussion of Lazarus's Heine translations in the larger context of translation in modern Jewish culture, see John Felstiner, "Jews Translating Jews," in *Jewish American Poetry: Poems, Commentary, and Reflections,* edited by Jonathan N. Barron and Eric Murphy Selinger (Hanover, N.H.: University Press of New England, 2000), 337–344. On Heine's Jewish identity in general, see S. S. Prawer, *Heine's Jewish Comedy* (Oxford: Clarendon, 1983).

34. This poem and these lines in particular will have an afterlife in the work of another Jewish American poet, Louis Zukofsky (1904–1978), who inserts this final speech in Lazarus's translation in the "Autobiography" section of his "Poem beginning 'The'" (1927). This work, created as a response to T. S. Eliot's *The Waste Land,* employs Eliot's collage-like form even as it creates a space for the Jewish modernist. By linking himself to Heine via Lazarus, Zukovsky creates a lineage of Jewish provocateur poets.

35. Heinrich Graetz, *Geschichte der Juden von den ältesten Zeiten bis auf die Gegenwart: Aus den Quellen neu bearbeitet* (11 vols.; Leipzig: O. Leiner, 1853–1876); in

English, *History of the Jews*, translated by Bella Löwy (6 vols.; Philadelphia: JPS of America, 1895), 536.

36. See, for example, Gilles Deleuze and Felix Guattari, *Kafka: Toward a Minor Literature*, translated by Terry Cochran (Minneapolis: University of Minnesota Press, 1986); and Henry Louis Gates, *The Signifying Monkey: A Theory of African-American Literary Criticism* (Oxford: Oxford University Press, 1988). For an illuminating discussion of the ways nineteenth-century German Jewish scholars anticipate contemporary multiculturalism, see Susannah Heschel, "Jewish Studies as Counterhistory," in *Insider/Outsider: American Jews and Multiculturalism*, edited by David Biale, Michael Galchinsky, and Susannah Heschel (Berkeley: University of California Press, 1998), 101–115.

37. See Alan Mintz, *Hurban: Responses to Catastrophe in Hebrew Literature* (New York: Columbia University Press, 1984); and David G. Roskies, *Against the Apocalypse: Responses to Catastrophe in Modern Jewish Culture* (Cambridge: Harvard University Press, 1984).

38. Emma Lazarus, *Selections from Her Poetry and Prose*, edited by Morris U. Schappes (New York: Book League, Jewish People's Fraternal Order of the International Workers Order, 1947), 35.

39. Merriam, *Emma Lazarus Rediscovered*, 132.

40. Salo Baron, "Ghetto and Emancipation: Shall We Revise the Traditional View?" *The Menorah Journal* 14 (June 1928): 515–526. See also Schorsch, *From Text to Context*, 376–388.

41. Michael Weingrad has suggested that another source for Lazarus's prose poem form may have been Charles Baudelaire, whose *Petits poèmes en prose* was published in 1869. See Michael Weingrad, "Jewish Identity and Poetic Form in 'By the Waters of Babylon,'" *Jewish Social Studies* (Spring/Summer 2003): 107–120.

42. For a discussion of Lazarus and Puritan typology, see Shira Wolosky, "An American-Jewish Typology: Emma Lazarus and the Figure of Christ," *Prooftexts* 16, no. 16 (1996): 113–125.

43. Readers will note that this same image from Isaiah will function centrally in Henry Roth's *Call It Sleep* (1934), which presents another version of the narrative of the birth of the "prophetic" Jewish American artist.

44. Lazarus's translation was printed alongside the Hebrew original in *The American Hebrew* (December 10, 1887): 74.

45. Nathaniel Hawthorne, *The Scarlet Letter* (New York: Bantam Classics, 1981), 75.

2. ECSTASIES OF THE CREDULOUS

1. The common spelling of the name of the town where Antin grew up is "Polotsk," not "Plotzk," as it was mistakenly printed in her first book.

2. For a discussion of Schindler, see Arthur Mann, "Solomon Schindler: Boston Radical," *The New England Quarterly* 23, no. 4 (December 1950): 453–476.

3. Mary Antin, *The Promised Land*, introduction and notes by Werner Sollors (New York: Penguin Books, 1997). Subsequent citations will be made in text.

4. Mary Antin, *From Plotzk to Boston*, foreword by Israel Zangwill (Boston: W.B. Clarke, 1899), 9.

5. Evelyn Salz, *Letters of Mary Antin* (Syracuse, N.Y.: Syracuse University Press, 2000), xiii. Subsequent citations will be made in the text.

6. Horace Kallen, "Democracy Versus the Melting Pot," *The Nation* (February 18, 1915): 193.

7. Randolph Bourne, "Trans-National America," *Atlantic Monthly* 118 (July 1916): 87.

8. For critical views of Antin over three separate generations, see Joseph Jacobs,

"An Orgy of Egotism," *American Hebrew* (May 31, 1912); Ludwig Lewisohn, "A Panorama of a Half Century of American Jewish Literature," *Jewish Book Annual* 9/5711 (1950–1951): 3–10; and Sarah Blacher Cohen, "Mary Antin's *The Promised Land:* A Breach of Promise," *Studies in American Jewish Literature* 3 (1977): 28–35. The reception history of *The Promised Land* is discussed by Michael Kramer, "Assimilation in the Promised Land: Mary Antin and the Jewish Origins of the American Self," *Prooftexts* 18, no. 2 (1998): 123–126.

9. Kramer, "Assimilation."

10. See Evelyn Salz, 2000; and Keren R. McGinity, "The Real Mary Antin: Woman on a Mission in the Promised Land," *American Jewish History* 86, no. 3 (September 1998): 285–307.

11. See Mary Antin, "A Confession of Faith," *Boston Jewish Advocate* (February 15, 1917): 5.

12. John Higham, *Strangers in the Land: Patterns of American Nativism, 1860–1925* (New Brunswick, N.J.: Rutgers University Press, 1955): 158–193.

13. See John Allen Gable, *The Bull Moose Years: Theodore Roosevelt and the Progressive Party* (Port Washington, N.Y.: Kennikat, 1978).

14. Jonathan Sarna, *American Judaism: A History* (New Haven, Conn.: Yale University Press, 2004), 137.

15. See Diane Lichtenstein, *Writing Their Nations: The Tradition of Nineteenth-Century American Jewish Women Writers* (Bloomington: Indiana University Press, 1992). See also Linda Kuzmack, *Woman's Cause: The Jewish Woman's Movement in England and the United States, 1881–1933* (Columbus: Ohio State University Press, 1990).

16. Josephine Lazarus, *The Spirit of Judaism* (New York: Dodd, Mead, and Co., 1895), 66–67. Subsequent citations appear in the text as SJ.

17. In addition to reflecting contemporaneous Reform apologetics, Lazarus's point might also be read in relation to recent scholarship emphasizing the "Jewishness" of Early Christianity—the idea, that is, that the "parting of the ways" between Judaism and Christianity was a much more complicated, protracted, and ambiguous process than traditional scholarship has suggested. See Daniel Boyarin, *Border Lines: The Partition of Judaeo-Christianity* (Philadelphia: University of Pennsylvania Press, 2004); and *A Radical Jew: Paul and the Politics of Identity* (Berkeley: University of California Press, 1994). It is instructive to consider the messianic and "enthusiastic" strains in American Jewish culture as recapitulating in some respects developments within early Christianity itself.

18. Quoted in Antin, *The Promised Land*, 299.

19. Antin's negative portrayal of the institution of the heder places her with numerous other late nineteenth- and early twentieth-century critics of East European Jewish life. See Steven Zipperstein, *Imagining Russian Jewry: Memory, History, Identity* (Seattle: University of Washington Press, 1999), 41–62.

20. Mary Antin, *They Who Knock at Our Gates: A Complete Gospel of Immigration,* with illustrations by Joseph Stella (Boston: Houghton Mifflin Co.), 139–142.

21. Jonathan Edwards, "Personal Narrative," in *Representative Selections,* with an introduction, bibliography, and notes by Clarence H. Faust and Thomas H. Johnson (New York: American Book Co., 1935), 60.

22. Walt Whitman, "Song of Myself," in *Complete Poetry and Prose* (New York: Library of America, 1982), 192.

23. See Harold Bloom, *The American Religion: The Emergence of the Post-Christian Nation* (New York: Simon and Schuster, 1993). Emerson and Whitman fit Bloom's model better than the more traditionally Christian Edwards, of course.

24. For a discussion of Abramovitsh's ambivalent portrayal of the shtetl, see "Introduction," *S. Y. Abramovitsh: Tales of Mendele the Book Peddler,* edited by Dan Miron and Ken Frieden (New York: Schocken Books, 1996).

25. Mary Antin, "Malinke's Atonement," *Atlantic Monthly* 108 (September 1911): 308. Subsequent citations appear in the text.

26. Mary Antin, "The Amulet," *Atlantic Monthly* 111 (January 1913): 36.

27. Paula E. Hyman, *Gender and Assimilation in Modern Jewish History* (Seattle: University of Washington Press, 1995), 10–49.

28. Quoted in Hyman, *Gender and Assimilation*, 29.

PART 2 (INTRODUCTION)

1. Quoted in Lederhendler, *Jewish Responses*, 109.

2. See Henry L. Feingold, *A Time for Searching: Entering the Mainstream, 1920–1945* (Baltimore, Md.: Johns Hopkins University Press, 1992), 24–33. See also Higham, *Strangers in the Land*, 300–330.

3. For useful discussions of Jews in post–World War I America, see Michael Alexander, *Jazz Age Jews* (Princeton, N.J.: Princeton University Press, 2001); Feingold, *A Time for Searching;* Deborah Dash Moore, *At Home in America: Second Generation New York Jews* (New York: Columbia University Press, 1981); Nathan Glazer, *American Judaism* (Chicago: University of Chicago Press, 1957).

4. See Michaels, *Our America*, 14.

3. "PILGRIM TO A FORGOTTEN SHRINE"

1. Ludwig Lewisohn, *The Island Within* (1928; Syracuse, N.Y.: Syracuse University Press, 1997), 263. Hereafter cited in the text as IW.

2. Mann wrote in his preface to Lewisohn's novel *The Case of Mr. Crump* that it was "in the very forefront of modern epic narrative . . . at every moment . . . both more and less than a novel; it is life, it is concrete and undreamed reality." Quoted in Ralph Melnick, *The Life and Work of Ludwig Lewisohn*. Vol. 1, *A Touch of Wildness* (Detroit, Mich.: Wayne State University Press, 1998), 551.

3. Harold Ribalow, *A Treasury of American Jewish Stories* (New York: T. Yoseloff, 1985), 142. For a discussion of Ribalow's role in the development of the category of Jewish American literature, see Jeremy Shere, "Jewish American Canons: Assimilation, Identity, and the Invention of Postwar Jewish American Literature" (Ph.D. diss., Indiana University, 2006).

4. Ralph Melnick, *The Life and Work of Ludwig Lewisohn*, 2 vols. (Detroit, Mich.: Wayne State University Press, 1998).

5. Steven Zipperstein, "The Lonely Passions of Ludwig Lewisohn," *The Forward* (25 June 1999). For another recent vote in favor of Lewisohn over the New York intellectuals, see Stanley F. Chyet, "Ludwig Lewisohn: A Life in Zionism," *The "Other" New York Jewish Intellectuals,* edited by Carole S. Kessner (New York: New York University Press, 1994), 160–190.

6. Ludwig Lewisohn, *Up Stream: An American Chronicle* (New York: Boni and Liveright, 1922). Hereafter cited in text as US.

7. See Amos Elon, *The Pity of It All: A Portrait of the German-Jewish Epoch, 1743–1933* (New York: Picador, 2002).

8. Ludwig Lewisohn, "Books We Have Made," *Charleston News and Courier* (July 5–September 20, 1903).

9. Quoted in Lederhendler, *Jewish Responses*, 105.

10. Ludwig Lewisohn, "Introduction," St. John de Crevecoeur, *Letters from an American Farmer* (New York: Fox and Duffield, 1904), xviii.

11. For an overview of the cultural scene in early twentieth-century New York, see Thomas Bender, *New York Intellect: A History of Intellectual Life in New York City from 1750 to the Beginnings of Our Own Time* (New York: Knopf, 1987) and Ann Douglas,

Terrible Honesty: Mongrel Manhattan in the 1920s (New York: Farrar, Straus, and Giroux, 1995).

12. Alfred Kazin, *On Native Grounds: An Interpretation of Modern American Prose Literature* (1942; New York: Doubleday, 1955), 135–136.

13. For background on the New Humanists, see Kazin, *On Native Grounds*, 197–238.

14. Eliot would later distance himself from what he considered Babbitt's excessively secular perspective. See T. S. Eliot, "The Humanism of Irving Babbitt," *For Lancelot Andrewes* (London: Faber and Gwyer, 1928).

15. The most comprehensive discussion of this group is Casey Nelson Blake, *Beloved Community: The Cultural Criticism of Randolph Bourne, Van Wyck Brooks, Waldo Frank, and Lewis Mumford* (Chapel Hill: University of North Carolina Press, 1990).

16. Alan Trachtenberg, *Critics of Culture* (New York: Wiley, 1976), 7.

17. A useful discussion of the rise of a modernist culture in opposition to the older genteel order is Frank Lentricchia, *Modernist Quartet* (Cambridge: Cambridge University Press, 1994).

18. Van Wyck Brooks, "The Fear of Experience" in *Modern Book of Criticism*, edited by Ludwig Lewisohn (New York: Boni and Liveright, 1919), 198.

19. Quoted in Douglas, *Terrible Honesty*, 49.

20. Ludwig Lewisohn, *Spirit of Modern German Literature* (New York: B.W. Huebsch, 1916), 61.

21. Ibid., 63.

22. See Charles Madison, *Jewish Publishing in America: The Impact of Jewish Writing on American Culture* (New York: Sanhedrin, 1976), 258–261.

23. There is a veritable dossier on the antisemitic statements of these two. See especially Joseph Epstein, "Mencken on Trial," *Commentary* 89, no. 4 (April 1990): 31–39; and Richard Tuerk, "The American Spectator Symposium: Was Dreiser Anti-Semitic?" *Prospects: An Annual of American Cultural Studies*, edited by Jack Salzman, vol. 16 (1991), 367–389. For a general overview of the position of Jews in the modernist imagination, see Anthony Julius, *T. S. Eliot, Anti-Semitism, and Literary Form* (Cambridge: Cambridge University Press, 1995); and Bryan Cheyette, ed., *Between "Race" and Culture: Representations of the Jew in English and American Literature* (Stanford, Calif.: Stanford University Press, 1996), especially the essay by Maud Ellmann. For a useful corrective to the now-standard view of T. S. Eliot as hostile to Jews, see Ranen Omer-Sherman, "Rethinking Eliot, Jewish Identity, and Cultural Pluralism," *Modernism/Modernity* 10, no. 3 (2003): 439–445.

24. H. L. Mencken, introduction to *Friedrich Nietzsche, The Antichrist* (New York: Knopf, 1920).

25. Ibid.

26. Quoted in S. L. Harrison, "Mencken Redux," *Journal of American Culture* 13, no. 4 (Winter 1990): 19.

27. Sinclair Lewis, *Main Street* (1920; New York: Signet Classics, 1998), 26.

28. For an excellent discussion of Jews in the American imagination and Lewis in particular, see Barry Gross, " 'Yours Sincerely, Sinclair Levy,'" *Commentary* 80, no. 6 (December 1985): 56–59.

29. Ernest Hemingway, *Death in the Afternoon* (New York: Scribner's, 1932), 53.

30. For a useful volume of essays tracing the myriad fantasies of "the Jew" in late nineteenth-century and early twentieth-century culture, see Linda Nochlin and Tamar Garb, eds., *The Jew in the Text: Modernity and the Construction of Identity* (London: Thames and Hudson, 1996). For a historical overview of the dynamics of philosemitism and antisemitism as they relate to nationalist movements, see Benjamin Ginsberg, *The Fatal Embrace: Jews and the State* (Chicago: University of Chicago Press, 1999).

31. Thomas Connolly, *George Jean Nathan and the Makings of Modern American Drama Criticism* (Madison, N.J.: Fairleigh Dickinson University Press, 2000), 27.

32. W. E. B. Du Bois, *The Souls of Black Folk* (Chicago: A.C. McClung and Co., 1903), vii–viii.

33. Du Bois, *Souls of Black Folk*, 60–74.

34. David Roskies, "S. Ansky and the Paradigm of Return," *The Uses of Tradition: Jewish Continuity in the Modern Era*, edited by Jack Wertheimer (New York: Jewish Theological Seminary of America, 1992), 243–244.

35. For a discussion of this episode in the context of the overall position of Jews in American universities at the time, see Susanne Klingenstein, *The Jews in the American Academy, 1900–1940: The Dynamics of Intellectual Assimilation* (New Haven, Conn.: Yale University Press, 1991). Klingenstein is inclined to view Lewisohn's response largely as histrionics, a self-serving declaration of pariah status rather than an honest depiction of the situation facing Jews in English departments in 1903. In Lewisohn's defense, one might say that from the standpoint of 1922, when *Up Stream* was published, this episode could be retrospectively highlighted as part of the pre-history of the later campaign against Jews and other foreigners.

36. The impulse to identify more strongly as a Jew precisely when one is attacked for being a Jew reflects a complex psychological process that is by no means easily explained. For a recent extreme case, far more dramatic than anything in Lewisohn's own life, see the interview with the Jewish former neo-Nazi skinhead John Daly, who moved to Israel and became a practicing Jew after he was nearly killed when his Jewishness came to light. "A Skinhead's Secret," in *Intelligence Report*, published by the Southern Poverty Law Center 122 (Summer 2006): 34–39.

37. Quoted in Melnick, *The Life and Work of Ludwig Lewisohn*, vol. 1, 280.

38. Feingold, *A Time for Searching*, 11.

39. Jonathan Sarna, "The Cult of Synthesis in American Jewish Culture," *Jewish Social Studies* 5, no. 1/2 (Fall 1998–Winter 1999): 52–79.

40. Quoted in David Singer, "Ludwig Lewisohn and Freud: The Zionist Therapeutics," *Psychoanalytic Review* 58, no. 2 (Summer–Fall 1971): 175.

41. Ludwig Lewisohn, *Mid-Channel: An American Chronicle* (New York: Harper & Bros., 1929), 129. Hereafter cited in text as MC.

42. Melnick, *The Life and Work of Ludwig Lewisohn*, vol. 1, 332–334.

43. Ludwig Lewisohn, *Israel* (New York: Boni and Liveright, 1925), 261.This is a good example of how the increased role of American Jews in the Zionist movement after World War I led to new directions in Jewish American literature. Waldo Frank was also appealed to by Zionist leaders, and his ensuing travels to Poland and Palestine were crucial in the development of his Jewish consciousness.

44. Naomi W. Cohen, *The Americanization of Zionism 1897–1948* (Hanover, N.H.: Brandeis University Press, 2003). See also Melvin I. Urofsky, *We Are All One! American Jewry and Israel* (Garden City, N.J.: Anchor Press/Doubleday, 1978).

45. Louis D. Brandeis, "The Jewish Problem and How to Solve It" (1915), *The Zionist Idea*, edited by Arthur Hertzberg (Philadelphia: Jewish Publication Society, 1997), 520.

46. See Stephen M. Poppel, *Zionism in Germany 1897–1933: The Shaping of a Jewish Identity* (Philadelphia: Jewish Publication Society, 1977).

47. For a discussion of the figure of the fugitive in American literature, see Philip Rahv, "The Native Bias," in *The Myth and the Powerhouse: Essays on Literature and Ideas* (New York: Farrar, Straus, and Giroux, 1965), 81–97.

48. Lewisohn's emphasis on the neuroses of assimilated Jews echoes the views of the influential Freudian psychoanalyst A. A. Brill, who treated Lewisohn after 1910. (See Melnick, *The Life and Work of Ludwig Lewisohn*, vol. 2, 216–218.) In a paper read before the American Psychoanalytic Association in 1917, Brill asserted that "the Jew is

disproportionately neurotic," which he explained both as a result of the inhuman treatment suffered by Jews throughout history and as a result of the theological idea of the Jews as the chosen people. Both of these factors have contributed, in Brill's view, to a heightened "racial self-consciousness." A. A. Brill, "The Adjustment of the Jew to the American Environment," *Mental Hygiene* 2 (April 1918): 230. For an overall discussion of Jews and the psychoanalytic movement in America, see Andrew R. Heinze, *Jews and the American Soul: Human Nature in the Twentieth Century* (Princeton, N.J.: Princeton University Press, 2004).

49. These stories may be found in the following collections: Philip Roth, *Goodbye, Columbus and Other Stories* (Boston: Houghton Mifflin, 1959); Bernard Malamud, *The Magic Barrel* (New York: Farrar, Straus, and Cudahy, 1958); Cynthia Ozick, *Bloodshed and Three Novellas* (New York: Knopf, 1976).

50. For an excellent discussion of possible responses to "Eli, the Fanatic," see Hana Wirth-Nesher, "Resisting Allegory, or Reading 'Eli the Fanatic in Tel Aviv,'" *Prooftexts* 21, no. 1 (Winter 2001): 103–112.

51. Stephen Ashheim, *Brothers and Strangers: The East European Jew in German and German-Jewish Consciousness 1800–1923* (Madison: University of Wisconsin Press, 1982); and Ritchie Robertson, "Western Observers and Eastern Jews: Kafka, Buber, Franzos," *The Modern Language Review* 83, no. 1 (January 1988): 87–105.

52. Ludwig Lewisohn, *Rebirth: A Book of Modern Jewish Thought* (New York: Harper & Bros., 1935), 299. Subsequent citations in text.

53. Ludwig Lewisohn, *Cities and Men* (New York: Harper & Bros., 1927), 11.

54. Ludwig Lewisohn, *The Story of American Literature* (New York: Modern Library, 1939), 113.

55. See Stanley F. Chyet, "Ludwig Lewisohn: A Life in Zionism," in *The "Other" New York Intellectuals,* edited by Carole S. Kessner (New York: New York University Press, 1994), 160–190.

4. MODERNIST FLASKS, JEWISH WINE

1. Daniel Aaron discusses Frank in his study of radical writers in America from 1912 to the early 1940s. See *Writers on the Left: Episodes in American Literary Communism* (New York: Harcourt, Brace & World, 1961), 284–287. For a more recent study, see Steven Biel, "Freedom, Commitment, and Marxism: The Predicament of Independent Intellectuals in the United States, 1910–41," *Intellectuals in Politics: From the Dreyfus Affair to Salmon Rushdie,* edited by Jeremy Jennings and A. Kemp-Welch (London: Routledge, 1997), 225–247.

2. Waldo Frank, *The Jew in Our Day* (New York: Duell, Sloan and Pearce, 1944), 92.

3. There is no biography of Frank. The sources I have drawn upon are Waldo Frank, *Memoirs of Waldo Frank,* edited by Alan Trachtenberg (Amherst: University of Massachusetts Press, 1973). Hereafter cited in text as M; Paul Carter, *Waldo Frank* (New York: Twayne, 1967); Michael A. Ogorzaly, *Waldo Frank: Prophet of Hispanic Regeneration* (Lewisburg, Pa.: Bucknell University Press, 1994); and Blake, *Beloved Community.*

4. On the relationship between Ethical Culture and Reform Judaism, see Nathan Glazer, *American Judaism* (Chicago: University of Chicago Press, 1989), 49; Jonathan Sarna, *American Judaism: A History* (New Haven, Conn.: Yale University Press, 2004), 132–133.

5. Waldo Frank, *Our America* (New York: Boni and Liveright, 1919), 87. Hereafter cited in text as OA.

6. Quoted in Bender, *New York Intellect,* 242.

7. As an indication of Whitman's status during this period, we might consider

the following recollection of Leslie Fiedler: "Even in the early 1930s only the most advanced of my fellow students were really familiar with that bulky, intricate work [*Leaves of Grass*]—and we were not quite certain whether or not we were supposed to admire it." Leslie Fiedler, *What Was Literature? Class Culture and Mass Society* (New York: Simon and Schuster, 1982), 87.

8. Ezra Pound, "A Pact," *The Selected Poems of Ezra Pound* (New York: New Directions, 1956), 27. Pound's poem was originally published in *Poetry* in 1918.

9. Frederick Jackson Turner, "The Significance of the Frontier in American History" [1894], *The Frontier in American History* (New York: Henry Holt and Co., 1920).

10. Quoted in Carter, *Waldo Frank*, 39.

11. Ibid., 49.

12. Waldo Frank, *The Jew in Our Day* (New York: Duell, Sloan and Pearce, 1944), 64.

13. Louis Ginzberg, *Legends of the Jews*. Volume Four: From Joshua to Esther [1913]. Trans. Henrietta Szold and Paul Radin (Baltimore, Md.: Johns Hopkins University Press, 1998).

14. Waldo Frank, *Rahab* (New York: Boni and Liveright, 1922), 15. Hereafter cited in text as R.

15. Waldo Frank, *Bridgehead: The Drama of Israel*, 217. Hereafter cited in text as B.

16. Susannah Heschel, *Abraham Geiger and the Jewish Jesus* (Chicago: University of Chicago Press, 1998), 18.

17. T. S. Eliot, *Selected Essays of T.S. Eliot* (London: Faber and Faber, 1934), 177.

18. This point might be reinforced by considering Frank's recollections of his friendship with Joyce himself in the early 1920s, when they had apartments in the same building in Paris. During their "midnight meetings" over wine, Frank came to realize that while Joyce's theme was "the disintegration of the self and of the society which produced it" (M 122), Joyce himself viewed this crisis from a bemused distance. In *Ulysses*, he had produced what Frank considered a false solution, a total picture that did not reestablish the grounds for active participation in the world: "The Joycean whole was a *completeness*," Frank writes. "Nothing remains to be said. . . . But I was beginning to learn that he did not share completeness, did not want to share it. Indeed sharing was alien to him. Joyce and I, although it was with affection, talked from opposite slopes of a great mountain, not seeing one another" (M 122). In Frank's view, Joyce remains the artificer, the master builder, who stands apart from his creation, unwilling to inquire into its viability as a language for healing the modern soul.

19. Much has been written about this moment in German Jewish culture. See in particular Michael Brenner, *The Renaissance of Jewish Culture in Weimar Germany* (New Haven, Conn.: Yale University Press, 1996); Robert Alter, *Necessary Angels: Tradition and Modernity in Kafka, Benjamin and Scholem* (Cambridge: Harvard University Press, 1991); and Peter Gay, *Freud, Jews, and Other Germans: Masters and Victims in Modernist Culture* (London: Oxford University Press, 1978).

20. Franz Kafka, *Letter to His Father*, trans. Ernst Kaiser and Eithne Wilkins (New York: Schocken Books, 1966); Gershom Scholem, *From Berlin to Jerusalem* (New York: Schocken, 1980), 10-11.

21. Jakob Wassermann's *My Life as German and Jew* (1921) describes with particular poignancy the difficulties of inhabiting his dual identity. Having imagined that he had written a novel "out of the soul of the [German] people," he discovered that he could not finally overcome "the prejudgement of [the Jew's] alien character" (qtd. in Brenner 133).

22. Frank's position here places him in a broader diasporist tradition in Jewish American culture. His praise of Jewish "abnormality" sounds almost identical, for example, to the impromptu discourse offered by the protagonist of Grace Paley's short story "The Used-Boy Raisers," published two years after Frank's book. Paley's Faith Darwin says, "I believe in the Diaspora, not only as a fact but as a tenet. I'm against

Israel on technical grounds. I'm very disappointed that they decided to become a nation in my lifetime. I believe in the Diaspora. After all, they *are* the chosen people. Don't laugh. They really are. But once they're huddled in one little corner of a desert, they're like anyone else: Frenchies, Italians, temporal nationalities. Jews have one hope only—to remain a remnant in the basement of world affairs—no, I mean something else—a splinter in the toe of civilizations, a victim to aggravate the conscience." Grace Paley, *The Collected Stories* (New York: Farrar, Straus and Giroux, 1994), 85.

5. CINDERELLA'S DYBBUK

1. Mary V. Dearborn, "Anzia Yezierska and the Making of an Ethnic American Self," in *The Invention of Ethnicity*, edited by Werner Sollors (Oxford: Oxford University Press, 1989).

2. See Louisa Levitas Henriksen, *Anzia Yezierska: A Writer's Life* (New Brunswick, N.J.: Rutgers University Press, 1988).

3. See for example the story "My Own People." In Anzia Yezierska, *Hungry Hearts*, introduction by Blanche Gelfant (New York: Penguin, 1997), 137–151. Subsequent citations in text as HH.

4. For a thorough examination of this relationship, see Mary V. Dearborn, *Love in the Promised Land: The Story of Anzia Yezierska and John Dewey* (New York: Free Press, 1988). See also Weber, *Haunted in the Promised Land,* 24–37. For a fictional retelling, see Norma Rosen's novel *John and Anzia: An American Romance* (Syracuse, N.Y.: Syracuse University Press, 1997). Also see Blanche H. Gelfant's introduction to *Hungry Hearts* by Anzia Yezierska (New York: Penguin, 1997), vii–xxxiv; and Carol B. Schoen, *Anzia Yezierska* (Boston: Twayne, 1982), 10–15.

5. J. Christopher Eisele, "John Dewey and the Immigrants," *History of Education Quarterly* 15, no. 1 (Spring 1975): 67–85.

6. Quoted in J. Christopher Eisele, 1975, 67.

7. John Dewey, *The Poems of John Dewey*, edited and introduced by Jo Ann Boydston (Carbondale: Southern Illinois University Press, 1977), 4–5. The same poem, with only the slightest variation appears in Yezierska's novel *All I Could Never Be* (New York: Brewer, Warren, and Putnam, 1932).

8. See Thomas C. Dalton, *Becoming John Dewey: Dilemmas of a Philosopher and a Naturalist* (Bloomington: Indiana University Press, 2002), 114–116.

9. Whitman, "Song of Myself," 1982, 50.

10. Anzia Yezierska, *All I Could Never Be* (New York: Brewer, Warren, and Putnam, 1932), 55.

11. See Walter Pater, *The Renaissance* (Oxford: Oxford World's Classics, 1998), 152.

12. Brander Matthews, "Up-Stream in America," *New York Times Book Review and Magazine* (April 9, 1922): 8.

13. Anzia Yezierska, "Mr. Lewisohn's 'Up Stream.' " *New York Times Book Review and Magazine* (April 23, 1922): 22.

14. Ibid.

15. For a reading of Yezierska and "ethnic realism," see Thomas J. Ferraro, *Ethnic Passages: Literary Immigrants in Twentieth-Century America* (Chicago: University of Chicago Press, 1993), 53–86.

16. Anzia Yezierska, *Bread Givers*, Introduction by Alice Kessler Harris (New York: Persea Books, 1975), 1. Hereafter cited in text as BG. In her biography of her mother, Jo Ellen Henriksen describes Yezierska's deliberate efforts, with the aid of her sister, to recreate her mother's syntax in English.

17. Matthew Arnold, *Selected Poems* (New York: Penguin, 1995). For a discussion of Arnold in relation to the Victorian crisis of faith, see J. Hillis Miller, *The Disap-*

pearance of God: Five Nineteenth-Century Writers (Cambridge: Belknap Press of Harvard University Press, 1963).

18. Anzia Yezierska, *Red Ribbon on a White Horse* (New York: Charles Scribner's Sons, 1950), 73.

19. It is interesting to note that these same lines from Arnold appear in another Jewish text written in the 1920s, Samson Raphaelson's "Day of Atonement," which formed the basis of the play and movie *The Jazz Singer*. Raphaelson's story charts out a narrative of rebellion and return that closely resembles *Bread Givers*. "Day of Atonement," *Everybody's Magazine* (January 1923): 44–55.

20. Irving Howe, *World of Our Fathers* (New York: Simon and Schuster, 1976), 486.

21. See William Toll, "Horace M. Kallen: Pluralism and American Jewish Identity," *American Jewish History* 85, no. 1 (March 1997): 57–74.

22. Horace Kallen, *Judaism at Bay: Essays towards the Adjustment of Judaism to Modernity* (New York: Bloch, 1832), 82.

PART 3 (INTRODUCTION)

1. See Wirth-Nesher, *Call It English*, 2006.

2. Irene Klepfisz, *Di feder fun harts* / The Pen of the Heart: *Tsveyshprakhikayt* / Bilingualism and American Jewish Poetry, in *Jewish American Poetry: Poems, Commentary, and Reflections,* edited by Jonathan N. Baron and Eric Murphy Selinger (Hanover, N.H.: University Press of New England, 2000), 320–336.

6. FROM HEINE TO WHITMAN

1. For a reading of the Popular Front agenda that informs Matthiessen's book, see Eric Cheyfitz, "Matthiessen's American Renaissance: Circumscribing the Revolution," *American Quarterly* 41, no. 2 (June 1989): 341–361.

2. Louis Miller, *Lider fun bukh: bleter groz* (New York: Yiddish Cooperative Book League of the Yiddish International Worker's Order, 1940), 203.

3. Anarchist thinker Emma Goldman relates an anecdote in her autobiography that reinforces this point. Describing a talk she gave in Montreal, she writes, "They were proud that I was one of their race. It was worth coming back to Montreal to reach their Yiddish hearts by the grace of the goi [*sic*] Walt Whitman," Emma Goldman, *Living My Life* (New York: Dover, 1970). Other Jewish writers who linked Whitman with socialist and Communist politics include Mike Gold; see his 1935 poem "Ode to Walt Whitman" in Walt Whitman's *Song of Myself: A Sourcebook and Critical Edition,* edited by Ezra Greenspan (London: Routledge, 2005), 82. For a discussion of Gold's poem and for other responses to Whitman from the left, see Alan Wald, *Exiles from a Future Time: The Forging of the Mid-Twentieth-Century Literary Left* (Chapel Hill: University of North Carolina Press, 2002).

4. For other discussions of the Yiddish response to Whitman, see Janet Hadda, "Di hashpoe fun amerike af der yiddisher literature," *Yivo-bleter* 44 (1973); Leonard Prager's "Walt Whitman in Yiddish," *Walt Whitman Quarterly Review* 1, no. 3, 1983: 22–35; and Rachel Rubenstein, "Going Native, Becoming Modern: American Indians, Walt Whitman, and the Yiddish Poet," *American Quarterly* 58, no. 2 (2006): 431–453.

5. For a useful correction to the view that Yiddish literature is solely the product of Jewish modernity, see Joachim Neugroschel's anthology *No Star Too Beautiful: Yiddish Stories from 1382 to the Present* (New York: Norton, 2002).

6. See David Roskies, *A Bridge of Longing: The Lost Art of Yiddish Storytelling* (Cambridge: Harvard University Press, 1995).

7. See Benjamin Harshav, *The Meaning of Yiddish* (Berkeley: University of California Press, 1990), 143–150. I am also expanding here on ideas raised by Ruth Wisse

in a series of lectures she delivered at the National Yiddish Book Center entitled "Abraham Sutzkever: The Uncrowned Jewish Poet Laureate," 1995.

8. H. Leivick. "Yiddish Poets," translated by Benjamin Harshav, in *American Yiddish Poetry: A Bilingual Anthology* (Berkeley: University of California Press, 1986).

9. Mani Leib, "To a Gentile Poet," *Penguin Book of Modern Yiddish Verse*, edited by Irving Howe, Ruth R. Wisse, and Chone Shmeruk (New York: Penguin Books, 1987), 138–139. In the Penguin anthology, Mani Leib's poem is translated by John Hollander, who renders the phrase "zing ikh oyf a fremder velt" as "I chant, amid the alien corn," lifting the phrase "alien corn" from John Keats's "Ode to a Nightingale." Hollander thus cannily inserts Mani Leib into the great tradition of English poetry, despite Mani Leib's ostensible claim to possess no tradition.

10. Bloom, *Anxiety of Influence*, 39.

11. H. Leivick, "How Did He Get Here? (Spinoza Cycle, No. 2)," translated by Ruth Whitman, in *An Anthology of Modern Yiddish Poetry* (Detroit, Mich.: Wayne State University Press, 1995), 111.

12. For a discussion of Prosopopoeia in the classical tradition, see Basil Dufallo, *The Ghosts of the Past: Latin Literature, the Dead, and Rome's Transition to the Principate* (Columbus: Ohio State University Press, 2007).

13. Abraham Brumberg, excerpt from *Journey through Doomed Worlds*, published in *The Forward*, June 13, 2003.

14. Irving Howe and Eliezer Greenberg, *A Treasury of Yiddish Poetry* (New York: Holt, Rinehart and Winston, 1969), 24.

15. See Marc Miller, "Heinrich Heine and the Development of a Canon of Modern Yiddish Poetry in America," in *Beyond the Modern Jewish Canon: Arguing Jewish Literature and Culture, A Festschrift in Honor of Ruth R. Wisse* (Cambridge: Harvard University Press, forthcoming).

16. For this survey of Heine's presence in Yiddish poetry, I am indebted to Sol Lipzin's article "Heine and the Yiddish Poets," in *The Jewish Reception of Heinrich Heine*, edited by Mark H. Gelber (Tubingen: Max Niemeyer Verlag, 1992), 67–76.

17. For a survey of the multiple and complex responses to Heine in Jewish culture, see *The Jewish Reception of Heinrich Heine*, edited by Mark H. Gelber (Tubingen: Max Niemeyer Verlag, 1992).

18. Nachman Syrkin, introduction to *Di verk fun Heinrich Heine* (New York: Farlag yidish, 1918), 7.

19. Ibid., 17.

20. See Dror Abend-David, *"Scorned My Nation": A Comparison of Translations of The Merchant of Venice into German, Hebrew, and Yiddish* (New York: Peter Lang, 2003).

21. For a reassessment of the overall significance of the "sweatshop poets," see *Proletpen: America's Rebel Yiddish Poets*, edited by Amelia Glazer and David Weintraub, translated by Amelia Glaser (Madison: University of Wisconsin Press, 2005).

22. Joseph Bovshover, *Gezamelte shriften* (New York: Frayer arbiter shtime, 1911), 67. Hereafter cited as GS. Translations of Bovshover are my own.

23. Harold Bloom, *Agon: A Theory of Revisionism* (Oxford: Oxford University Press, 1982), especially 224–232.

24. Heinrich Heine, *Songs of Love and Grief,* translated by Walter W. Arndt (Evanston, Ill.: Northwestern University Press, 1995), 213.

25. For a survey of translations of Whitman, see Prager, "Walt Whitman in Yiddish."

26. Leonard Prager and A. A. Greenbaum, *Yiddish Literary and Linguistic Periodicals and Miscellanies* (Darby, Pa.: Norwood Editions, 1982).

27. See, inter alia, Israel Jacob Schwartz, *Unzer lid fun Shpanye* (New York: Idishe Kultur Gezelshaft, 1931); *Khaim Nakhman Bialik-shriftn, yidish* (New York: Yidish

Natsyonaler Arbiter Farband, 1946); *Sefer ha-Shabat* (New York: Natsyonaler Arbeter Farband, 1947).

28. See James Perrin Warren, *Walt Whitman's Language Experiment* (University Park: Pennsylvania University Press, 1990). See also Paul Zweig, *Walt Whitman: The Making of a Poet* (New York: Basic Books, 1984).

29. Aaron Glants-Leyeless, "Shvarts, der amerikaner," *Zukunft* (December 1961): 468.

30. Ibid.

31. Quoted in *Leksikon far der nayer yidisher literature,* edited by S. Niger, S. Charney, Yakov Shatski (New York: Altveltlekhn yidishn kultur-kongres, 1956), 568.

32. Israel Jacob Schwartz, *Kentoki* (New York: M.N. Mayzel, 1925), 5. Subsequent citations are noted in the text as K. All translations are mine, except where I have consulted Gertrude W. Dubrovsky's translation, *Kentucky* (Tuscaloosa: University of Alabama Press, 1990). References to this work cited in text as GD.

33. The phrase *Columbus's country* was a common expression in Yiddish, almost always used in a quasi-ironic sense, as if to deflate the grandeur of America.

34. For a discussion of Asch's *Keyn Amerike,* see Mikhail Krutikov, *Yiddish Fiction and the Crisis of Modernity, 1905–1914* (Stanford, Calif.: Stanford University Press, 2001).

35. Harshav, *The Meaning of Yiddish,* 142–143.

36. H. Leivick, "To America." In *Jewish American Literature: A Norton Anthology,* edited by Jules Chametsky et al. (New York: Norton, 2000), 287.

37. Reuben Ludwig, *Gezamelte shriftn* (New York: Y.L. Perets shrayber-fereyn, 1927).

38. Quotations from Ludwig's "Symposium" in English are taken from my translation of the poem in *Tikkun Magazine* 18, no. 5 (September/October 2003): 57–59.

39. Ibid., 58.

PART 4 (INTRODUCTION)

1. For a description of this event, see Irving Howe, *A Margin of Hope* (New York: Harcourt Brace Jovanovich, 1982), 273–275. For a number of responses to the event and to Arendt's book more broadly, see "Eichmann and the Jews," *Partisan Review* 31, no. 2 (Spring 1964): 253–283. See also Alexander Bloom, *Prodigal Sons: The New York Intellectuals and Their World* (Oxford: Oxford University Press, 1986), 329–331.

2. Hannah Arendt, *Eichmann in Jerusalem: A Report on the Banality of Evil* (New York: Penguin, 1980).

3. According to one common view, Eichmann's trial (along with Arendt's response to it) marked a transitional moment in the history of American responses to the Holocaust—a moment when the Holocaust began moving from "silence" to "salience" in the public consciousness. See Alan Mintz, *Popular Culture and the Shaping of Holocaust Memory in America* (Seattle: University of Washington Press, 2001), 11–14; Peter Novick, *The Holocaust in American Life* (Boston: Houghton Mifflin Co., 1999), 134–142. For a contrasting view, which sees more continuity than rupture in this history of American response to the Holocaust, see Hasia Diner, "American Jewry and the Confrontation with Catastrophe," *American Jewish History* 91, nos. 3–4 (2003): 439–464.

4. Robert Lowell to Elizabeth Bishop, October 27, 1963, in *The Letters of Robert Lowell,* edited by Saskia Hamilton (New York: Farrar, Strauss and Gireaux, 2005), 438.

5. In his 1959 collection *Life Studies,* Lowell evokes Jews at a few interesting moments. In his prose memoir "91 Revere Street," he writes movingly of his great-great grandfather, Major M. Myers, a German Jew who had served in the war of 1812. In "Memories of West Street and Lepke," about the period Lowell served in prison for being a conscientious objector, he recalls spending his time "jammer[ing] metaphysics

with Abramowitz," presumably a Jew, who was whimsical and wise, with a purchase on higher truths. Even Lepke, the condemned murderer on his way to the electric chair, becomes somehow exemplary as a model of forbearance in a cruel world. Such moments in Lowell's oeuvre suggest that by the mid-1950s it had become possible even for the quintessentially WASP poet to imagine the Jew as an exemplary figure, whose speculations in a world as confining as a prison yard offered a glimpse of freedom, humor, and hope. See Robert Lowell, *Life Studies* (New York: Farrar, Straus and Giroux, 1959), 57. For a discussion of the figure of the Jew in postwar American poetry, see Hilene Flanzbaum, "The Imaginary Jew and the American Poet," *ELH* 65, no. 1 (Spring 1998): 259–275.

6. Much has been written about the "Jewish American Renaissance" in postwar America. On the one hand, there are innumerable essays and reviews by critics who might themselves be considered part of this renaissance. See inter alia Irving Howe, "Introduction," *Jewish-American Stories* (New York: A Mentor Book, 1977); Alfred Kazin, "The Jew as Modern Writer," in *The Commentary Reader,* edited by Norman Podhoretz (New York: American Jewish Committee 1966); Alfred Kazin, *Book of Life* (New York: Delta Books, 1971), 125–161; and Leslie Fiedler, *Waiting for the End: The Crisis in American Culture and a Portrait of Twentieth Century Literature* (New York: A Delta Book, 1964), especially chapters 5 and 6. Such works may of course be read as "primary" sources, since these writers embody trends in postwar Jewish American literature themselves, and their critical writings are also adventures in self-exploration. Among the most useful "secondary sources" (though I recognize that the boundaries separating these genres are permeable), I would include Mark Shechner, *After the Revolution* (Bloomington: Indiana University Press, 1987) and *The Conversion of the Jews* (New York: St Martin's, 1990); Norman Finkelstein, *The Ritual of New Creation* (Albany: State University of New York Press, 1982); Ruth Wisse, "The Jewish American Renaissance," in *The Cambridge Companion to Jewish American Literature,* edited by Hana Wirth-Nesher and Michael Kramer (Cambridge: Cambridge University Press, 2003); and Murray Baumgarten, *City Scriptures* (Cambridge: Harvard University Press, 1982).

7. Irving Howe, *Jewish-American Stories,* 13.

8. Grace Paley, *The Collected Stories* (New York: Farrar, Straus and Giroux, 1994), 13.

9. See Hana Wirth-Nesher, *Call It English: The Languages of Jewish American Literature* (Princeton, N.J.: Princeton University Press, 2005).

10. Irving Howe, "This Age of Conformity," *Partisan Review* 21, no. 1 (March–April 1954): 7–33.

11. See Ruth R. Wisse, *The Schlemiel as Modern Hero* (Chicago: University of Chicago Press); and Sanford Pinsker, *The Schlemiel as Metaphor: Studies in the Yiddish and American Jewish Novel* (Carbondale: Southern Illinois University Press, 1971).

12. Bernard Malamud, "Angel Levine," in *The Magic Barrel and Other Stories* (New York: Farrar, Straus, and 1958).

13. Alexander Bloom, *Prodigal Sons: The New York Intellectuals and Their World* (Oxford: Oxford University Press, 1986), 170.

14. Irving Howe, *A Margin of Hope: An Intellectual Biography* (New York: Harcourt Brace Jovanovich, 1982). Subsequent citations in text as MH.

15. Mark Shechner has discussed various postwar Jewish writers as searching for alternatives in the wake of de-radicalization. Shechner has usefully sketched out some of the directions Jewish writers and intellectuals took during those years, including their interest in alternate therapies, Wilhelm Reich, and so on. What I am adding to the picture are the ways in which specific engagements with Jewish culture and memory also absorbed some of these energies. See Mark Shechner, *After the Revolution.*

7. "MY PRIVATE ORTHODOXY"

1. This project was described by a number of the speakers at a memorial service for Kazin held at the 92nd Street Y in New York City in 1998. It has also been described to me by Kazin's widow and literary executor, Judith Dunford, and his son Michael Kazin.

2. Bernard Rosenberg and Ernest Goldstein, eds., *Creators and Disturbers: Reminiscences by Jewish Intellectuals of New York* (New York: Columbia University Press, 1982), 208.

3. Alfred Kazin, *Starting out in the Thirties* (Boston: Little Brown, 1965), 3–4. Hereafter cited in text as SOT.

4. Kazin later described the situation of Jews during the years he was writing *On Native Grounds* in these terms: "I started young, at a time when there was still a lot of open anti-Semitism. I knew as a matter of course that it wouldn't be easy to get certain jobs. I naturally didn't try to become a professor . . . don't think people today realize quite how much the situation has changed towards and about Jews. New York in the thirties was hard on blacks and Jews. Jews then were substantially a lower class." In Rosenberg and Goldstein, *Creators and Disturbers,* 197–198.

5. Ibid., 196.

6. See Alfred Kazin, *On Native Grounds: A Study of American Prose Literature from 1890 to the Present* (1942; New York: Doubleday, 1955). Subsequent references will be to this edition and cited as ONG.

7. Kazin to Mark Van Doren, 1/22/42. Van Doren Collection, Columbia University Rare Book and Manuscript Library.

8. Russell Jacoby, *The Last Intellectuals: American Culture in the Age of Academe* (New York: Basic Books, 1987), 90.

9. *New York Times,* June 12, 1936: BR 26.

10. Alfred Kazin, *New York Jew* (New York: Knopf, 1978), 4. Hereafter cited in text as NYJ.

11. "Under Forty: A Symposium on American Literature and the Younger Generation of American Jews," *Contemporary Jewish Record* 7, no. 1 (February 1944): 3.

12. Such sentiments, coupled with the less hostile, but only slightly more partisan views of the other writers, elicited harsh criticisms from many readers of the symposium. See Anita Norich, "'*Harbe Sugyes*/Puzzing Questions': Yiddish and English Culture in America During the Holocaust," *Jewish Social Studies* 5, nos. 1–2 (1998–1999): 91–110.

13. For two highly critical treatments of the New York intellectuals' response to the Holocaust, see Ruth Wisse, "The New York (Jewish) Intellectuals," *Commentary* 84 (November 1987): 28–38; and Midge Decter, "Socialism and Its Irresponsibilities: The Case of Irving Howe," *Commentary* 74 (December 1982): 25–32.

14. Alfred Kazin, "In Every Voice, in Every Ban," *The New Republic* 110 (January 10, 1944): 45.

15. See, for example, Varian Fry, "The Massacre of the Jews," *The New Republic* (December 21, 1942): 816–819; or an editorial entitled "The New Zionism," printed on March 8, 1943: 303; or "What Hope for the Jews?" from April 26, 1943: 554–556.

16. For a useful discussion of the implications of the Holocaust for philosophy and ethics, see Josh Cohen, *Interrupting Auschwitz: Art, Religion, Philosophy* (London: Continuum, 2002).

17. Such a view contrasts with the way Ziegelboim is portrayed in a commemorative volume published in Yiddish just after the war. Here he is commonly referred to by his party name, *Khaver Artur* (comrade Arthur), and while his devotion to "the folk" is constantly evoked, the rhetoric throughout remains stridently Marxist. See *Zigelboym-bukh,* edited by Y. Sh. Herts (New York: Farlag Unzer Tsayt, 1947).

18. For a reading of *A Walker in the City* that focuses on the motif of Americaniza-

tion, rather than return to Jewishness, see John Paul Eakin, "Kazin's Bridge to America," *South Atlantic Quarterly* 77 (Winter 1978): 45–61.

19. Howe, 1982, 275.

20. Elliot Cohen, introduction, *Commentary* 1 (1945): 2.

21. I am indebted to Richard Cook for this point.

22. Alfred Kazin, *A Walker in the City* (New York: A Harvest Book, 1979), 51–52. Cited hereafter in the text as W.

23. Sigmund Freud, *Civilization and Its Discontents*, translated by James Strachey (New York: W.W. Norton & Co., 1961), 18.

24. For a reading of the implications of Kazin's formal innovations for the genre of autobiography, see Robert Philipson, "Kazin's Modernist Autobiography: *A Walker in the City*," *Studies in American-Jewish Literature* 10, no. 3 (Fall 1991): 182.

25. Interestingly, this is precisely the dichotomy that Thorlieff Boman put forth a few years after the publication of Kazin's book as a way of distinguishing Greek and Hebrew thought; see *Hebrew Thought Compared with Greek* (Philadelphia: Westminster, 1954). Boman argues that the Greeks and the Hebrews possessed distinct conceptions of truth, evident in their emphases on different senses: since the Greeks value logical thinking, a truth that is "unveiled," their expressions for "to know" all derive from "to see." For the Hebrews, who according to Boman value "psychological understanding," truth inheres in the subjective response to God. Hence, "[f]or the Hebrews, the most important of the senses for the experience of truth was his hearing (and various kinds of feeling)" (206). Erich Auerbach's famous discussion of Homer alongside Genesis further reinforces this view (*Mimesis* [Bern: A Francke, 1946]). To locate Kazin alongside these scholars is to identify a common mid-century tendency to define Judaism via a distinctive epistemology. For a discussion of visuality in American literature, see Josh Cohen, *Spectacular Allegories* (London: Pluto, 1998).

26. We should note that Psalm 95 figures prominently in the Epistle to the Hebrews, as a warning to the Jewish Christians in Jerusalem to avoid the fate of their Jewish predecessors. See Hebrews 3:7; 4:7. Indeed, Kazin may very well have developed an interest in the Psalm from reading the New Testament, rather than from his prayer book. If so, this use of Psalm 95 might reflect yet another instance of the Jewish American writer relocating or returning the Christian revision of Judaism back to its original Jewish context: in *A Walker in the City*, the Psalm inspires a return to Jewish loyalty.

27. In his essay "The Education of Alfred Kazin," Robert Alter identifies several moments in *A Walker in the City* when Kazin seems to get some aspect of Judaism "wrong." Kazin "remembers" Jews walking to synagogue every night wearing prayer shawls, when this could only have occurred once a year, on *Kol Nidre* evening; he recalls the "liturgical refrain" on the kosher butcher shop window that reads "*Kosher Bosher*" (in reality the sign would have read *Basar Kasher*); and he transcribes a Hebrew phrase as "*Beneshalelem*," as if he were unaware that the phrase is "*Ribono shel olam*." For Alter, these mistakes all indicate that Kazin is not really as connected to his Jewish past as he claims to be; his "memories" are a blend of invention and counterfeit Judaism. My proposal, by contrast, is to read Kazin's "mistakes," particularly his "misquoting" from the prayer book, as creative misreading. See Robert Alter, "The Education of Alfred Kazin," *Commentary* 65 (June 1978): 42–49.

28. We might read Kazin's "editing" of the prayer book alongside the patterns of Jewish revision described by Arnold Eisen in his book *Rethinking Modern Judaism: Ritual, Commandment, Community* (Chicago: University of Chicago Press, 1998). See in particular the chapter "Nostalgia as Modern Mitzvah," 156–187.

29. Alfred Kazin, *Contemporaries* (Boston: Little, Brown, and Co., 1962), 296.

30. Quoted in Hana Wirth-Nesher, "Introduction," in *New Essays on Call It Sleep*, edited by Hana Wirth-Nesher (Cambridge: Cambridge University Press, 1996), 3.

31. Henry Roth, *Call It Sleep* (New York: Farrar, Straus and Giroux, 1991), 64.

32. For these insights into the connection between *A Walker in the City* and *Call It Sleep*, I would like to thank the participants in my seminar "Jews and American Culture," given at the University of Michigan in the fall of 2005: Alexandra Hoffman, Joshua Lambert, Patrick Barry, Alex Beringer, Angela Berkley, Jennifer Lapidus, and Rebecca Wiseman.

33. See Steven Kellman, *Redemption: A Life of Henry Roth* (New York: Norton, 2005), 124–140.

34. See Alfred Kazin, *Bright Book of Life* (New York: Delta Books, 1971), 125–161.

35. Kazin, "The Jew as Modern Writer," 41.

36. I have described Kazin's form of Judaism as a "Romantic Judaism," a phrase some would regard as an oxymoron. Consider Leo Baeck's essay "Romantic Religion," which characterizes "Romantic religion" as one in which "tense feelings supply its content, and it seeks its goals in the now mythical, now mystical visions of the imagination." Baeck applies this definition to Christianity, which he polemically contrasts with the structured and morally grounded Judaism. From Baeck's perspective, Kazin would appear to be sundering Judaism from its ethical moorings, the sine qua non of the Jewish religion. It is precisely this sort of critique that Cynthia Ozick will later levy at Allen Ginsberg, another "apostate" Jewish writer (also drawn to Blake and Whitman) in her essay "Towards a New Yiddish." Nevertheless, it is precisely his Romantic sensibility that enables Kazin to imagine himself back into the framework of Judaism and Jewish history. See Leo Baeck, *Judaism and Christianity,* translated by Walter Kaufman (New York: Meridian Books, 1958), 190.

37. Alfred Kazin, *God and the American Writer* (New York: Knopf, 1997), 257.

38. Lionel Trilling, *The Opposing Self* (New York: Viking Books, 1950), 127.

39. Saul Bellow, *Herzog* (New York: Viking, 1964), 201.

40. Allen Ginsberg, *Kaddish and Other Poems, 1958–1960* (San Francisco: City Lights, 1986), 8.

41. Ibid., 27.

42. For discussions of the role of the *Kaddish* prayer in postwar Jewish American literature, see Hana Wirth-Nesher, "Language as Homeland in Jewish-American Literature." In *Insider/Outsider: American Jews and Multiculturalism,* eds. David Biale, Michael Galchinsky, and Susannah Heschel (Berkeley: University of California Press, 1998); and Maera Y. Shreiber, "Jewish American Poetry," in *The Cambridge Companion to Jewish American Literature,* edited by Michael P. Kramer and Hana Wirth-Nesher (Cambridge: Cambridge University Press, 2003).

8. THE JEWISH WRITER FLIES AT TWILIGHT

1. Mark Yudel and Chaim Gold, "Introduction," *The Great Dictionary of the Yiddish Language* (New York: Yiddish Dictionary Committee, 1961), 510.

2. Ibid., 3.

3. Uriel Weinreich, "A Story to Tell," *New York Times,* June 10, 1954: B22.

4. See Benedict Anderson, *Imagined Communities: Reflections on the Origins and Spread of Nationalism* (London: Verso, 1983).

5. Jeffrey Shandler, *Adventures in Yiddishland: Postvernacular Language and Culture* (Berkeley: University of California Press, 2006), 1–30.

6. Quoted in Edward Alexander, *Irving Howe: Socialist, Critic, Jew* (Bloomington: Indiana University Press, 1998), 13.

7. Alexander Bloom, *Prodigal Sons: The New York Intellectuals and Their World* (Oxford: Oxford University Press, 1986), 133.

8. Quoted in Alan M. Wald, *The New York Intellectuals: The Rise and Decline of the Anti-Stalinist Left from the 1930s to the 1980s* (Chapel Hill: University of North Carolina Press, 1987), 321.

9. See Alexander Bloom, *Prodigal Sons;* Alan Wald, *The New York Intellectuals;* and Richard Pells, *The Liberal Mind in a Conservative Age: American Intellectuals in the 1940s and 1950s* (New York: Harper & Row, 1985).

10. "Our Country and Our Culture," *Partisan Review* 19, no. 3 (May–June 1952): 284.

11. Irving Howe, from "Our Country and Our Culture," *Partisan Review* 19, no. 5 (September–October, 1952): 575.

12. Stuart D. Hobbs, *The End of the American Avant Garde* (New York: New York University Press, 1997).

13. See Lionel Trilling, "On Teaching Modern Literature," in *Beyond Culture: Essays on Literature and Learning* (New York: Harcourt Brace Jovanovich, 1965), 3–30; and Leslie Fiedler, *What Was Literature? Class Culture and Mass Society* (New York: A Touchstone Book, 1982).

14. This episode is discussed in detail in Edward Alexander, 1999, 54–57.

15. Irving Howe to Lionel Trilling, March 22, 1949, Trilling Papers, Columbia University Rare Book and Manuscript Library.

16. A widely circulated anecdote has it that one of Trilling's senior colleagues questioned the young professor's qualifications because of these three affiliations.

17. See Alan Wald, *The New York Intellectuals,* and Gerald Sorin, *Irving Howe: A Life of Passionate Dissent* (New York: New York University Press, 2003).

18. Irving Howe, *Sherwood Anderson* (Stanford, Calif.: Stanford University Press, 1951), 244.

19. Irving Howe, *William Faulkner: A Critical Study* (New York: Random House, 1952), 26.

20. Irving Howe, "On the Horizon: An Unknown Treasure of World Literature," *Commentary* (September 1952): 270.

21. Irving Howe, "Eliezer Greenberg," *Yiddish* 3, no. 2 (Spring 1978): 4.

22. Irving Howe to Aaron Kramer, June 28, 1973, Aaron Kramer Papers, Special Collections Library, University of Michigan.

23. For a discussion of the role of gender in Howe's construction of Yiddishkayt, see Irena Klepfisz, "Introduction," *Found Treasures,* edited by Frieda Forman, Ethel Raicus, Sarah Silberstein, and Margie Wolfe (Toronto: Second Story, 1994).

24. Howe is quoting from Maurice Samuel, "Who Can Translate Yiddish?" *Commentary* 9 (June 1948): 34–39.

25. Abraham Joshua Heschel, *The Earth Is the Lord's* (New York: Farrar, Strauss & Giroux, 1949), 18.

26. For a useful discussion of new ways the shtetl was conceived of in postwar America, see Steven Zipperstein, *Imagining Jewish History* (Seattle: University of Washington Press, 1999), 16–39.

27. According to the YIVO rules, this would be spelled "yidishkayt." I will keep Howe's spelling, since I am using the term with his specific meaning. Howe's use of this term is slightly misleading, perhaps, since contemporary Orthodox Jews use it as synonymous with religious Judaism, but the term has also gained broad currency with Howe's meaning.

28. This oft-cited line appears in the preface to Hegel's *Philosophy of Right* (1821). See *The Philosophy of Hegel,* edited by Carl J. Friedrich (New York: Modern Library, 1954), 227.

29. Walter Benjamin, *Illuminations,* translated by Harry Zohn, edited by Hannah Arendt (New York: Schocken, 1969), 87.

30. For a discussion of the relationship between Benjamin's "The Storyteller" and his more pro-modernity essay "The Work of Art in the Age of Mechanical Reproduction," see Eugene Lunn, *Marxism and Modernism: An Historical Study of Lukacs, Brecht, Benjamin, and Adorno* (Berkeley: University of California Press, 1982), 170. Though

their intellectual pedigree is often markedly different, there are a number of fascinating parallels between the New York intellectuals and the Frankfurt School, including a tendency to be highly critical toward the products of mass culture.

31. For a discussion of the question of what Howe and Greenberg include and what they leave out, see David Roskies, "The Treasuries of Howe and Greenberg," *Prooftexts* 3, no. 1 (1983): 109–114.

32. Another expression of this overall impulse was the publication of *Anthologie de la Poésie Négre et Malgache* (Paris: Presses Universitaires de France, 1948), compiled by Léopold Senghor, one of the founders of the Negritude movement.

33. Eliezer Greenberg, "The Literature of Small Peoples: A Special Problem," unpublished manuscript of talk delivered in Dublin on June 8, 1953. See Eliezer Greenberg papers, YIVO archives.

34. Irving Howe, *The American Newness: Culture and Politics in the Age of Emerson* (Cambridge: Harvard University Press, 1986), 54.

35. Irving Howe, *The Critical Point: On Literature and Culture* (New York: Dell, 1973), 187. Hereafter cited in text as CP.

36. Irving Howe, "Tevye on Broadway," *Commentary* 38 (November 1964): 73.

37. Howe, *World of Our Fathers* (New York: Bantam, 1976), 596.

38. Irving Howe, "American Jews and Israel," *Tikkun* 4 (December 1988): 74. See also Irving Howe, "The End of Jewish Secularism," *The Anne Bass Schneider Lecture in Jewish Studies* (New York: Hunter College of The City University of New York, 1993).

39. Howe, introduction to *Jewish-American Stories*, 16.

40. See Morris Dickstein, "Ghost Stories: The New Wave of Jewish Writing," *Tikkun* 12, no. 6 (November/December 1997): 33–36. See also Donald Weber, "The New New-World Voice," *The Forward* (June 4, 2004): 11.

41. I am indebted to Josh Lambert for this typology of contemporary Jewish American writing. For a useful study of contemporary Jewish American fiction, see Andrew Furman, *Contemporary Jewish American Writers and the Multicultural Dilemma: The Return of the Exiled* (Syracuse, N.Y.: Syracuse University Press, 2000).

42. Simon Rawidowicz, *State of Israel, Diaspora, and Jewish Continuity* (Hanover, N.H.: University Press of New England, 1997), 53.

43. Ibid., 55.

44. Hana Wirth-Nesher explores the relationship between Bellow's translation of "Gimpel the Fool" and *Seize the Day* in Hana Wirth-Nesher, "Language as Homeland."

45. John Felstiner underscores a similar point in his essay "Jews Translating Jews," in *Jewish American Poetry: Poems, Commentary, and Reflections,* edited by Jonathan N. Baron and Eric Murphy Sellinger (Hanover, N.H.: Brandeis University Press, 2000), 337–344. He describes how Howe and Greenberg's *Treasury of Yiddish Poetry* paired leading Jewish American poets with Yiddish poets: John Hollander with Moyshe-Leyb Halpern, Mani Leyb and others; Adrienne Rich with Celia Dropkin, Kadya Molodowsky, and Dvorah Fogel; Stanley Kunitz with Israel Emiot; and Jerome Rothenberg with Melech Ravitch. This process of pairing poets might be imagined as one in which the American poet is introduced to his or her Yiddish prototype(s). The American poet is admitted, on the authority of Howe and Greenberg, into a literary tradition defined as Jewish. This approach creates a view of Jewish literary history as a continuous process of revision, translation, and migration—a *goldene keyt* or "golden chain" that connects the generations even as it seems in perpetual danger of dissolving through mistranslation or fanciful reinvention.

46. Bernard Malamud, *Talking Horse,* edited by Alan Cheuse and Nicholas Delbanco (New York: Columbia University Press, 1996), 80.

47. Ibid.

48. Irving Howe, *World of Our Fathers* (New York: Harcourt Brace Jovanovich, 1976), 596.

49. Philip Roth, *The Anatomy Lesson* (New York: Farrar, Straus, and Giroux, 1983), 74–75.

CONCLUSION

1. For Rich's own account of her reclamation of Jewishness, see "Split at the Root: An Essay on Jewish Identity," in *Blood, Bread, and Poetry: Selected Prose 1979–1985* (New York: Norton, 1986), 100–123.

2. Adrienne Rich, "Sources," in *Your Native Land, Your Life* (New York: Norton, 1986), 18.

3. David Biale, "Preface: Toward a Cultural History of the Jews," in *Cultures of the Jews,* edited by David Biale (New York: Schocken Books, 2002), xix.

4. Marnie Parsons and W. Roger Williams, "Man of Sorrows," in *The Hebrew Prophets: Visionaries of the Ancient World,* edited by Lawrence Boadt (New York: St. Martin's Griffin, 1997), 30–31.

5. The creation of a "prophetic Judaism" has of course been a central strategy of Reform Judaism, which beginning in early nineteenth-century Germany and America laid claim to the prophets as avatars of "universalism" and "ethical monotheism"—often as part of modern rhetoric of *apologia* for Judaism. But while the turn to prophecy in Jewish American literature might parallel and even in some cases reinforce this development, I am reading this turn in literature as a forceful critique of the status quo rather than as some capitulation to a bland "ethical monotheism." I would also emphasize the American dimension of this turn to the prophetic tradition. See James Darsey, *The Prophetic Tradition and Radical Rhetoric in America* (New York: New York University Press, 1997).

6. E. L. Doctorow, *The Book of Daniel* (New York: Random House, 1971), 314.

7. Ibid., 319.

8. Tony Kushner, *Angels in America: A Gay Fantasia on American Themes* (New York: Theater Communications Group, 1993).

9. An analogous sort of move might be traced through the major transitions in the history of English poetry: Milton completed *Paradise Lost* after being released from prison by the newly restored Charles II, in despair at the failure of the English Revolution; he then turned to *Samson Agonistes,* based on Judges, to further ruminate on this failure. And one might explain the turn to prophecy in English Romanticism as a way of responding to the disillusionment in the wake of the French Revolution. I am indebted to Ori Weissberg for this point.

10. R. W. B. Lewis, *The American Adam: Innocence, Tragedy, and Tradition in the Nineteenth Century* (Chicago: University of Chicago Press, 1961).

INDEX